Gqimm Shelele

Sin'bingelele emakhaya, e'koleli,
e'bhedlela naphakathi emajele.

Greetings to everyone at home, at schools,
in hospitals and even inside the various prisons.

Gqimm Shelele

THE ROBERT MARAWA STORY

AS TOLD TO
MANDY WIENER

MACMILLAN

First published in 2022
by Pan Macmillan South Africa
Private Bag X19
Northlands
Johannesburg
2116

www.panmacmillan.co.za

ISBN 978-1-77010-825-7
e-ISBN 978-1-77010-826-4

© 2022 Robert Marawa and Mandy Wiener

All rights reserved. No part of this publication may be reproduced, stored in or introduced into a retrieval system, or transmitted, in any form or by any means (electronic, mechanical, photocopying, recording or otherwise), without the prior written permission of the publisher. Any person who does any unauthorised act in relation to this publication may be liable to criminal prosecution and civil claims for damages.

All photographs courtesy of the Robert Marawa personal collection.

Editing by Tlou Legodi
Proofreading by Sean Fraser
Transcription by Qhawekazi Phelakho
Design and typesetting by Triple M Design
Cover by publicide
Front cover photograph by Xavier Saer

Prologue

I ripped off all my clothes and threw myself onto the cold tiles in the apartment, desperately trying to cool down my body temperature. I was sweating, overheating, anxious, irritable. I didn't know what to do with myself. I stood up, bouncing between the couch, the bed and the floor. The pain was getting worse, a shooting pain. I could handle pain but this was something else. This wasn't normal. I lay down on the tiles again. Anything to help soothe the heat.

My phone rang. It was Pelisa, one of the PAs from SuperSport. Where are you? You are late for the meeting with the advertisers.

It sounds like you're dying? Yes, I think I may be dying.

I was going mad. I was 35 years old – surely, I couldn't be having a heart attack. But this wasn't normal. I had to do something. The heat. The anxiety. The pain. I reached for my phone and called S'thembiso. I need an ambulance, I told him. At your apartment in Rivonia. Urgently.

At the hospital, there was a team of doctors and nurses holding me down, numbing my groin area. They had done X-rays and were trying to push through a stent. The monitors were beeping. I could hear absolutely everything happening around me. At one point I heard a nurse say, 'We are losing him,' and the beeping on the monitor slowing down. I could hear them arguing about what should happen next.

I thought I was dying. All I could think about was that I hadn't told my family what was happening. All those things that you are taught about the Angel Gabriel coming to pick you up, all of that started racing through my mind. How was I going to leave the earth like this?

I was listening to everything going on around me but I couldn't say a word. The minute they started inserting the stent, I could feel it moving up through my body. There was a sense of hope that the stent would get to the blocked artery in time for it to open and to get the blood circulating. The clock was ticking.

As the stent was about to reach my chest, the doctor warned that I would experience a sharp pain and the nurses literally had to hold my arms and feet down. The pain was so severe. You can stab me a gazillion times and I'll be okay. The pain of a heart attack is unbearable.

Then there was just relief. The artery was open. It felt like I had won the jackpot. I took a deep breath and thought, thank God. I had come so close to death.

My 2008 heart attack was a wake-up call about my future, but it also gave me a chance to stop and reflect on my life.

1
Farm life

At the meeting of two roads that descend from either side of a valley, deep in rural KwaZulu-Natal, is a small homestead made up of a few simple structures. The paint is peeling, the signs advertising Coca-Cola, washing soap and mealie meal are faded, and there are potholes on the streets.

Grassland stretches in every direction, punctuated by the occasional knot of trees or family compound.

Fort Louis is a trading station set on a quiet farm in eNkandla. The sounds of animals are heard more than the voices of humans. The air is clean, crisp and fresh at night and during the day.

A stream runs through the valley and each road out of the settlement leads uphill.

This is where I lived with my family from the age of three. My parents owned the convenience store, a general dealer on the farm, serving surrounding districts. The nearest large town was Vryheid, about an hour and a half's drive.

Our home was nothing special. It was an asbestos and tin-roofed structure. It's what we made of it that ensured it was special, working the land. But that was home. That was where we lived.

My parents had their own bedroom. As did my oldest sister, Nomvula. And then there was a double-bunk bed in a separate room. Gugu, the second-born, was on the bottom of the bunk bed and I was at the top. One Christmas Eve when I was about seven I fell off that top bunk and cut my chin open. There was a spare room for visitors before my younger sister, Vanessa, was born, after which she relocated to the carpet in my parents' room, initially. We ended up swapping because I was the only boy and I got my own room.

Farm life was simple. There were cows, sheep and chickens. We subdivided the chicken run to have some for home and others for sale. The ones with the white feathers were the ones we sold and the rest we fed and kept for our own purposes. We sold chickens at the shop but on Sundays people could buy from our house. I had to run out into the rain, catch one and hold it, tie the feet, catch another one and then sell it for five rand, ten rand or whatever the chicken was worth at the time. I also had to learn how to milk the cows. I went into the stable with the farmhand. His name was Cadalo, like the blackjack plant, and I grew up under his guidance. He looked after the farm and made sure that I knew how to milk a cow and shear a sheep.

I would take the bucket full of milk back to the house and cover it with a white tablecloth, which was then used to sift the milk so that all the dirt remained behind on the cloth, and then we would make cream. We would put the wool into sacks, tie them up and send them off to the factory.

That became part of every day. It wasn't even a chore.

Milking happened at a certain time. I rounded up all the cows, brought them back and counted if all of them were present. Then I reported to Dad how many calves had been born so that we could increase the headcount. We took the livestock to the dip. It was a little journey on the road. We needed to make sure that none of the cows ran off and that the same number returned home.

There was also planting of mealies, vegetables and fruit. We grew everything.

That was farm life.

Families were very scattered in our area, so I didn't have many friends. eNkandla is vast; you don't have next-door neighbours. If you have a neighbour, you're pointing somewhere, there up on the hill, at a homestead far away.

I also found that because my family owned the local store, other kids tried to be nasty because I was that boy from the family that was running the shop. They caused trouble with me and I didn't want to get into mischief.

I was always pretty comfortable in my own space. I would kick a soccer ball or ride my bicycle on my own. That was my entertainment. I kicked the ball around all by myself. There was a wall and I learnt how to tap without dropping the ball and I had to pass to myself. I cycled a lot. I ran around in the space that I had. Once in a while, there would be one or two kids around and we would hold a little tournament.

As a boy, my dream was to be a policeman or a firefighter after my dad bought me toy cars with battery-operated sirens.

The blue lights were a powerful sign of authority and I wanted to be that authority.

During the week I went to the local farm school called Woza Woza. Every Friday the boys would bring good-quality cow dung from home and the girls would bring two-litre bottles of water. We would do the ukusinda. It was a cleaning process to polish the floor.

The cow dung could not be dry because if it was, then it was only good for making fire. If the cow dung was still slightly moist, then that's what you would bring. The girls used water to moisten the dung.

It was as if we were plastering a wall, but on the floor, with a sweep of the hand. And then we would allow it to dry and the floor would be sorted. By the time all of us came back on a Monday morning, it had settled in nicely and we were rocking a beautiful floor in the classroom.

Life was simple and very rural. But my dad had genius ideas to liven things up.

He would put on a horse-racing event. A 'Durban July on the farms'. In general, he was big on betting and on the horses, but this was a competition called Oswenka. All the city gents from Joburg, the migrant labourers who had come back home to the farms, would be in their suits. There was a competition to see who had the best suit. So Oswenka would come to display what they were wearing in front of the judges, and show the inside of their jackets. If someone had a waistcoat, he was the man. They had style and were wise from living in the hostels in Jozi. They showed off their shoes and socks. That was farm entertainment.

Despite us not having the attractions of city or township life, if there was a birthday to be had, it was celebrated. Dad made sure that when he came back from Vryheid he had bought cakes from Checkers. We would get candles and put them on the cakes. We blew out the candles and ate sweets and drank cool drink.

Milestones were recognised and celebrated. That made my family what it was. My parents were loving and our home was happy and we celebrated that. I was always there with a camera to capture the moment. I became the default cameraman.

2
Family connections

Marawa is not a common surname. It's not like a Mkhize or a Dlamini, which are widespread. There are very few Marawas around. My dad, Frank Marawa, was a Motswana from Klerksdorp. He grew up in a township called Jouberton, outside Klerksdorp, in a section called X31. That's where he lived for the bulk of his life until moving to KwaZulu-Natal.

On my father's side my standout memory is that my ouma was very tall. She was the only woman I knew at the time who wore a size-nine shoe.

Dad lived a simple township life. There were many hardships as they did odds and ends for income. My father had four or five brothers, all of whom he outlived. They sadly passed away. It was a hard life.

My father was an avid sportsman. He played golf because he was a caddy in Klerksdorp. Even before Tiger Woods exploded, he was a Tiger Woods fan because he was able to identify his talent. He even wrote to the Tiger Woods Foundation and they sent my dad signed memorabilia from Woods.

He knew golf inside out and he had golf clubs. When we lived on the farm in Fort Louis, I would see these sticks in the

I was really sick. When I went to the clinic, they said I must go to Nquthu. I had pre-eclamptic toxemia which is high blood pressure. I must rest. I mustn't go to the shop where we were working. I must take it easy. Otherwise, it's either the child's life or my life that would be lost. At that time, there was no checking whether one would have a boy or a girl. But I knew because of the signs that it was a boy. There was a big-boned nurse who used to say when she was on duty she delivered only girls. I used to keep quiet. This is a boy, I knew it. It was a smooth delivery. I was very happy. I didn't want a girl because I already had two girl children. I was very happy to have a boy and I think I spoiled him rotten because he was a boy. My husband went to the registrar's office while I was still in the labour ward in Vryheid and gave the baby his names without even asking me. He was very much into American history and that's why he named him Robert Kennedy. I was annoyed because here am I in pain and all that, and he doesn't even come to ask me. My name for him is Themba. Everybody knows him as Themba. That was my hope after my beloved girls. And he's still my hope.

When I was very young my parents moved to Fort Louis in eNkandla. My grandfather had become chairperson of the board of the KwaZulu Finance Corporation and he had contacts in food retail. He pushed for my parents to move to Fort Louis and take over the trading store there.

be friends and he just kept on coming and coming. He told me he was a Motswana from Klerksdorp. And so, I don't know how it happened, but it happened. We got engaged and then I called off the engagement. There was an anonymous letter sent to me saying that if I was really a bishop's daughter, I shouldn't marry this person. After that I don't know how many people came from Klerksdorp and flowers were sent. He would send priests and teachers and everybody to tell me what a good person he was. We ended up getting married in 1964.

At first, they lived in Klerksdorp and my sisters Gugu and Nomvula were born there. My father was a buyer at one of the Spar franchises in Stilfontein, a mining town near Klerksdorp. Dad struggled to get a promotion because of his race and he was frustrated that white men kept being brought in and were appointed above him. With help from my grandfather and his influences, he was able to secure a business in Vryheid and my parents moved to a township called eMondlo.

My grandfather made that possible and my mother gave up nursing to start this journey with my father. She sacrificed her career for the two of them to start this unknown chapter.

I have no recollection of that place because it was the very earliest stages of my life. I was born in Vryheid Hospital in a very Afrikaans town. There was a section where black families could go for medical treatment and that's where I came into the world. My mother recounts my birth:

My first memories in life are from eNkandla. It is big and homesteads are far apart. Fort Louis is kilometres away from kwaNxamalala, which is where former President Jacob Zuma is from. I didn't even know he lived in that area until he gained prominence in our politics. But later on, when we both lived in Johannesburg, every time we saw each other we would say, 'Hey, mkhaya, mkhaya.' When Mr Zuma was staying in Hillbrow he drove a green Camry. I was a student and staying in Yeoville. I would see him driving his green Camry in Hillbrow and we were homeboys from eNkandla.

Fort Louis was an opportunity for both my parents to ensure a better life for themselves and their children. There was a drive in my father because he had grown up not having much. He felt he could achieve things that he had only dreamt about and would make him feel proud. Putting up the trading store and bottle store elevated him to see himself as a businessman. At that level, he could have a degree of power and authority and access to influential individuals. Later on in life, Chief Buthulezi and King Goodwill Zwelithini had a very good and close friendship with my dad.

Because of all of those things and knowing that Bishop Zulu was the one who made it possible for us to be at Fort Louis, my father became religious and closely involved in the church.

The church was on a farm so there wasn't a proper big building with an orchestra and organs. It was a structure that's called a church because there's a roof and we all went and congregated there. My parents took it upon themselves to change people's lives. They served pensioners free soup and bread while they were queuing for many hours for their pensions. And when the business started growing and there was access to money, my father built two Anglican churches, in Ngqamboshane and Emhlathuze. The churches had stained-glass windows and you could walk in and see Mary and the angels, and the cross. My father liked music and he wanted the church to have a choir. He was a fan of the Mormon Tabernacle Choir and had recordings of Louis Armstrong. He drew inspiration from these musicians and formed a choir, recruiting people from within the congregation to join.

My father received his matric but didn't study further than that. Everything else about him was self-taught, but he was a very proud man and that was the level of his own sophistication. He wanted to see other people flourish and was a very generous person.

The business grew, with both my parents contributing their skills. My mom looked after the shop and the bookwork. And my father was a go-getter and a great negotiator. He would drive to Vryheid on the gravel road, buy goods for the shop and load them into the truck. He was able to manoeuvre his way by virtue of being multilingual. He spoke Afrikaans fluently because all the people he had caddied for on the golf course had been Afrikaners. He could speak to the farmers and get them what they needed, so he became that darkie who was loved by the Afrikaners in Vryheid.

Dad was Dad. He was the head of the house but he also gave my mother space to perform her functions at the shop the guidance and the inspiration that he brought with him. As a young boy on the farm, I rarely spoke and was more of a listener and an observer. My grandfather was so wise and when he spoke, and what he spoke, always made sense.

He was a major part of how my mother and father landed up on the farm at Fort Louis.

My mother trained as a nurse at Sir Henry Elliot in uMtata (now Mthatha) and then did her midwifery at King Edward Hospital. She got a position as a qualified nursing sister at Ladysmith Provincial Hospital.

Mom tells the story of how she met my father:

After being on duty in the morning at seven, I finished my shift at twelve. I was sitting in the lounge of the hospital reading my book and there was this man there. I wouldn't say he was handsome or anything, just a man. I didn't even look at him or anything. I just knew somebody was there. In the meantime, I suppose he was looking at me. He greeted and I answered. I continued reading because I like reading novels and then he came over and apologised, asking if I knew this person. He had a letter in his hand. It was one of the nurses there and he asked if I could please deliver it for him. I agreed and went back to my book and he kept on looking at me and then he walked out. After that, whenever I was off, he was there telling me as soon as he saw me, he liked what he saw. I kept on pretending he wasn't there. But he put in too much pressure. I said we could bag at home but I had no idea about golf.

My father's life and his career prospects changed considerably when he met my mother and moved to KwaZulu-Natal. A nurse, born into a reputable religious family, my mother's name is Lynnette Phumlile Marawa, daughter of Bishop Alpheus Hamilton Zulu, bishop of the Anglican Church. She is from the Zulu family – oMageba, oNdabezitha, oSithuli.

On my mother's side, the family history is very politicised and religious. Bishop Alpheus Zulu, my grandfather, was highly educated – he was a schoolteacher in uMlazi and achieved a BA degree with a distinction in Social Anthropology from the University of Fort Hare. After he received a calling from God, he became a priest in the Anglican Church. He ultimately became the Bishop of Zululand and Swaziland, and in the early 1960s he was elected president of the World Council of Churches. Throughout his time as a religious leader, he experienced pushback from the government but he was an advocate of passive resistance and did not condone violence.

Together with Chief Albert Luthuli, he co-founded the Natal Bantu Cane Growers' Association that helped families become self-sufficient by growing small food gardens. Chief Luthuli and Bishop Zulu both joined the African National Congress in the same year but later, after retiring from the diocese, my grandfather went to the Inkatha Freedom Party and became its national chairperson. He believed in the party's mission statement of non-violence. Prince Mangosuthu Buthelezi immediately made Bishop Zulu the Speaker of the House. He felt that he couldn't lose the knowledge that my grandfather had and

7

things that added up to building my ultimate respect for her.

I suppose every lovely, beautiful marriage also has a side that is a struggle, which as kids you don't know about at the time because you're just seeing Mommy and Daddy. But then later in life, as you sit and you talk and you interact, you fully appreciate the struggle. Once you've seen it, you realise that we could have lost them or they could have walked out or there could have been so many different variables. But because I was too naïve, we just thought Mommy and Daddy were always there.

Being the only boy among three sisters had its pros and cons.

Nomvula was the firstborn and with that came the fact that she was honest and supportive; and she has a very sweet, soft, gentle and understanding side. Like my mother, she became a nurse first, and then she went on to further her studies and attain two Masters degree. As the firstborn, Nomvula has always had all our backs and she has always cared for all of us. She was the de facto leader, the one who loved to study and wanted to achieve and set the example for us.

Gugu was the second born and she and Nomvula formed a close bond because it would be some time before I, and then Vanessa, came along. The two of them became close and shared their experiences, their journeys, their secrets and their disappointments. Gugu and I would become close later on, bonded by our mutual love for sport.

I was born third and then six years later came Vanessa. So, while our two older siblings were close, Vanessa and I were similarly allied. I was proud and protective over her, although them just from the photo. Keep in mind that television was not a thing then; we were listening to games on the radio and not watching them.

My father started that for me and my obsession grew over time and fuelled my love for the game.

We were seen as the farm people when growing up, especially among my family. We were looked down upon because everybody else lived either in the township or in the city. We were not always involved much in the extended family.

I always felt like we were on the bottom rung. We woke up to cows and chickens and there was always that classism from an early age. Cousins said to us, 'It is so boring. What do you guys do? Where do you go to?' and so on.

My mother and I have a similar nature, perhaps partly because we also share the birth month of March. She was always a quiet person, choosing to observe rather than being outspoken or controversial. She always chose peace. She has a beautiful, loving, gentle soul. She describes me as being soft-spoken and soft-hearted so we are similar in that way.

She was an immense protector of all of us, though there were times when she was also very sharp. Mom gave up her twelve-year career as a qualified nursing sister and her job at King Edward Hospital to start this whole new journey with my father. It was courageous of her to do that.

It was only my dad and mom in the shop running the business. She sacrificed more than most, whether it was within her personal space as a mother or as a wife. It's all part of the when she was little, I was scared to pick her up because I thought I would drop her.

Vanessa went to crèche and primary school in Vryheid. She attended Nardini Convent School and my mother drove up and down to take and fetch her. She had a different experience from her older sisters because she was learning to swim and competing in galas and did ballet, which she became very good at. She was the first to go to a multiracial school, so doing all these things was foreign to the rest of us in the family. But we supported her and she excelled.

I suppose that all four of us as siblings were separated by the fact that we were all at different boarding schools and we couldn't make a connection. In the same way, we couldn't connect with our parents because we only saw them four times a year during the holidays.

But the love and the bond of the family were there throughout.

As a boy, home was a loving and happy environment, but my existence on the farm was all I really knew. Before long, my parents realised that Woza Woza farm school wasn't going to get me far. They began to look around through the Anglican Church and my grandfather became involved too. The priest got word that there was a gap at a convent school called Little Flower. My parents didn't know any better, so at age six, I was packed off to boarding school, leaving farm life and Fort Louis behind.

3
Number 196

My father steered his car through the gate and up the tarred road across the red-brick paving into an open parking area in a courtyard in front of the Little Flower School in Eshowe. The drive had taken us around two and a half hours on a mix of gravel and tar roads. To the left I could see a building that I soon found out was the dining room; and to the right were the dormitories.

All I had known in my short six years of life was my rustic farm school with its cow-dung floor. I took in what lay before me – the lawn, the grass, a large brick-and-mortar building – and I was overwhelmed. This was a proper place. I was moving a step up.

Along with me on this journey I had brought a small trunk. Written on the side in paint was the number 196. That was my allocated number at Little Flower.

We had been given instructions where to buy every single piece of clothing, every item of uniform, and even what trunk to purchase. Everything was perfectly structured. For days my mom and the lady who was helping us in the kitchen were sewing labels with the number 196 onto every item of

I had to start from scratch with my education because the sisters realised that we hadn't really learnt much at that farm school. I started with the basics and ended up being at Little Flower for seven years. It was hard core.

If you had a weak bladder, for example, and you wet your bed, the nuns removed your normal mattress. Then you'd have to go and weave yourself what they called a grass mattress. You would put a whole lot of hay together and stitch it up. That would become your mattress so you could wee all you wanted while you were sleeping. Thankfully, my bladder control was great, so I never had the misfortune of being pricked by hay at night while trying to sleep.

That was the kind of shame we had to endure. That was our reality.

At night when we were asleep, the boys would put a piece of paper between your toes and set it alight. You would wake up to your toes burning. It was cruel.

We all had duties and responsibilities. We looked at the duty list to find out whether we were cleaning the veranda or the toilet. The worst one was if you were the honey boy, removing crap from the septic tank.

If you had to do septic-tank duty, you were called the 'honey boy'. You would take an empty mealie sack, cut it so that you could put your head through the bottom and cut holes for your arms. You would wear that and be given a wheelbarrow and a shovel.

There were two septic tanks side by side. You would open the two tanks. There was the wetter, drooly crap on the

Across from me was a boy whose name I later learnt was Lucky Mbuyazi. He had cleared his bowl and had finished eating. He could see that I was not enjoying this meal. I offered him my bowl because I was done. 'Sure,' he said, 'bring it my way.'

Instinctively, I knew that I had to make sure the sister didn't see this transaction taking place because I was supposed to eat my food. He pushed his bowl halfway into the middle of the table. I lifted my bowl up to flip it over to pour the tomatoes into his bowl and as I did that, he pulled his bowl towards him and all my boiled tomatoes spilled onto the table.

The sister came straight over to the table and Lucky sank me. 'Sister. Look at this new one here.'

I hadn't been at the school an hour and this was my first experience. I was sitting with my lunch splashed all over the table. The sister shouted that I must gather all my food back into the bowl and I must use my hands to do it. Lucky was laughing, watching me scrape the tomato slop into my bowl with my hands, and then I had to finish every last bit of it.

I'll never forget Lucky Mbuyazi and what he did to me on that first day at Little Flower. It was only the start of what was to come.

I quickly realised that this was not going to be a normal existence and I had to adjust. How Lucky treated me with the tomatoes became my reality. Many kids came from families that were difficult or broken. The boys could be hard and cold. And I understood the explanation for the 196. We were never names. We were just numbers.

the number. The Sister checked that I had the keys for the padlock and I was told to say goodbye to Dad.

My father sat me down to bid me farewell and it dawned on me that he was leaving. All of a sudden I could see his face had changed. He had felt the impact of the fact that he was leaving his only son in this environment and he would be driving back to Fort Louis on his own. He didn't show much emotion, but his face transformed. There were no tears and he didn't say anything profound. He just said goodbye.

He got into the car and drove off. Later in life, my mother told me that he had broken down in the car and cried as he got in to start the engine. Here was this masculine guy who used to be a boxer and exercised in the gym, literally crying.

I didn't cry. I was more curious and intrigued that I was going to be with other kids. I thought this could be a great place. I didn't know what to expect from the nuns but they seemed lovely.

As it was lunch time, I was ushered into the dining room to join the other boys for the meal. There was a long white table with benches on either side and there were ten boys on one side and ten on the other. Each boy had a silver-coloured bowl placed in front of him, filled to the brim with boiled tomatoes.

Each kid was sitting there with a spoon, eating out of their silver bowls. Half of them had finished eating by the time I sat down. I was given my bowl and took one spoonful. I was on the verge of throwing up. I had never eaten this in my life and it was the most disgusting thing I had ever come across. I couldn't even comprehend how terrible it was.

clothing, even the pairs of socks. It couldn't be written on the item with a marker pen; it had to be stitched on with red cotton. Then it was all locked in the trunk that was sitting beside me as I stood in the courtyard.

A nun appeared, looking like an image that we had been taught from the Bible. She was draped in white and I thought she had come from heaven. All the nuns at the school were white, and mostly German. There was Sister Thoma and Sister Elizabeth and so on.

I was nervous and didn't know what was about to happen. I had been told I was going to a boarding school, but no one had explained the concept of boarding to me. All I knew was that we had packed enough clothes to last me a very long time, which meant I was going to be staying behind when my father drove off. I was not going back home with Dad. Logic told me I was there to stay; otherwise why would they be sewing all of this 196 into the clothes in my trunk?

'Hello, Mr Marawa,' the sister greeted my father. 'I assume this is Robert.'

She was very polite and very welcoming. My dad was multilingual so he could converse with her in English. My little bit of farm English that I'd been taught was neither here nor there. It was pretty much nonexistent. They spoke and I didn't understand much of what she was explaining. I was just looking around and watching the kids go through to the dining room. We had arrived just in time for lunch.

My trunk was placed with all the others. Mine was clearly marked with the brush-painted 196 on the side. No name, just right-hand side. On the left-hand side was the stiffer formation of the crap.

As the honey boy, it was your duty to shovel the crap into the wheelbarrow. You often got splashed with shit. That's why you wore the sack and not your clothes. You pushed the wheelbarrow from the back of the building to the orchard where the shit was used as fertiliser for the grapefruit and bananas and guavas and all the other fruit growing there.

You had to keep going back and forth until the tanks were at a level that the nuns were happy with and then you had done your job for that session. Others would be working in the pigsty, cleaning it up, feeding the pigs, making sure they were okay. Funnily enough, we hardly ever got any pork or bacon from there. That delicacy was reserved for the nuns.

I was between the ages of six and thirteen during this time. I never complained about it. I just assumed this was how life was supposed to be and it was okay. My parents knew no better. For them this school was an upgrade.

It was only later on in life when I started to relay these stories to my parents that they were shocked. Every time we told stories about Little Flower people thought we were making up stuff.

I didn't realise until I was out of that environment what we were enduring. It didn't sound like it was a school that catered for kids as young as five. But it was our lived experience. It was harsh. It was like a reformatory.

When I look at it now, I always say you can drop me in Mogadishu and I will survive because of all the life skills that were drilled into me in that school.

They literally had something called The First Bully. You needed to know who was the boss of the bullies. If you thought you could beat up that guy, then you challenged him to a fight. The kids would form a ring and the two of you would get into the middle and fight. If you could beat up The First Bully, then you became The First Bully. Then you were the man, you were in charge. There were some brutal fights, with lips cut and teeth getting knocked out.

When I look at it with hindsight, I see how it helped shape me because I had to learn how to be independent, not to rely on anybody else, but be self-reliant, defend myself, fight for myself, and offset any form of bullying that happens in most schools.

There were some children who were day scholars too. We had a guy called Joshua who ran from Nkwalini to Eshowe. It was around 30 minutes each way and he would jog every single day to get there. When we woke up to go for breakfast, Joshua was already there, seated, the first person to arrive at school. Then he had to jog back. There was no transport. So, there was that level of craziness that was happening. It was always extreme.

I think my personality and perspective were moulded at that school because of the raw nature of life and what it was. You had to figure things out and there was no guiding figure. I learnt to get on with things. I never made a fuss about anything.

We were given boiled cabbage leaves to eat and we thought nothing of it because we didn't know any better. We thought how to swim, we could have started in the shallow end and walked through the water and started with using my legs.

There was none of that. It was just straight to the deep end. Boom. Gone.

S'thembiso was one of the naughtiest kids at Little Flower. He was always pulling pranks. I don't recall him ever apologising for it and that's because he found it so funny. I don't think he took it seriously as it's just not in his nature. We have stayed good friends despite it. He's been married twice and I've been the best man and MC at his weddings. I have kept away from swimming since then and I realised how quickly things can change in water.

I still don't know how to swim today.

I was a shy child so I never spoke much. I was never talkative or expressive. I was always very introverted and subdued.

I went to church enough times at Little Flower to have churched myself for the rest of my life.

We lined up outside the chapel from five o'clock in the morning, making sure that everyone was quiet before we were allowed to go in. When it was Easter, we went to chapel but we also had to go through the different stages of the crucifixion. Then it was rosary season, so we had to go through the rosary every night. 'Hail Mary, full of grace, the Lord is with thee. Blessed art thou amongst women ...' Every single day. Rosary. Up until you finish it, up until the end, we all had to pray en masse doing it.

We also had to go for confession. We went to chapel and

there was a little box where the priest sat inside. They burnt incense and we had to write down our sins. Whatever it was that we had deemed to have been a sin, we had to write on a piece of paper with our name and then go put it in a 'fire', which wasn't really burning these papers.

I think they were trying to trick us to confess not only to God, but for them to know what we had been doing. We were being open to God from a spiritual perspective, but they were also trying to figure out what we had been up to.

I think it was great nourishment for me coming from a religious family, although it was a Catholic church and we were Anglican. It was the same God and the same crucifixion. But it was a lot of going to church and a lot of praying. And the behaviour of the children was the exact opposite of how so-called religious people should act.

I don't resent or blame my parents at all for sending me to Little Flower. They thought they were doing what was best for me. It was really my father who wanted me to go there and my mother regrets not pushing harder against him. She had been in boarding school herself so she knew how bad it could be. But my mother was always there for me and would come to visit even though the sisters told her it unsettled me. She was always there to support me.

I still have a photo of my birthday at Little Flower and my mom had brought me a cake. There is Sister Elizabeth in the background but it was my mother who had brought the cake. She was that mother who, regardless of what it was, was there to support me. My dad was the one who dropped me off on which comes more like a haunting flashback, is of my experience with swimming.

There was a community pool in Eshowe and we had to walk there from the school. Especially on hot days or if it was a Saturday, the nuns would arrange that we go and splash around and play in the water.

It was my first encounter with water like this. I didn't know the art of swimming. It had never been taught to me. When I saw people floating in the water and flapping their arms, I thought it came naturally. A friend of mine, S'thembiso Nzimande, was a playful, naughty boy and he told me that I should come with him to the deep end of the pool because he was going to teach me how to swim.

I was convinced, so I got in the water. Before I knew it, I started sinking. I went down and down and down. All I remember was seeing stars. My nose and ears filled with water. I just kept going down. What I was experiencing was drowning.

I could hear the noise in the background. Boys were laughing. They were well entertained. S'thembiso had told me he was going to show me how to swim but there was nobody nearby to help. I was drowning and nobody was coming to save me.

Suddenly two boys appeared and dragged me out and laid me down on the side of the pool. I had taken in so much water. I didn't know who those boys were but they saved my life.

I have never forgotten that incident. Whenever I see a pool, I have that flashback. If S'thembiso had wanted to teach me this was how life should be. There was a big avocado tree at the school, so we would go and shake it in the hope that an avo or two would fall. We would take the unripened avo and wrap it up in newspaper, dig a hole and bury it, hoping that no one had seen us. That was the kind of life skill that we learnt. Every week or so we would go and check on the avo to see if it had ripened and was ready for eating.

Once it was nice and ripe, we would take it into the dining room. We would be given plain bread to eat with nothing on it. We would slice up that avo and pile it up on the bread and we would call it a mountain. Everyone would look at your delicious slice of bread and this mound of chopped-up avo and it would make you feel so good. We were excited about small things like that because they were big things to us at the time. Avocado was a status symbol. Not everyone had access to it but if you were smart enough to go in and grab it, you could get it.

Those were things that couldn't be taught in the classroom. If we didn't have avo then it was a packet of Marie biscuits that became a delicacy. If you could afford to buy them, then at breakfast you would take a couple of those Marie biscuits, dip them in tea and then place them on top of your bread. We would build it up until the whole packet was finished. That's what we called the castle. There was a competition to see who had the biggest castle, but it was just Marie biscuits and bread. We were having fun with it. The situation was crazy but that was our reality.

One of the recurring memories I have of Little Flower,

day one but he didn't visit much after that. My mother always tried to step up and make it as livable as possible. When I look at that photo, it reminds me of just how present she was in my journey.

Little Flower will always be that place that shaped me. Taught me. Tortured me. I made very good friends, several of whom I have managed to keep into my adult life. Friends like S'thembiso Nzimande – he was number 187 – and Diliza Mbete – he can't remember what his 'prison number' was.

As hard as it was when I look back, I don't blame anybody for the experience. My parents wanted to get me out of Woza Woza. There was a big jump, and it was a big jump into hell. You either stuck it out or you left. It was a jump that I think I needed. I don't think my life would have turned out the way it has if it wasn't for Little Flower and the discipline and hard work. It taught me to be streetwise more than anything.

Those lessons would be so useful later on in life when I ended up being plagued by people trying to control me. The lessons I learnt at Little Flower taught me how to absorb but also how to silently fight back or be a step ahead in terms of understanding and learning what went on in people's mind and what they intended to do.

I learnt how to keep my survival instinct on alert all the time. I don't think I would have managed if I had gone to a softer school.

Maybe the man above knew all of these storms I was going to face and the hurdles I was going to have to overcome later on in life given my career choice. I have encountered people who were very cruel, very crude, very sinister in what they would try to do to offset my career. With that grounding, always being one up on them has helped me a great deal.

4
Saturday afternoons

I fiddled with the knob of my small grey radio, the sound of crackling adding to the expectation of the boys gathered around me. It was just before three o'clock on a Saturday afternoon and we were done with our chores for the day. Everyone had gathered at our favourite spot, the concrete seats that caught the very last rays of the afternoon sun.

The air was as full of static as the radio was as I turned the dial to Radio Zulu. It was derby day and everything was on the line. Chiefs supporters were on one side of the circle, the Pirates boys on the other. The banter and singing were already in full swing. My little radio gifted to me by my father took pride of place in the centre. It was the gateway for us boys, gathered together on a schoolground in Eshowe in Natal, into the brilliant buzz and excitement of Orlando Stadium hundreds of kilometres away. The radio brought football to life. The radio became a stadium.

Koos Radebe's voice cut through the tension. 'Kwesikamaminzela isigodi.' He would transport us to Orlando. As the fans arrived, he would keep quiet, leaving the microphone to pick up the ambient noise. All he would say was, 'Zafika izihlwele.'

GQIMM SHELELE

The fans have arrived. That was powerful.

For the young boys gathered around the radio, our minds went to that big place in Soweto where thousands of football fans had gathered. The screaming, the shouting, the singing. Every kid gathered around that small box was so quiet you could hear a pin drop. But when there was a goal, the victorious boys would run in every direction to celebrate, imagining they were the players on the pitch who were basking in glory. The losers would sulk in anger.

That was the beauty and the power of radio.

In the end, that little grey radio became my protective shield because everyone wanted to listen to it; they made sure that the space was always protected. That's all they wanted and it was an escape and a release for all of us.

My dad realised that football was my real love and he had bought me that little FM medium-wave radio. It had an aerial that you had to yank out and I listened to Radio Zulu, which is now Ukhozi FM.

That's where my love and appreciation for radio began. I could tell you the line-up, whether it was Cyril Bongani Mchunu aka Kansas City or Joshua Mlaba, Malindi kaNtuli; all of those greats then became part of my life and my journey.

On Saturdays we woke up and made our beds in the dormitories, ensuring that the hospital corners on the bed were neat and tidy. We competed in sports like athletics against other schools. It was also a big day for doing cleaning duties at Little Flower.

I would know if he talked about Jimmy Joubert. That he was a white guy who also played cricket; he was a big, tall guy because Koos nicknamed him 'Brixton Tower'. I didn't even know what Brixton Tower was but I knew it was a tower, so this guy must be tall. The descriptions were raw and direct and there was no mistaking what he was describing. Later on in life, when I got to see Jimmy Joubert, I was like, okay, this is the Brixton Tower.

Phillip Mangethe was completely different to Koos Radebe as a commentator. He mainly covered the games in Durban while Koos was in Johannesburg.

If they were playing in Umlazi, Bab'Mangethe would describe that Patson 'Sparks' Banda is keeping goals ngale kojantshi wesitimela. Ujantshi wesitimela is a railway line that heads towards Umlazi hostel. Literally, he was referring to the railway line but figuratively he meant he was keeping goals away from the net.

He used minute details to describe the scene, and he used them repeatedly as he laid the foundation or as he was calling the game before it kicked off.

Koos was about the pace and the hype and the build-up. It was clarity of voice, the description of the players. He would talk about Marks Maponyane's pace and speed. He would describe how Marks was wearing a white wristband that he used to wipe off his sweat, so that became his trademark, 'Go Man Go' Maponyane. He always emphasised the nicknames. 'Go Man Go Maponyane, Go Man Go Maponyane.' Immediately you knew that this is a fast guy, very pacy, can't

If you cleaned the toilets, Saturday was the day when they had to shine. If you were cleaning the verandas or the tarmac or whatever it was that you were doing, Saturday was the day when everything had to be spic and span. Once all of that was done and we had run the athletics races and played football and gone to lunch, the afternoons were for relaxing.

Everybody knew that 3pm was the start of a football game. Everybody would be waiting and anticipating the match. They would make sure that my radio was working and had batteries. They relied on it. There was no excuse for the batteries to be flat.

At two or three minutes to the hour, Koos Radebe would come on. He was really unmatched. He's the one person who made me love commentary. His brilliance shone in the short time that he had to paint a picture.

His descriptions were so powerful; they were like magic. We had no idea what a stadium looked like but it felt like we were in the stadium.

Everybody was waiting for kick-off and then, boom, the game was on. If there was an early attempt at goal within the first minute, the boys would scream and shout and physically push you.

'No, no, you are Kaizer Chiefs, you move away. Hey, Orlando Pirates, no, come to this side. You, you are on the wrong side.'

We formed boundary lines over a radio. Koos would fire away. He described the football players and because radio is the theatre of the mind, I never knew what certain players looked like but I could describe them from the commentary.

touch him, he evades the tackles, jumps over the opponents when they try to slide tackle him.

Koos was a world apart from anybody who touched the microphone. It's best captured in a song by The Winners called 'We Are Number One'.

Radio was boss. I always wanted to be on television doing sport, but I respected radio so much that I never, ever imagined myself being on radio because of the excellence of the people I grew up listening to. I never, ever thought I would walk anywhere near a radio station because all my major heroes were from radio. From a radio commentary point of view, number one was Koos Radebe. Number two, Kansas City. Number three, Joshua Mlaba, Malindi kaNtuli, Bhodloza Nzimande. All of those people were my childhood heroes.

When I was thirteen, I heard that Kansas City was going to be at a music concert in Newcastle with Rebecca Malope and other artists. I begged my parents to go to Newcastle, wherever Newcastle was. So, they made a plan with one of the guys who was a regular taxi operator in the area to take me there. I went and it was almost like a rock star walking in when I saw Kansas City. That is how enamoured I was with him because I really respected his craft. I admired what he did on radio, the entertainment factor, the delivery. I didn't know what radio was supposed to sound like, but whatever he was doing, he was doing it 100% right.

Sundays were also part of my radio journey. On Sundays at 12 midday there was something called *Zakhala Izingcing*. Let the phones ring. It coincided with the church bells ringing at

Little Flower and the nuns had told us that was the time when the angels flew past overhead. On the show, people would phone in, send dedications, and then the main thing would be asking for a particular song. They would ask Kansas City to play a song, and he would play it for them. It was a wow thing. Whatever song you wanted, you asked for it, and he delivered.

Radio was the thing for me all the time.

Television became what I picked up and what I liked and what I mimicked. But radio was way beyond and above impossible. That was where my fascination with radio started – with that small, grey radio my dad bought for me to listen to football.

During the holidays, I went home to Fort Louis. I arrived to find a pile of newspaper clippings that my mother had diligently been keeping for me.

There was an occasional bus that transported people between Natal and Johannesburg. When that bus came through, my parents would get the newspaper, albeit it three days old. My mom and dad both loved reading. We may have been out in the bundus but we loved to read.

The *Sowetan* was a massive publication and it was huge when it came to football. Mom kept the *Sowetan*, the *Sunday Times* and *City Press* for me. Then, whenever I got home for school holidays, I went through the whole stack of newspapers. I put the latest at the bottom and the oldest at the top so I had the chronology of the transfers and news correct. I went through them in that order.

5
Half in, half out at Hilton

At the end of a road eight kilometres from the village of Hilton, on an escarpment above Pietermaritzburg, are large wrought-iron gates.

Behind these gates is Hilton College, which looks northwards across the wide sweep of the Umgeni Valley to the Karkloof Falls on the horizon.

This is the official description of Hilton College, the prestigious boarding school my parents chose for me to attend for secondary education.

The school follows the English public-school tradition and is steeped in history. With its main Cape Dutch-style building, the manicured avenues and vast playing fields, Hilton couldn't have been further from my reality on the farm or in Eshowe.

Little Flower was a feeder school to another high school in Eshowe called Sunnydale, so the expectation was that I would go there. But my father's circumstances had changed and he had begun interacting with other businessmen and his world had opened up. He had been negotiating with the Spar group to come and juice up the little farm store that we owned. He had also been speaking to other businessmen from

My main focus was always on the sports pages and reading and updating my soccer knowledge. I read guys like Sy Lerman, who was also very prominent in the magazine called *Sharpshoot Soccer Mirror*. There was Louis Mazibuko, Sibusiso Mseleku, Molefi Mika and Sello Rabothata. When you saw their names attached to a story then you knew you were in the right zone; they always delivered. They literally educated me in the world of sport, even before I met them. Sbu Mseleku was the journalist who coined the name 'Bafana Bafana' for the national team.

My mother kept those clippings for me religiously and I will always be indebted to her for that.

would ask: 'What is that?' or 'Where is that?' and I would have to describe it.

In 1987 when I started, there were very few black kids at Hilton. The ratio was minuscule and it was a unique experience to be among a handful of black boys at a mostly white school. Three guys were there on a scholarship: Bonga Chiliza, Mzamo Khuzwayo and Khwezi Zondi. It was frowned upon if we spoke isiZulu or another vernacular language. The three of them also didn't have a great grasp of the English language so they were also laughed at and ridiculed because of how they spoke. They were from Umlazi, Kwamashu and Claremont respectively, and they didn't care what white people thought of them. They were academically gifted and I loved that about them. Chiliza and Khuzwayo ended up getting academic ties. Chiliza is a professor of Psychiatry at UKZN and Khuzwayo is a board member at Hilton.

I think about how a lot of similar kids were lost in a system that didn't work for them, but these three were saved and were able to hone their academic talents and become massive successes.

The only boy I knew at Hilton was Diliza Mbete. He had bolted from Little Flower because he and his brother, Bongani Mbete, couldn't stand being there. After two years at Little Flower, they couldn't cope and said this is too much, cheers. The universe reconnected us. Diliza was in my class and Bongani was in the standard above us. At least there was someone I knew who I had already been friendly with at Little Flower. He had gone to the UK in the interim to better his education. They were well-to-do because their father was a doctor in the Transkei. You could also tell from how he spoke that he was more refined and he would chat with the white boys. Meanwhile, I was rough and in the eyes of many of the boys, probably still smelling of cow dung.

Initially, I hung back because there was a lot to take in at Hilton. I don't remember having an immediate friend. I recall making it up as I went along.

Even the dining room was overwhelming. There was all this food and fresh bread rolls and you could dish up for yourself. Having gone from hiding avocados underground to apples being used to decorate the food. I couldn't believe it. Meals were even finished off with a little bit of dessert. It was five-star treatment.

The dining room was also overwhelming because I didn't know anyone. I drifted towards the other darkie kids who were there and started to have conversations with them. There was a black boys' table in the dining room. We tried to find some commonality. The three of them, Chiliza, Khuzwayo and Zondi, were highly intelligent but they were like me in that they didn't really know much about sports except soccer. So, what were we supposed to do?

We found comfort in being together because we were all staying in different houses and involved in different activities, but we could come together at the dining-room table. I was in Falcon House. Khuzwayo, Zondi and Chiliza were in Ellis House. When we got together it was an opportunity to talk about our experiences. We weren't complaining or trying to myself to fit the place. I never felt inadequate to be there. Yes, I felt isolated, especially since I hadn't been exposed to different racial groups in this way.

I also remained a mystery to a lot of the other kids because I never gave them a sense of who I was or what I was about. I was constant in how I did my day-to-day business. I was never trying to be loud or important. I was learning new things along the way and being exposed to new things. I was eating posh food that I had never eaten before. I had been sent to the school and I had to make it work. If I didn't know something, I learnt about it. I wasn't just being educated in the classroom but also outside of the classroom. A lot of the other kids knew about these things. But I never felt inadequate to be there.

First-years at Hilton were called 'Poops'. Like many other boys at boarding schools, the first years were at the beck and call of the matrics. If they sent us somewhere, we had to go. We couldn't walk on the grass; we had to walk on the pavement. We couldn't cut corners around a building. The first-team rugby players would come and throw their dirty rugby boots at us and we would have to clean them. All of these things were foreign to me. I wondered why I had to polish and shine somebody else's smelly boots.

These things would probably have made sense to kids who had brothers in the system or if people had spoken to them about it. They knew what to expect if they were a Poop.

It was tradition but it also felt like they wanted those boys coming in to first year to feel their wrath. As a newcomer to wage war or riling each other up; it was about commonality of experiences and the like.

Hilton had many layers. There was the visual splendour and then there was the deeper reality of it. Once you looked past the superficial stuff on the outside, you had to go deeper into the actual meaning of it. It was a real culture shock for me.

These kids understood each other from a life perspective. They had a shared lived experience.

There were one or two white kids who had also grown up on a farm. I couldn't work out whether they were being condescending or well meaning, but they would come and greet and say, 'Sanibona, ninjani?'

I experienced racism for the first time at Hilton but I didn't know it was racism. Up until that point my only experience of racism had been at the Wimpy in Vryheid, where black people weren't allowed to sit down in the restaurant. You could only order takeaways.

I didn't know what real racism was. I just knew we were all different kids. This was the first time I had to deal with proper white children. There had only been one white kid at Little Flower, but this was the first time I had to live in an environment like that, in the same living space as white boys.

The environment made me feel like I was half in and half out. I was never entirely 'in'. I had to prove myself beyond just to be there. I never tried to force my way or try to make friends. My constant was that I was okay being in my own space. If friends come along, they would come along and if they were genuine then friendships would develop. But I never changed

Skinstad was in the scrum with me and he ended up becoming a Springbok captain.

In a short period of time, I had to learn a sport I had never been exposed to. I was briefed in terms of what I needed to do and, because I was adaptable, I could do it. As long as I wasn't in the water, I was happy. We played well and got good results and I was a regular member of the second team.

There was racism on the rugby field, though. There was always a K-word here and there when we were playing against Maritzburg College and similar schools because they were not really institutions that accepted black kids. When they encountered black kids on the rugby field, it was an opportunity for them to have a sense of rage. They wanted to slap us and sort us out. They were being exposed to what Daddy or Mommy would call a kaffir. You could tell there was a personal vendetta, some extra spice reserved for a game between Hilton and Maritzburg College.

They put in extra effort to pummel you if you were the black kid. There was always a concerted effort to make us black kids feel like we shouldn't be playing the sport.

It was built up into hatred. Rugby is a sport that requires you to be fired up and that extra spice was really race fuelled. I heard other boys talking about how they were targeted or what was said to them at the time. And there was always nothing we could do. What was I going to say? I would just be accused of lying.

It became a talking point for us around the dinner table. We identified who was responsible and then we would have our own little bit of revenge in the return game against that team. We would get payback with a knee to the ribs or give them some extra in the ruck.

The non-angry side of me appreciates the opportunity I had to go to one of the top schools in the country. I appreciate that I had a learning experience that is in many ways second to none. The learning was holistic – both in class and outside the classroom. It required me to keep my eyes open constantly because these were kids who had very privileged backgrounds. They knew a lot about things I didn't know about.

I am appreciative of what my parents had to sacrifice to pay those school fees. And I don't regret going to Hilton. It was extreme going from Woza Woza to Little Flower to Hilton. It was the kind of experience I needed to test me.

My eighteen-year-old self was quiet and reserved; I was just discovering girls, but in love with sport.

I was always the quiet, shy guy and I watched and observed more than I spoke. I found it difficult to try to engage and I think that was almost my shield because the other kids didn't really know how to approach me. I was not unfriendly, but I was protective of my space. I held on to the little pocket of friends that I had. I never pushed anyone away from trying to enter my space or trying to understand what I was about.

Being the quiet, shy kid, I needed something that was going to open me up and studying speech and drama provided that outlet.

Speech and drama helped me work on being more

together forever. So, we did get to know each other's families very well and there was a close connection.

We used to have deep conversations because I don't like shallow chats. We wrote letters to one another. I would buy a chocolate and tuck it into an envelope and add a lyric from a popular Luther Vandross song.

When I left high school, Mbali also went to pursue higher education and we lost contact. But we did reconnect again recently.

When I matriculated from Hilton in 1991, I took the decision never to go back to the school and I have not returned since. I didn't go back for our twentieth school reunion because I wasn't interested. I wasn't bothered. I just thought, stuff it.

Hilton didn't give me what I thought it would. I thought it was a school that would bring people from all walks of life into a shared space. I have thought about it a lot and maybe I was angry at not being able to play football when I would have loved to play it.

So, why couldn't we play football? In the absence of any clear explanation, was the perception about playing football linked to it being a majority-black sport? Sure, kids must be exposed to as much as they can, but also don't suppress people who might have a particular natural sport talent.

As an example, we had Bobby Skinstad, Wayne Fyvie, Hentie Martens and Gary Teichmann at Hilton. They were very good at rugby. But it is equally likely that there would have been other kids who would have been brilliant at football. They

Socially, I found my crew with The Three Musketeers aka The Mooi Boys.

It was my late friend, Aubrey Ndlovu, and Bothata Molotlegi, who is a prince from the Royal House of Bafokeng and me. Bothata was an athlete and he was very fast. He and his brother broke all sorts of records in athletics. We became friends and, with Aubrey, we became known as The Mooi Boys. At socials at St Anne's or any of the other girls' schools, the three of us always tried to look sharp and comb our hair in a certain way. I never really took all that to heart because I wasn't seeking attention or validation. But even today when I bump into girls from back then, they will refer to The Three Musketeers or The Mooi Boys.

My first love was a girl from St Anne's. Her name was Mbali Mthembu and we dated for a number of years. You always remember your first love. She was the first person who I developed any real feelings for. I remember not wanting to go back to school but feeling hopeful because I might have an opportunity to see her at a social.

At the time, I didn't know it was love and I didn't know how to understand or define it. I suppose it was puppy love, but I developed genuine feelings for her. She was very reserved and wasn't trying to be a popular girl. She was a beautiful person on the outside and in her heart. She was well brought up and well mannered. If I think of high school then I think of that relationship.

With first love came the idea that we were going to be

could have played for the national team, gone overseas and had wonderful careers. But a decision was taken that still makes absolutely no sense to me.

Think back to Little Flower and how we all sat crowded around my little radio listening to the football commentary. We were all hooked on the sport but we didn't have the luxury of seeing it being played until much later on television. Our minds were creating the images for us. We were fixated. But we were never given the opportunity to actually play the sport.

I know you go to school to learn, but sport is a major part of this. Kids even get scholarships and bursaries based on how well they play. Hilton gave rugby players from Treverton and Cordwalles and Cowan House bursaries based on being brilliant rugby players. But there was an imbalance with the absence of an opportunity to be given a bursary for being an excellent footballer.

It never sat well with me and still doesn't. I also don't think that, at the time, the parents fought hard enough to give football the prominence it deserved.

Now there is football at Hilton because there was a concerted push for it to happen. Mr Celo Mbanjwa played a key role in driving football at the school and it was Mr Silva Pillay who fought hard for it to be an official sport.

I'm told that it was around 2003/4 when the first low-key games began, but it was only in 2007 when the official current match kit was adopted and it became an official school sport. By 2008 the 1st XI had their own match kits as well.

Businessman Sandile Zungu has poured money into it. In

2019, the Zungu Soccer Stadium was opened at Hilton College. Clubs such as Mamelodi Sundowns and Maritzburg United have gone to train using the facilities at Hilton. But it's been a battle. There was resistance from the board of governors and many of the old boys.

This is why I say that it is a brilliant school, but towards the end of my stay, I questioned many things that helped me to formulate my position. Prejudice had crept into the schooling system and it was not only coming from the kids.

This is why Aubrey and I would literally be told to our faces by a teacher that we would never amount to anything in life. Maybe it was because I didn't understand something in class or we might not have done well in a test, but that was not helpful in building our confidence.

We went to Physical Education and all the kids were swimming, but the black boys would be struggling. Swimming was not something that we did recreationally. I drink water, I wash in it, but that's it. The PE teacher would tell the black boys to dip our feet in the water and to watch, and maybe we could learn from watching.

They could see that we were struggling. What stopped them from ensuring there were swimming lessons for those kids who needed them?

Here I am today, a grown-ass adult, and I can't swim. I can go in the pool, I can walk around in the shallow end. But I can't swim a stroke of any kind because there was an assumption that I wasn't supposed to learn how to.

We do have to place it in the context of the time, in the

early 1990s under apartheid rule. But at the time when I was there, it was a racist school.

My experiences of racism on the rugby field, for example, opened my eyes to the reality of what was going on.

When I reflect, I realise why, when I got the opportunity to be a broadcaster, I really understood the issues around transformation in sport and rugby specifically. The experience of playing against other schools opened my eyes to the treatment that black kids would get.

Later on in life, when I was on radio, we formed the 'The Room Dividers' with Thando Manana, Lawrence Sephaka and the late Kaunda Ntunja to openly talk about transformation and associated issues, and how we could make progress on these issues and move forward. We pushed the minister of sport to focus on transformation because it was not only about quotas. If I had not gone to Hilton College, I would not have really cared about it or taken as much interest in transformation as I did.

I made a point of dealing with issues of transformation by bringing them to the table because I had seen the consequences of a lack thereof and I understood why certain kids didn't get far in sport. It was because those sports were not transformed enough to allow a talented black player to get ahead in life. They messed boys around and moved them from one position to another and they would get completely frustrated, to the point where they wanted to quit the sport.

So many excellent black kids have tried to explore the

talent that God has given them, only to be denied an opportunity simply because they happen to be black. Look at Sandile Nomvete – he was a mightily talented tennis player. He was at St Charles and could have gone and played at Wimbledon or wherever but he was stuffed around. He was exposed to playing tennis, he excelled and he got his colours and represented the province, but then his gift for the game wasn't supported post-schooling. A lot of kids get awarded bursaries or scholarships and that never happened for him. When that happens to a talented kid, they lose hope and the appetite for success. He became a very successful businessman in the end and is now the CEO of a property fund. It's the same struggles of the Serenas, Tigers and Lewis Hamiltons of the world. There's no expectation for you to do well.

Obviously, there has been a huge change in what Hilton is about and there has been transformation in many areas. There are definitely more black kids there now than when I was there. In my time at the school, you could literally count the black kids on one hand.

I have spoken to Bob Skinstad about what things were like then and I think he understood. What I always admired about him was that he was very open and transparent and I enjoyed engaging with him. He was not that kid who would put any prejudice ahead of anything. He spoke very openly.

It was five years of being at a school that contributed a great deal towards foundationally bringing me to a particular place and making me who I have become. It made me highly opinionated the system, it felt like bullying. But these things just happened. I didn't go home and tell my parents what I was going through because it was simply the way things were. I accepted it because I could see all the other first years were experiencing the same thing.

I also felt a degree of isolation because my parents weren't able to come to watch me play sport on the weekend like other boys. Their parents would make the time to come and watch their kids play in a tennis tournament or hockey matches or rugby games. My parents were all the way out on the farm and would have had to drive hours and hours to get there to watch their kid play 40 or 80 minutes of rugby. There was no resentment because I understood our situation. There was absolutely no way that my parents would be able to come to the school to watch me play anything.

One of the harshest realities was not being able to play my favourite sport that I loved and lived for – football. Hilton didn't offer football at the time. I complained bitterly to my parents. How could they have sent me to a school where I couldn't play football?

After all those years of listening to the commentary of games on radio, growing my knowledge from the recordings that my mom had made and reading all the newspaper clippings that she had kept for me, I had been looking forward to going to a high school where I could play the game. It was my main intention.

Then I arrived at this school where football didn't exist.

There had been no negotiation. There was simply no football.

We found a way of playing the game, though. We asked the boys from Michaelhouse because they were a bit more open to it. The Michaelhouse boys formed a team, and the Hilton boys formed a team but we also played with the kids from the local village. It wasn't an option at Hilton College so we had to find another way.

I played rugby and basketball. I also tried hockey because it looked similar to football but with a stick, but that wasn't going to last. There was a lot of experimenting. I would have loved to play squash but all of these things came with expensive equipment.

While the doors were shut to football, I was able to nurture my love for basketball. It developed because there was no other option. In my second year playing for the first team, I was made the captain. I went on and played for the Natal Midlands and was selected to represent the province. It was a dream fulfilled and my prominence at school did rise because I got colours for basketball, which was something I had never thought would be possible. I was always mindful of what I saw as my limitations coming into an environment like Hilton.

My parents were doing the best they could just to get me to school so I couldn't accuse them of not being supportive. If I was gifted and talented at basketball or rugby, I could only show them photographs when I was home and tell them about it.

As far as rugby was concerned, I was a tall, skinny chap and figured out quickly that I belonged in the scrum and should play lock. I ended up playing second-team lock. Bob pavements and all these different houses and gardens that are well maintained. It looked like something out of a fairy tale.

There wasn't a piece of paper or an empty can on the ground. Everything was spotless. It was a massive culture shock. I was too nervous to take anything in and I remember almost nothing about that day.

I didn't know what to expect. To use a sports analogy, I didn't know anything besides football. So, you talk to me about hockey? I don't know what hockey is. Talk to me about tennis? I don't know tennis. I don't know what rugby is. I don't know how to play cricket. I don't know how to swim.

Besides being overwhelmed by the aesthetics and everything I could see in front of me, the English I had learnt at Little Flower was a very different kind of English. It was more slang than English, like our own dialect. We had created words and terminology that ordinary people out there in the world didn't know. 'You know, hey, I'm going pozzy,' and pozzy was home. There were all these words that were thrown in that made no sense in the normal discourse of life. I got to Hilton and now there was a different kind of English being spoken.

Most of the boys had been to Cordwalles or Treverton or Cowan House for primary school. For many of them, it was a family tradition to go to a certain school for primary school and then go on to Michaelhouse or Hilton College. Most of them knew each other from being at the same school or competing against each other in sport.

And there I am coming from the unknown Little Flower. When they asked me what primary school I had been to, they the KwaZulu Finance Corporation and they had been discussing where they were sending their children to school.

They were obviously rich individuals so they had spoken about Thomas More College and Hilton College.

I first went to write an entrance exam at Thomas More. I passed and they were willing to take me, but my dad had heard enough about Hilton to convince him that it was the better option. Anything outside of Little Flower seemed like heaven, but being at Thomas More and seeing the kids playing football really appealed to me. Football was life. But my father chose Hilton.

He said well done for passing at Thomas More, you did very well, they are willing to take you a year early but Hilton is a good, strong Anglican-based school, their results are good and they've got a bigger spectrum of sports and options. I accepted it because I didn't know any different. There was no way I would have known anybody who would have gone to Hilton, considering my background on the farm. I wasn't offered a bursary – it was the farm store that put me and my three sisters through school.

I didn't know anything about Hilton, so my first day was very intimidating. I have a photograph of that first day – I'm dressed in my uniform with my black blazer and black-and-white, striped tie and my mother is walking a step behind me in a beautiful dress. My sister Nomvula was there too; she was the one behind the camera capturing the moment.

It was very intimidating. You drive in and there are these spanking, white buildings and well-manicured lawns and about certain things, and then later on in life I have used the microphone to fight the battles that I know other parents are fighting or other kids who are at the school might be fighting.

I may not have played a role in changing the school when I was there, but I have taken a more holistic view and I see my experiences at Hilton as a tool that has helped me to shape the conversation on a national platform.

I did not articulate it at the time by referring directly to my experiences at Hilton, but they gave me the motivation and context for the broader conversation and battle. For example, when I was asked to anchor the 2007 Rugby World Cup in France for SuperSport, I turned down the opportunity. It was because of my strongly held views about rugby and having to endure five years of the sport. I was also intentional about bringing football to the forefront and giving it more prominence in broadcasting.

At one point I was asked to go back to the school to address assembly. I don't think I even responded to the invitation. I took a very cynical look at it and thought, how dare you make my high school experience something that it wasn't? At Hilton, I was repeatedly told that I was an ultimate loser in life; and we had fun poked at us and we were excluded.

I had forged my way through life, pursuing my career and my talent, and then they found this was an opportune moment to say, 'Oh, please come back, please come and deliver a keynote speech and address us at assembly.'

How am I supposed to feel? Am I then going to submit my

speech beforehand to be verified so that you know what I'm going to speak about? Or are you just going to say, 'Robert is here'?

I understand that I could have used that opportunity to be honest about my experiences. But I didn't think the event, which was the celebration of the school's 150 years, was the appropriate occasion. The honest talk would not have been a sweetheart conversation. I would have had to shake things up and not portray the school in a way that camouflaged the truth. I wasn't going to give the talk that everybody wanted to hear and clap to. Giving me an opportunity to speak now would be an occasion to speak openly about my experiences. It's not about throwing stones at the school. It's about better understanding the time when I was there and unpacking some of the observations and injustices that didn't make sense to me.

6
Broadcasting beginnings

Each time I came home from school for the holidays I was greeted by a pile of recorded VHS tapes.

While I was at boarding school, my mother recorded all the football games for me. We had a poor-quality little television with an outside aerial, but she did her best. I had taught her how to press record, but sometimes a tape ran out and nothing recorded. It was hit and miss.

Every night, as a family, we got down on our knees and my father led us in collective prayer. Once we were finished praying, everyone went to sleep. But I stayed up and watched the games that my mother had recorded for me.

I would literally watch the entire 90 minutes of a game and I was fascinated. If it was Chiefs and Pirates, I watched from beginning to end, and in my mind acted as if it was a brand-new game that was happening live. I got emotionally involved. I got to know the players, and I learnt to understand the dynamics and appreciate the rules of the game. It was my football learnership.

My sister Gugu was also up one night, reading novels, and she saw that I was still awake. She came and sat with me and we chatted about what I was watching. I explained who was playing and she watched for a bit.

She became a regular feature and started sitting through more and more of the football games and asking more and more questions. She got hooked on the sport and her knowledge of the game grew. My viewing became her viewing too. I couldn't start a game without her being there.

On Saturdays, we closed the shop at 1pm, which gave my dad time to watch the game at 3pm. All three of us had a keen interest in what was happening and we watched together. Gugu genuinely became hooked and she developed a passion for sport. She started doing soccer and cricket updates for Radio Zulu, which is now Ukhozi FM.

When I was in high school, my father brought a home a camcorder with a VHS tape that you could pop in and out. I became obsessed with it. If there was a cousin getting married in Klerksdorp or it was my sister's twenty-first birthday, then I was the cameraman.

I recorded the videos and everyone was excited. We all sat and watched and it was a big deal.

This broadcasting thing was hovering around on the periphery of my life.

If I was done helping at the shop and I had free time, I laid out the tripod, mounted the camera, turned it in my direction and took one of the newspaper clippings that my mom had saved for me and I pretended to be a newsreader. The newspaper clipping was my autocue.

I practised reading and then I picked up the last sentence and delivered it to the camera. I was working to get the fluidity right. I would rewind and then watch it back and look at how I could improve. I would try again and correct the mistakes and improve my delivery. I had no one helping me so I had to frame and crop myself.

This was my own personal mission. My sisters weren't involved. I remember once my father walking in when I was in the middle of delivering my bulletin; he just looked at me with a funny expression on his face and walked out.

I wanted to be a sportscaster and I was willing to put in the hours practising, doing whatever it took to make me good enough.

I recorded the audio track onto a TDK cassette on a radio. Then I recorded myself on camera. I got past hating the sound of my voice played back to me and I kept going. Reading and recording and reading and recording. I used the newspaper for content to deliver and then I moved on to the back pages and delivered sports bulletins.

I would play it back and see how close I was to the final product.

My aim was to be as close as possible to what Martin Locke was doing on TopSport or what I saw Ahmad Rashad do on *Inside Stuff*, the NBA basketball show. They both really inspired me and I wanted to be as good as them. I never wanted to imitate Martin but I used his poise, delivery, facial expressions as guidelines.

My mom remembers how I used to obsess over the camera

and how she recorded the games and kept clips for me:

> *He loved the camera. His dad had a big camera that he used to take overseas. He used to go to New York, and he loved jazz and he used to take pictures there. So, Robert would take the camera during Christmas when we were all at home and he would be interviewing everyone. It would be a fun Christmas Day because we're on our own really at Fort Louis. We didn't have neighbours or anybody. We saw other families and other human beings in the shop. I used to record the games and keep them so that when he comes on holiday he'll see all of them as they used to be. It was my way of showing love for him. He was the only boy and I cared for him because I had already cared for the two girls and they were older. So, he is my little only son going to a rough boarding school at that young age. I was feeling for him.*

I had so much respect for radio that I just never thought myself capable of being on air. It wasn't an option. But television was something that I aspired to and I was willing to practise as hard as necessary.

All that practice ultimately paid off in my future. I was unknowingly following the principle described by Malcolm Gladwell of 10 000 hours of practising something to become proficient in it.

All the elements built up over the years. Listening to those stadium and the smells were very pleasant.

One stall was selling skopo, sheep's head, trotters, chicken feet. It was all dripping in cooking oil that had been used a gazillion times. People didn't care. They just wanted to eat and it smelt so good. There was another selling amagwinya and another selling atchar.

The main thing that people really loved was meat. There were big brisket steaks grilling and they were flying out of the stalls. People were eating and drinking. The smell of ganja was thick in the air. You would see a chap rolling a joint in front of you, smoking, passing it on and everyone was jolly and happy.

Sure, there was rivalry, but there was something about the stadium atmosphere that was electrifying. There was anticipation, there was banter back and forth; people insulted one another, but there was no animosity, no fighting.

I could hear the speakers from inside the stadium and I distinctly remember, because I had listened to so much radio, it was the voice of Treasure Tshabalala. Treasure was the MC for the day and he was announcing that the venue was full and couldn't accommodate any more people so those outside the stadium had to head home. He said the game would go ahead but no one else could get in, whether they had tickets or not. It was chaotic because we were trying to leave as instructed, but more people were arriving who were pushing to try and get in.

After travelling all that way, and even having tickets, we ended up listening to the match from outside the stadium. It was heartbreaking. That was my first experience of being at a stadium, but they shut the doors and we couldn't watch the games on my little radio, Mom keeping the newspapers for me, doing the recordings on VHS of the games, practising with the camcorder, understanding the players and building my knowledge of the game.

Sport is what happens – you can't script that. All of the knowledge I brought to my career were things I had learnt between the radio, the newspapers and the VHS tapes.

It all eventually fell into place. It was the realisation of a dream.

When I was in high school, Gugu took me to watch my first football game in Johannesburg. We caught the Greyhound bus from Dundee to watch the Bob Save Super Bowl final between Kaizer Chiefs and Orlando Pirates at Ellis Park. I must have been around eighteen at the time.

We had bought the tickets already but we didn't expect the magnitude of the game. There was the intrigue and allure of going to watch a live game in person as opposed to being a farm boy and always seeing and hearing it from a distance.

Gugu and I arrived at Ellis Park stadium and there were thousands of people outside desperately wanting to get inside. We could hear the noise of the fans; the stadium was packed.

People were dressed in the outfits and overalls of their clubs' colours. They were playing those big longhorns – vuvuzelas were not a thing at the time. There was a lot of singing, groups singing together, faces being painted. There were all sorts of creative designs.

Then there was the food. Stalls had been set up outside the

game. I was so close to the action and wasn't able to get in.

We could hear the reactions from the crowd. It was a weird experience. Thankfully, the game was a draw so they had to replay and everyone who had tickets could come back again. It was a bittersweet first experience for me.

Experiencing the magic of being at a stadium as a teenage boy was special. That close-up experience ignited things in me. I had always wanted to play football. I even believed I would play at Wembley Stadium one day. It wasn't a realistic dream, but being at Ellis Park and experiencing what was going on made me imagine what it would be like to be a football superstar. Imagine having all those people coming to watch you play.

Footballers became idols and the fans were all at the stadium to scream and shout and sing your name. It made me imagine what it would be like to be on the field and have people screaming whatever nickname they had given me. Imagine becoming a hero simply because of your God-given talent to play football.

But I had lost five years of not playing football at high school, so how on earth was I going to skip and run to being a pro? I knew I had missed out on the formative years of acquiring the skill and techniques and just the basics of playing the game, but for a short while that afternoon I lived my dream.

7
University days

When I finished matric, I thought I wanted to become a lawyer. It was a combination of instinct and what I had seen on television. I liked the idea of putting forward and advancing arguments, finding legal ways of defending individuals.

The reality was that I was never going to be a scientist or a historian or a geographer. I had no passion for test tubes or Bunsen burners or working out the meaning of pi. While I was quiet, I loved a good solid argument and putting across a point of view among friends.

I signed up for a law degree at Wits University.

My dream of being a broadcaster never disappeared. It was something I still hung onto. But it didn't occur to me to study journalism. Maybe I was naïve, but I just thought that I wanted to be a sportscaster and be on television.

It was an internal dream and not something that I shared with anybody else, not my mom and dad and not my siblings or anyone. This was my dream. Like all parents at that time and in that era, it would have been difficult for me to explain to them that I just wanted to be on television. I knew that

I needed something that was education driven because they believed strongly in empowering all of us with education so that we could achieve whatever we wanted to.

That's why the lawyer argument worked. It gave me the ability to go study at Wits University and get access to Johannesburg. But I never verbalised to anyone that I wanted to be a broadcaster. They could see that I had an interest from what I was doing with the camera that my dad had bought. They could see that I was recording and filming and doing pieces on camera and they could watch it back. But I never actually articulated it to anyone.

But I never stopped working on the dream. I never stopped recording or reading the old publications. My mom still kept the newspapers for me and I kept practising. To keep the peace in the house I said I wanted to go study law.

It was 1992 and I was excited to move to the city. It was daunting too, arriving in Joburg with its high buildings and everything that came with the City of Gold. I had a little bit of experience, having visited Soweto before with my friend Aubrey, one of The Three Musketeers, who stayed in Orlando West, near the old Maponya supermarket.

That had been my first taste of township life so I had an idea of what to expect and what city life was all about. We used to leave Orlando and go to the city and take a walk down Small Street into the Carlton Centre. There we went to the movies and I saw all these things I had never encountered before. At that age we were so impressionable and that used to be a fashionable gathering place to go check out girls, to have a date and to go to the movies.

My parents wanted me to be in a more structured environment so I went to stay at res at the Ernest Oppenheimer Hall (EOH), which was near the Wits Business School. You had to cross a highway and skim through the back of Jubilee Hall to get to campus, so it was a little walk away.

I was independent, but it wasn't the independence of staying in my own apartment. Arriving at EOH, I had never drunk alcohol before, believe it or not, so I was in for a rude awakening. We were the new kids, the 'freshers', and when you arrive in your first year in a university set-up, you were given a taste of real life.

On the first day the seniors had set up a welcome party. There was this big black dustbin and these guys were emptying bottles of five-litre Autumn Harvest into the bins. They were pouring bottles and bottles in and they were chucking Fanta Orange in with it. They were mixing up a potent concoction.

The first-years were given a plastic cup and we had to go and dip our cup into the bin and take a drink. It was not like I had a choice. We had to do it. I never knew what getting drunk was before that. I never knew what alcohol tasted like and this was my first encounter with alcohol at res and at university.

I remember quite well in the end, when I had to go back to my room I was so finished. I had the key in my hand and I had to go to my room, E10. I just made it up the flight of stairs and kept trying to fit my key into the keyhole and I couldn't open the door. So, I passed out on the floor outside my room. I was done. Other kids were busy throwing up around me; they were all smashed.

I passed out and all I could remember was that the first-years had to wake up at 5am to go on a 10-kilometre run. It was from one extreme to another, recovering from drinking a dustbin full of alcohol and then going for a 10-kilometre run in the same clothes from the night before. That was orientation week.

Fortunately, I was a good long-distance runner, so despite not feeling well and having passed out on the cement floor the night before, I ran and finished in the top two. My reward was more drinks.

Orientation week was crazy. It was a new world. We had been semi-wrapped in cotton wool so that was the first realisation from my side that independence was really kicking in. There was nobody to complain to and this was the new life I was facing. The reality was a rude awakening.

I was carrying on with the journey of studying, which meant choosing subjects and getting into the hard work of university.

For three years, I studied a BA LLB with Film and Drama as one of my majors. It was a strange combination, but one that also spoke to my dream of broadcasting. It also helped to diversify my mind and I got to learn about something completely different to law.

We had excellent lecturers, like the late Maishe Maponya and Professor Zakes Mda. There were people in our class who ended up becoming something major in their careers, such as

Moshidi Motshegwa and Hlomla Dandala. Vusi Kunene and Rosie Motene became big superstars on television after leaving university. That was the calibre of people who were there. That spoke to how good the teaching was, that so many ended up fulfilling their passion and starring in telenovelas and films.

In my third year, the OJ Simpson murder trial started and it really reinforced my desire to be a lawyer. I had a little television in my room and the trial was shown on late-night television on SABC every single day. I was watching Johnnie Cochran and Robert Kardashian and his entire team. I was fascinated and watched all night. I was hooked and I didn't want to miss a single minute.

All the detail still sits in my mind, of Marcia Clark and her delivery. It's like it happened yesterday. That reminded me of why I wanted to do law and I was excited because I was learning first-hand and not from a movie. This was a real-life court case. Of course, the jurisprudence was different in South Africa from that in America but it didn't really matter to me.

I was watching a real wily lawyer in Johnnie Cochran doing what he was supposed to do – defending his client and doing it in a brilliant manner. He was dealing with the jury in the way they were supposed to be dealt with, piecing together the evidence, smashing the prosecution's case left, right and centre. I knew then that I was on the right path and I was doing what I was supposed to be doing. I went into my lectures with more passion and enthusiasm and excitement, knowing that when I graduated, I would be in a courtroom defending people and putting together legal arguments.

My main focus when I was at Wits was obviously to graduate. That was important from a family perspective because that was the expectation. I had been sent to Johannesburg to study law at a premium university.

8
Love for the game

For the first time in my life, when I was at res at university, I had an opportunity to play football. Signing up to play the game I loved was one of the first things that I did. I was finally able to reunite with the game that was taken away from me for so many years.

Here was another chance for me to be a footballer. But I knew that, having not played the game for so many years, I wouldn't be the superstar that I thought I could be. I played in midfield but then drifted into more of a defensive position but I wasn't brilliant at all. I played from a social perspective, knowing I was never going to fulfil my Wembley dream. I played with the guys from EOH against other men's res teams and clubs like the Italian team.

We played at Milpark Stadium and a couple of the guys we played with went on to play professional soccer. I also became friendly with Christopher Bongo, who was a Congolese striker training with Orlando Pirates at the time. He was a friend who had equal passion for the game and somebody I could go to the stadium with to watch live matches.

outspoken. The shy guy needed to move to one side and the more vocal, confident guy who could stand in front of people and talk needed to come out. I had a very good teacher, Mr Geoff Thompson, and I learnt a lot about diaphragmatic breathing and how that helps with speech and projection and pronunciation.

I learnt to find a different space to enjoy and express myself by participating in plays and drama. As I grew up, I was still a shy human being and I was able to enhance myself by getting on stage and doing things with performing arts. By acting out a role on stage I could assert myself.

I suppose subconsciously that was also me preparing myself for a life in a public space. Without that grounding and being able to go on stage and perform all of the plays that we had to perform, it would have been difficult for me. Growing up on a farm, I was not as expressive or confident as I could have been. It gave me the confidence to get up on stage in front of people. It helped to shape me for my broadcasting career.

That was one positive to take away from Hilton, my interaction with Geoff Thompson and how hard we worked. He knew his job. He was not somebody who looked at you and passed judgement. I think he had a job to do and he fulfilled it. He was a happy, jolly person with a deep, rich voice. It made me think that one day I could have a powerful voice like him.

Over time, my mindset changed and I started to engage more in a positive way. I started to do more introspection and look at how I could improve on the sports field or how I could better my results academically. But with interpersonal relationships with other kids, I always struggled. I put on a brave face and I was learning to understand other cultures as I went along.

While I was at Hilton, I got to understand white culture better and gain insight into a few of the Indian kids who were there too. I understood little pockets of these cultures, but I didn't really want to engage in a meaningful way. There were occasions when one of the kids invited me to dinner with their parents. I remember once going to a white boy's house in Pinetown. It was a culture shock. The mother and father and all the kids were sitting around the table and this boy my age said he would have a Castle Lager. I was astonished that he was drinking alcohol with his parents at the table. It was the first time I had experienced this. At home, we went and fetched drinks for the adults but we never sat around a table and asked for an Amstel.

The same thing happened when our housemaster, Mr Strydom, invited us to his house when we became prefects. His wife cooked for us and he asked what we wanted to drink. I was conservative and asked for a Coke. All the other boys were asking for Castles and Amstels and he brought the drinks to them. As I got over my initial shock, I learnt that it was part of an open discourse – their parents would rather they had a drink openly around the dinner table, as opposed to a kid who drank secretly in his room or behind a building, downing a six-pack and drinking themselves into a stupor. It was a culture of learning the art of drinking rather than overdoing it in secret.

The atmosphere in the taxi was crazy from the minute we climbed in at Noord Street. Everyone was dressed in makarapas, scarves or team jerseys. Some were carrying horns, blowing them out the window. I couldn't afford a jersey so I was just wearing a regular shirt. There was no shouting 'short left' because we were all headed to the same place, FNB Stadium. There was so much singing the driver couldn't even play his music.

Some had climbed into the taxi with their Bells or Viceroy – the 'cellular', as it became known. Others had bought their loaf of bread, hollowed out the inside and slipped in a nip to smuggle the alcohol into the stadium. Once inside they would pull out their bottle and have a good time.

There were guys rolling their zols on their laps, getting it ready and prepared for when they climbed off the taxi.

It was a cacophony of colour and action and sound and smell.

Often it was me, my friend Christopher Bongo and another friend Babalwa Mneno who headed off to games at FNB or Ellis Park together. Ellis Park was often more affordable because it was within walking distance of Doornfontein.

If we were heading to Ellis Park, we caught a double-decker bus and stopped at Fontana on the way. Everyone would be walking in the same direction and singing songs and the vibe was electric. Inside the stadium, the noise was just crazy. It's a completely closed stadium so it's so loud.

For years, I had only ever heard or seen the end product on television or radio, so experiencing this in person was always a novelty.

Walking to our seats in the 'extra strongs', I would gasp at the sight of a player like Howard Freeze warming up on the pitch. I had only ever seen him in magazines or on television. Freeze is one of the greatest defenders Kaizer Chiefs has ever had. Because of his defining features, you could always identify him with his semi-afro.

My game started when the players walked on to the field to warm up. I spotted the different characters and referees and looked at what form they were in.

I was like a kid in a candy shop in anticipation of what was to come. Because of my fascination with the game, I noticed every tiny detail. I identified each player, who was fit and who wasn't. It was captivating.

These were people who had been my heroes and here I was seeing them in person. I felt like I knew them personally from following them for so long and here they were, right in front of me.

I had learnt through the descriptions on radio and visualising each of them, what they looked like. I watched the focus and intensity of the warm-up drills. I appreciated that this was the real deal; this is what I had been watching from home all of these years.

I could feel the tension in the stadium. There was an air of anticipation. The players would disappear and return wearing their match jerseys, the referee with the ball in his hand.

Nothing beats what a football game brings to life. I got to experience that so many times and the feeling has never ever changed. Football then was and still is a pure and true religion.

It was an honour and a privilege to be in that space. I knew that I hadn't made a mistake about my love of football. It wasn't a gimmick. It was real and true and genuine.

There was just something about the game that sparked something inside of me.

I think for many black families, it was politics and it was football, and in between there was music. For me it was just about the football on the field.

Later on in life I learnt about the different layers of the game – I grew to understand more about the administration, the public relations, the marketing, the running of the game.

My love for the game changed over the years when I began to see the injustices and the politics of it all.

But in those years, as a fan, my love for the game was raw, naïve and beautiful.

9
Fate or good fortune?

It was the middle of the week and I was studying in my room at EOH. I took a break from the books and switched on Metro FM. Vusi Letsoalo had a midday show at that time and he was broadcasting from the SABC's Auckland Park headquarters. It was a stone's throw away from campus.

All of a sudden I heard he was interviewing Aaliyah.

This was 1994/1995 and Aaliyah was in town. She had just released her debut album *Age Ain't Nothing But a Number* and was doing a PR tour. Her mother was accompanying her because she was only fifteen.

I used to read up a lot on hip hop and RnB. I was always fascinated by the stories of how some of the record companies made it or the Johnson family got to own *Ebony* magazine. I was reading *Right On* and *Word Up* magazines and snapping off posters. As a high-school kid, I put pictures of Salt 'n Pepa and other hip hop stars on my walls.

I knew the story of Aaliyah. She was still then an up-and-coming star, but she had made a bit of a name for herself.

So, when I heard Vusi Letsoalo chatting to her on radio, I

was like, 'What? Are you crazy?'

I knew the SABC wasn't too far away from me so I decided to walk to the studio and go meet Aaliyah in person. I literally just took a walk. There was this human being and I liked her music, I was a fan of hers as an artist and I wanted to do whatever I could to at least be within sight of her. I didn't even know where Metro FM was at the time.

I walked into Radio Park at the SABC and went through the security process to get into reception. I just thought I would try my luck. As I walked in, I saw three people walking out across reception leaving the building. It was Aaliyah, her mom and a bodyguard/driver.

There was one of the greatest young artists in the world at the time and she was walking towards me and I had no idea what I was going to say. It was clear she had not reached super stardom because there was no one else to see her; no one was going crazy trying to get her autograph. Cellphones weren't a thing so there were no selfies. But no one really seemed to know who she was.

They were just casually walking through. Out of respect, I stopped her mother and asked her how she was, introduced myself and told her that I loved her daughter's music, that I had read about her.

I could tell that she was a bit surprised because they hadn't got much traction from South Africans because no one had mobbed them in reception. It was just me who had walked in and come to greet them.

I ended up having an impromptu chat with Aaliyah. She

was chilled. I could tell she had a bit of swag, wearing sunglasses. She was dressed up, but she was very cool. We chatted about her album, what new material she was working on. I hadn't even listened to the end of the interview with Vusi because I had dropped everything and left my room so I had no idea if I was repeating what he had asked.

I realised that I hadn't even brought a pen or piece of paper with to get her autograph. How was I going to prove to people that I had met Aaliyah? I scrounged around in my pockets and the only bit of scrap paper I had on me was an ATM slip. I asked her driver for a pen and Aaliyah signed her autograph on my ATM slip. She scribbled 'Love Aaliyah' in a tiny corner of the paper.

I kept that slip for years in the back of a framed photo. But somehow I lost it over time.

That was my first real encounter with a global superstar.

I walked away surprised that people didn't know who she was. But more so, I was quietly satisfied with myself because I had followed my gut instinct to take the initiative and go find her. I had the courage to approach her. I've never been afraid to approach people because of who they are or their celebrity status.

I've always seen human beings as being all the same. You can be a president, you can be a security guard, you can be anything. You are human. We breathe the same air. We will have a conversation. That has always been my take. If I really feel the burning desire to do something, if it's just to say to somebody, thank you, you've made a difference, we appreciate what you're doing, I would do it.

That was also my first experience of being inside the SABC. Little did I know that soon I would be back in the building, searching not for a superstar singer, but for my own dream to be fulfilled.

In the early 1990s in South Africa, there was an advert on television and in magazines for a really popular soap brand. The face of the soap was a drop-dead gorgeous woman. Damn, she was so beautiful, the kind of beauty you would fantasise over, almost like a Naomi Campbell. Just wow! I would flip through *Pace* or *Drum* magazine and I would come across this advert and be mesmerised by her. She was a woman I dreamt about being with one day.

By the time I moved to Joburg and went to res, I didn't have much experience with women, having only had one relationship in high school. I was nineteen and open to exploration!

As a side hustle as a student, I joined Bon Models, a modelling agency in Joburg. I was told that I should do it so I gave it a try. I was at varsity with Paul Phume and we played basketball together. He was with Bon and went on to make it as a male model; he became Mr South Africa and Mr Carlton Centre. There was a trend of men doing this and entering pageants. So, he encouraged me to do it. I wasn't interested in becoming a Mr Something-or-other or doing pageants, but I was interested in getting some side gigs.

I signed up and took taxis to castings when I could and I began to get some work.

On one of the first castings I went to, I was still inexperienced and wasn't quite sure how everything worked. I walked into a reception area and saw quite a long queue of models. Everyone had a number that they had been given. I was trying to work out what was going on and looked around for someone to speak to.

I turned to my left and sitting there on the side was this magnificent woman. My God, I thought to myself, it's her. What on earth was happening? It was the soap ad lady! Right before me. My eyes were popping out.

I greeted everyone, including her, and asked somebody to help me with what was going on. She was a megastar so she didn't really need to speak to me. I sat down, awaited my turn as everyone went in one by one. I couldn't stop thinking about her. It was like my spine was sweating. No, this can't be. I was in total disbelief and kept looking in her direction. I just never thought I would ever meet this person or see her in the real world. Here she was literally metres away from me.

They called my number and in I went, thinking that by the time I came out of my casting, she would be gone and I would probably never see her again. I had lost my opportunity to even speak to her. I can't even remember how the audition went because I was so distracted.

I walked out the casting room and, to my surprise, there she was, still seated in the same position. She was waiting for a friend to finish their audition. I was so shy but I had to seize the opportunity. I somehow found the courage and confidence to go over and greet her.

I was expecting a negative reaction because she was such a superstar. But we started chatting. I told her that I was new to castings and told her that I had seen her ads on television. I was so tongue-tied and I didn't really know what I was saying, but she wasn't dismissive at all. She was actually listening to me.

It didn't even occur to me to ask her out. I was so spellbound and speechless, in awe and admiration of her. I was happy with just having met her. I was even happy to walk away and never see or talk to her again.

But she asked me how she could contact me! No one had cellphones then, so I told her we could meet up again some time and she could phone the call box in the res. She gave me the number of the apartment where she was staying at the time.

It was such a magical and surreal moment. I didn't care if I never went to a casting again in my life. Imagine admiring a Naomi Campbell from afar, then going to Europe and the first person you bump into is her. She actually gave me the time of day and we exchanged numbers and had a chat.

I didn't tell anyone about it. It was just internal jubilation. I think my internal organs had turned inside out. For two days I played it cool and then I called her. I didn't want to come across as being overwhelmed by having met her.

We agreed to meet for coffee at Three Sisters in Hillbrow. That was *the* place at the time. It was a swanky, cool spot with chairs on the pavement, opposite Alex Hair. I wasn't sure I could even afford a teabag. We sat, chilled, talked. She had a glass of wine and smoked. We actually connected. She was the most strikingly beautiful woman I had ever encountered, with or without make-up on.

There was chemistry and energy. I could sense that there was attraction on both sides. But I also knew my chances were slim. I was a nobody and she was a superstar.

We agreed to meet again and she suggested that Friday that we go to the Holiday Inn in Hillbrow. We could chill there.

I was trying to contain my excitement. I headed back to res and my feelings were shooting through the roof. I was about to hang out properly with this person I had been admiring through a television set.

So, the day approached and Friday came and I took my excited self to Holiday Inn. We sat in the restaurant chilling and relaxing. Little did I know that she had booked into the hotel.

She suggested we go and chill in her room. And that, ladies and gentlemen, was the beginning of the end.

My head was spinning. To this day I don't even remember the detail. But the gorgeous soap ad lady, who I had been admiring all this time, was the lady who took my virginity from me.

It really was a Jim comes to Joburg moment. I wasn't experienced enough to even know what a box of Durex was about or how it should be used. She was very kind and gentle, but I'm sure she realised that this one is wet behind the ears but trying to disguise it.

I think in the end there was a genuine connection. But it

was obvious that she was older than me and more experienced in her life journey.

I saw her again a few times and then her career took her overseas a lot. She would occasionally get in touch when she was back in the country. We had a mutual respect for one another. I have no idea where she is today or where her career has gone.

But this was a crazy thing to happen to me. A lot of what happened to me in terms of what I aspired to do was just presented to me. I don't know if it was karma or fate, or if it was me just going after what I wanted and aspired to. I'm quietly spiritual and the things that I desired when I was far away were coming true in Johannesburg. Including the person who took my virginity.

That experience with the soap ad lady definitely gave me confidence. I also did more and more castings and got to know some of the select models that were really making it in the country. I was literally a nobody in Joburg and suddenly all of these things were happening for me. Maybe it was fate, maybe it was God listening to me. But things were happening.

10
Simunye, we are one

My main focus when I was at Wits was obviously to graduate. There was a heavy workload and it took its toll, but it never dampened the notion of becoming a lawyer. I kept that focus and still had the fascination with breaking down cases, how evidence was gathered, how a defence was built and representing an accused.

In my final year of my degree, I was awarded a scholarship to continue my studies in the UK. It was called the 1820 Settlers Foundation Scholarship. The idea was that I would go and study entertainment law abroad, which was a balance of my two parallel aspirations of being a lawyer and doing something within the television and sports space.

There weren't many entertainment lawyers in the country at the time and I thought there was a need, considering how many artists end up being poor at the tail end of their careers. I wanted to focus on their plight and their well-being and how to secure life after fame. I imagined I could represent sportsmen and musicians.

I was halfway through my final year and I only had a few half-year courses left to qualify and finish my degree.

But on the backburner I was still stoking the fires of broadcasting. Radio wasn't an option for me because it just seemed beyond me. I didn't even join the campus radio station, although I would listen to Voice of Wits (VOW) in the canteen.

I was still practising with my dad's video recorder when I went home. It was a bulky thing that I had to strap over myself and work with a tripod so I couldn't take it with me to campus. I would go and be the cameraman at family events or at church.

My fascination with sports on television continued. I watched TopSport with my idol Martin Locke and learnt from him and how he anchored. I watched how he engaged the experts, seamlessly transitioning, drawing information out of them. I watched *Mabaleng* and how at halftime in a football match, they broke away to horse racing at Turffontein, which I always found a bit strange.

I just watched Martin closely – he had so much power and knowledge and charisma and creativity. Sports is not staid and serious like the news. It gives you the latitude to put your personality in the forefront and on display.

I always thought Martin was a great master of that. I learnt so much from just watching him as a viewer, consuming what he put out. It all inspired me, driving me closer and closer to doing what he did.

I wanted to be a sports presenter at the SABC.

So, one day, towards the end of my degree, with my future on a scholarship to the UK set out, I saw an advert pinned to the notice board in the canteen at Wits. It was a flyer looking for presenters at the SABC.

There was a problem, though. The deadline for tryouts had passed. My heart sank. I had missed my opportunity by one day.

It was 1996 and there was only TV1, TV2, TV3, CCTV and NNTV. The SABC decided to reorganise its three channels to make them more representative of different language groups. It was two years since the democratic government had come in to power and the net effect was to reduce Afrikaans as a medium.

The new channels that were launching were SABC1, SABC2 and SABC3.

The main driver across all three channels was the revolutionary introduction of continuity presenters. Every station was going to showcase the imaging of that particular channel and they were hoping that the presenters would be superstars and they would be a mix of young, funky-looking people to shore up each channel. They wanted specific language speaking people on each of the channels.

The advert that I had seen was for continuity presenters for these new channels.

Between the adverts for DJ Oskido playing at a men's res that weekend and a search for a newsreader at VOW, or whatever was topical that week, was the flyer for the SABC needing presenters.

I couldn't believe that I had missed the chance and auditions had closed the day before. I often didn't pay any attention to that notice board so it was just by chance that I had taken a look.

I wasn't completely disappointed or disheartened because I knew I was going to try anyway. I was going to go and present myself at the SABC and try my luck.

'To hell with this, I'm going,' I told myself. I wasn't sure what I was hoping to find or gain because I could see that the tryouts were shut. It was game over. But I took a walk to the SABC anyway.

I presented myself at the television reception and asked them where they were holding the auditions. The woman at the counter confirmed that the auditions had closed. I paused for a long time and asked her if she was sure. Was she sure, sure, sure? Did they really have the people that they wanted?

She told me that a lot of people had been in and out all week, coming for auditions, and she was certain that the producers had found who they were looking for.

I was taking my time, hanging around, and a woman who had worked on the auditions was walking past and overheard our conversation. She had come to the reception desk to sign someone in and could hear what we were talking about.

This woman asked me if I was there for an audition and what language I spoke.

I told her that I spoke isiZulu and English. She introduced herself as Celeste and told me she had been conducting the auditions. What a stroke of luck or good fortune or Godly intervention!

She said that last she checked that morning, they had been struggling to fill some gaps and one of those was a male who could speak isiZulu and English. She asked if I was able to wait and if I was in a rush. Of course I wasn't, so I sat myself down.

Thirty minutes later she came back and the stern look on her face from earlier had been replaced with a smile. I could tell that I was a lucky bugger. They still had a gap.

Celeste had asked the crew to set up in studio so I could come through for an audition. She asked if I had read an autocue before. No, I had not. I had never done any work on television.

The technical guys set up the cameras and the autocue and Celeste took me through to the studio. I followed her through the long corridors of the SABC, my heart pounding. I was in disbelief. I could see one or two familiar faces that I recognised from television, a newsreader or a presenter.

This was the closest I had ever been to realising the dream. This was the headquarters of television. The SABC was the broadcast hub. This was what we consumed nationwide. I was walking where Riaan Cruywagen had walked for many years.

It dawned on me as I was following Celeste what the magnitude of this was. I was just hoping and praying that I would be able to do something that they would be happy with. This was an opportunity of a lifetime.

We got into the lift and I couldn't focus on what was going on. She pushed a button and I was just thinking, where am I going, will I be up to it, could I do it? Could this shy guy come out of his shell and deliver what was expected of him?

Finally, we walked into the studio and a controller, Bheki, was running the desk in the control room. There were monitors and feeds coming in and it was impressive. I greeted a few other people who were there. There was a camera and a chair.

The studio was lit up. Someone came to mic me up and sat me down on the chair and I was briefed. They told me the vision for SABC1, that it was going to be a young, funky, energetic, trend-setting station.

I was just a student wearing normal clothes, jeans and a loose shirt. I wasn't a fashionista and have never been about labels or designer wear.

They explained the whole process of the autocue and how it all worked. They finalised the script, included my name, and ran through it with me. It was half isiZulu and half English. It was written to accommodate for dual presentation. 'Welcome to the brand-new SABC1 channel. Welcome to Simunye.'

The rest was a blur because I was so nervous. They handed me the dongle that controlled the autocue. It was a little string with a black knob at the top. I checked through the script and told them when I thought I was ready.

I could hear Bheki asking Celeste if we were ready for the first take. She said they should record. She was in the studio directing and taking instructions from the controller.

Boom. I did it in one take.

They looked at each other and said should we do one more? Bheki said he didn't think it was necessary. Celeste walked into the control room and said they would take the recording to Keith Pfeiffer, who was in charge of the rebrand and conceptualising the launch of the new channels. He was the one who would make the final call. He was responsible for the fine balance of making sure that there was a presenter of every gender and race and it was all mixed.

Celeste asked how she could get hold of me and I told her there was a call box on my floor at res. I told her to ask for Robert at J10 and I gave her an estimated time during which I would be available. They were getting closer to the launch date and the only space that was left was this one, so there was urgency to get it finalised.

She walked out and I left the building, making the walk back from the SABC to res. I was overwhelmed, excited and nervous. It was the first time I had been in the studio. I had actually been in the space where the magic happens. Whether I clinched the job or not, I had a taste of the thing that got me excited. I was in the space that I had always dreamt of being in. Even though it was a tiny studio with just a chair and lights and an autocue.

The big question was, would I be a part of it going forward?

Celeste and I had agreed on the best time for the following day that she should call me to give me the good or bad news. I thought I would be having a sleepless night, but the call came in later that afternoon.

I was in my room at res and someone knocked on my door and told me I had a call on the phone box.

Keith had made up his mind.

'Welcome to SABC1!'

Keith had watched the audition and didn't even hesitate, she told me. He was convinced that I should be part of the line-up. He wanted me to launch with Camilla Walker, who was bilingual in English and isiZulu.

I had a foot in the door of my bigger dream of being a

sports broadcaster, but I wasn't even thinking of that. I had this immediate development to deal with.

What had I got myself into? I hadn't even spoken to my mom or dad or sisters. I was just going about my achieving my dream of being on television and doing sports. I was potentially going to be on television for something else.

How would my dad feel about this? He was very strict and I had a law degree to finish. I also had a commitment to the 1820 Settlers bursary scholarship that I had to fulfil. I needed to graduate so that bursary could kick in. Would my dad warm up to the idea? I was confused and wasn't sure I had done the right thing.

I had gone about it all very quietly and I didn't share the news with anybody. Not even the other kids at res or my friends. This was my journey. I just walked back to my room from the call box. I was beyond excited about the possibility of something new. I was going to be a part of a new innovation and a new journey. There had never been anything like this in the country.

I was cautiously excited though, because I was still worried about having to phone home. I'm not one to get overly enthusiastic or disappointed; I'm always lukewarm, somewhere in the middle.

Deep down inside I had a feeling of contentment. I had made the right move. I was getting closer to what I wanted to do. It was a step in the right direction towards achieving my bigger goal.

We were all gathered together, this group of us who had been selected to be the faces of Simunye as continuity presenters. A great deal of thought and consideration had gone in to how we would dress, what music would be played, what the look and feel would be. There would be monthly promos promoting us so those had to be planned.

Keith Pfeiffer knew exactly what he wanted. They had paired us up with other presenters and they explained how the launch would run. The clothing would be supplied and we would have to match with our partners too. Everything had to be crisp and sharp. This was television.

I was just ready to get on with the job and see where it would take us.

But, first, I had to tell my parents. I decided that my mother was the safer option to talk to. She was supportive of what I was doing but there was a concern that it was going to disrupt my studies. She didn't want me to give up the varsity work. I assured her that it would not disrupt varsity and I would work shifts around lectures. Mom gave me her full support.

I did have to speak to Dad before the launch happened. I couldn't let him find out by seeing me on television. We had an uncomfortable conversation on the phone. He explained that he was paying a lot for university, that I had a scholarship to honour, we had already shaken hands and signed the contract. I told him this was something I wanted to do; it was the beginning of a journey that would create a career for me. I told him that I knew he was disappointed and irritated but he had to try to trust me.

He didn't object and tried to lend support. So, I had the green light to go ahead.

The launch was at Gallagher Estate and it was a huge event. I was nervous as hell. There were millions of people watching. This was to be an enormous turnaround of the SABC's properties. There was a great deal of expectation because it had been hyped so much. Keith was a marketer extraordinaire so there had been so much coverage in the newspapers and magazines.

I had to manage my nerves and the butterflies. I created an imaginary family in my mind to speak to. There was a father and a mother and a sister and these were the people I would be talking to. I couldn't think about the millions of people who would be watching. I would lose it. I couldn't mess up the journey before it had even started.

Fortunately, Camilla and I had struck up a lovely rapport. She had worked on Radio Zulu before and she was a novelty because she was a blonde, white lady who grew up in KZN and spoke isiZulu fluently. We shared stories and she told me about her experiences. 'Oh, yes, I knew Kansas City' and 'Ey bengimazi Kansas. You know, I knew him. And he was so kind to me. I knew Joshua Mlaba, yes, I knew Malindi kaNtuli,' and she was rattling off all these names of radio personalities that I was in awe of. I'd never met these people. That became a beautiful hook because here was someone who had access to all these guys.

There was also just great energy between us and we found a commonality that centred us and we trusted each other. She was just a very easy-going person and she laughed a lot. If she made a mistake, she just laughed it off and moved on.

So here we were, ready to go. The world was waiting. We had to carry the broadcast.

For the opening link, Camilla and I had worked on the script together. We had changed a few things and we would alternate between English and isiZulu. We had rehearsed and we were as ready as we could be.

We had double checked, double rehearsed, triple rehearsed, quadruple rehearsed. We were getting a flow; we had established an energy. We had our earpieces in. We were watching the monitor.

The countdown began. My back was soaked with sweat. I felt like I had been in the gym for an hour. Adrenaline pumped through me. I was trying not to show it on camera. I was trying my best to be cool, calm and collected.

We went live and then we were done! All I remember hearing at the end of the first link was people clapping in the control room. We hadn't messed up. We were done and it was out there. We just sat back in the chairs and recovered for the next fifteen minutes. We were just taking it all in.

My mother was excited. She was genuinely emotional about it. My father, despite the initial hesitancy, was very proud.

He was trying to stay firm that I should finish my studies and get an education, but he was proud that the Marawa name was on everybody's lips and people were talking about it. I could see that the pride was there.

I felt that I was finally on the journey I wanted to be on. I will always remain grateful to Keith Pfeiffer for giving me that chance. He guided me and polished me so much, told me where to tighten up. He had a great deal of faith in my potential and he was able to work with a raw farmboy student who had come to Joburg. He had the patience to get the best out of me and give me the confidence to believe I could do it.

I had been given a massive opportunity and my journey was underway.

11
Finding fame

We had absolutely no idea at the time how the concept of continuity presenters would explode. In a way, we were the first batch of on-air personalities that achieved celebrity status in South Africa. It was something new that hadn't been tried before and it gained us almost instant fame because of how well marketed it was. We were in people's homes and our faces were in magazines on a daily basis. We were all given some form of profile. It was on a crazy scale. It really was a frenzy.

It was aspirational. We portrayed what other kids aspired to be, almost in a modern-day Instagram famous kind of way. People wanted to associate with us.

We couldn't go to a shopping mall without people rushing out of stores to come and cheer at us. People wanted to hug us and shake our hands and get us to sign body parts. Going to a restaurant wasn't the same any more. Managers came and gave us special treatment. It got to a stage where people instantly recognised us. Life changed in many ways. It was really madness. We were on posters on people's walls. What I had been doing with posters of Aaliyah, people were now doing with us. We were being asked to attend events and to appear on *Selimathunzi*. We would go to Sun City to record Simunye promos as a group. We did music videos. We danced the Macarena. We recorded 'African Dream' surrounded by candles. There was nothing we didn't do.

Naturally, I'm fairly reserved and not one to be on a popular platform so I felt exposed. It felt invasive in a way, like I wasn't being given space. But also, as a young person, I was excited by the recognition. I also appreciated how proud people were of me, particularly based on my background coming from eNkandla, and from a farm. People said to me that they never thought someone coming from rural KZN could become as famous as me. That was overwhelming.

My friends were mostly mature enough to understand. You get friends that either understand or don't. Friends invariably were supportive, but it takes its toll because it gets to be a little bit too much hanging around and waiting while people ask for photographs or autographs.

I was never rude and dismissive of fans. I've always wanted to give of my time and space and, in the industry, it requires a level of patience. I know other people are very rude and they dismiss their so-called fans, but I've never been that way inclined because I always see it as losing nothing by giving 30 seconds of my time to take a photo, to make somebody's day and I'm happy.

I was also a kid who wanted to meet the Kansas Citys of this world. And I would have given my left leg to do so. I would have given my kneecap. I would have given anything to meet

Kansas City, to take a photo with him. Now here is somebody who feels the same about me. How can I dismiss someone like that?

The social media and digital space wasn't what it is today. There were fan letters written to us that arrived in the post. Women inserted photos of themselves and offered their phone numbers and asked to meet. It was overwhelming again because I couldn't believe people would take their time and energy to do that. They were probably just taking their chance as well. Shooting their shot.

I never really took advantage of women throwing themselves at me. I've always said I love to work hard for what I get. So, as a so-called typical man, it was ideal to be a hunter as opposed to just somebody throwing themselves at you. And then what happens afterwards? You know you haven't worked hard for it, or you haven't been given the run-around for it. That is more meaningful than somebody who just throws themselves at you. There might have been situations where it looked tempting because the person was a pretty lady, but I never took advantage of that because I always knew there would be repercussions.

I started to go to more events and parties and there was a culture of having a couple of drinks. I would have a cider because I always thought whiskey or brandy was something for older people in the household. That's what my uncles would drink. I always shied away from that because I thought it was not for me. So, it was Hunter's Gold or Bernini. I realised that if I drank too much I would be sick, which was never a great feeling, so I drank minimally.

But the nightlife crept in through my very good friendship with Prosper Mkwaiwa. He was originally from Zimbabwe but came to live in South Africa. Most of my friends around that time were from Zim, because when I arrived at res from KZN I was confused about language. There were people speaking Sesotho, Setswana, Xitsonga, Tshivenda, you name it, and despite my dad being Tswana, I couldn't communicate with people who didn't speak isiZulu. So, my default friends were those from Zim who could speak isiNdebele, which is similar to isiZulu.

At res they probably thought I was from Zimbabwe but it didn't bother me because I was able to communicate, share jokes and have common things to talk about with my group of friends.

Prosper and I connected and he became a very good friend and confidant. He had a car so he would pick me up from res on weekends and we went out. He also had access to funds; he had the currency, so we went to parties and events.

He introduced me to what was then the Hillbrow nightlife. There was a predominantly coloured nightclub called Pink Cadillac, then there was Razzmatazz, which is where the likes of DJ Oskido played and where Boom Shaka was formed. Within the Razzmatazz set-up, Oskido then spotted these kids, Junior, Theo, Thembi and Lebo, and then we saw right in front of our eyes how Boom Shaka was born.

I love music. I'm not a dancer. So, I did a lot of sitting, watching, just observing. I loved to watch people jazzing at

Pink Cadillac and the live performances at Ground Level, where artists like Dr Victor would play. We were in such close proximity to the artists and they were accessible to us.

Prosper grew in the music industry as a promoter and he was taken up by the bright lights of Johannesburg and had a desire for 'celebritydom'. He was Mr Party Man and our friendship grew over time too. He knew where everything was happening and I tagged along. My growing prominence also worked in his favour. He dated Tina Jaxa, who acted in *Generations*, and I got to know other people in the industry through him. He ended up dating Kelly Khumalo and I got to know her; we were from similar backgrounds in KZN and I got to know her sister Zandi.

I'll be very honest; I never took drugs at all. The thing I feared the most was just a simple cigarette. My friends smoked zol or cigarettes, but I could never start smoking. I feared becoming dependent on it.

The party and celebrity life never took over for me. I had read a lot about the rise and fall of sportsmen and celebrities. I had been watching and learning and didn't want to fall into the same trap. I still had a dream to fulfil. I wasn't going to let the so-called fame go to my head because I wasn't yet doing what I wanted to be doing.

I still wanted to fulfil my dream of anchoring sport in South Africa. That was it. So, that was my driving point. That was what I helped to shield me from anything else because I was not overly excited by telling people that the news is coming up next because they knew that the news was coming up next. I always knew that I don't want to just be a continuity presenter.

Meanwhile, I was spending more and more time working at the SABC growing my broadcasting career and less and less time on my studies.

I was a couple of half-year courses away from finishing my degree. I never just woke up and decided I'm going to drop out. I think I tried to balance the two, but it became quite clear that I was never going to conquer the juggling act. The demands on the television side became more, the demands on my time to go and shoot and be available increased, and then we did roadshows that required travelling.

It was gradually peeling away from university and studies. But there was still the question of the scholarship. I was supposed to go do an entertainment law degree as a postgraduate student in the UK. Obviously, that wasn't going to happen. But everything had been confirmed.

The only way I could spin it to my parents was that I had an opportunity to get first-hand practical experience by being involved with this opportunity that had been presented to me at the SABC. Once I had learnt about the intricacies of the industry, then I could go to the UK and study entertainment law and understand the theory behind it.

They bought it because in the end they had no choice because the process was already underway. They were also swayed by the response from family members, cousins, uncles, nephews, nieces who were proud of my newfound fame.

My mother recently found the letter I had sent them titled 'Dear Parents' in which I told them about my decision to pursue a career in broadcasting. She recalls:

I don't remember well how I took it at the time, but to me, I think as long as something is permanent and will put money on the table or, as they say in English, bread and bacon on the table, I don't think these days you mind. In our day, it was either a teacher, nurse, lawyer, bookkeeper and so on. And now remember, there was no television in South Africa with the old Afrikaans government. They didn't want it because they didn't want us to learn too much what's happening on the other side of the world. So even then, as a parent, all you want is permanency for your child and that he is able to get something of whatever he chooses to do. That's how I saw it, but I don't know how my husband took it. I think he liked it because later on he would phone into the radio station and change his voice!

They were equally proud of the family name, especially from my father's side, gaining countrywide exposure. Now they knew that there was a Marawa who is in this industry. That made it difficult for them to be hard on me because they were equally supportive but also equally proud to see what was happening.

I always promised that I would finish the degree because it was already something that they had spent money on to put me through the first three years.

I regret not finishing it and I still want to finish it. I really do. It's like driving from Joburg to Durban and then you off-ramp at Mariannhill but never actually get to Durban.

I needed half a year to put all those half-year courses together, but the problem was continuity presenting was just the tip of the iceberg.

My broadcasting career was about to take off and I wouldn't just be introducing soap operas and news bulletins. The world of sports was about to open up for me.

12
Nation builder

It was 1996 and South Africa was just a few years into returning from sporting isolation. On the back of the magic of the 1995 Rugby World Cup victory for the Springboks, Bafana Bafana had made it through to the final of the Africa Cup of Nations in our own back yard.

My friends and I had managed to get tickets for the final at FNB Stadium and it was like a dream come true. Just being in the stadium watching the game live was special to me.

I was already a continuity presenter for the SABC, but I wasn't in the sports world yet. The idea was to become the sports anchor for the broadcaster, but my genuine love for football meant that I had to buy tickets myself.

The first AFCON game I had been to was SA versus Ghana and the stadium had been packed. The game was sold out and our group of friends sat on the upper tier of the half-finished FNB Stadium. It was incomplete and it didn't go all the way around yet, so we sat on the very top bit. We were just grateful to be able to see top-level football being played.

Every time I went to the stadium, it gave me more of that feeling of wanting to be in that space where football and broadcasting happened. It was a memorable game purely because it was the first time I was watching the skills of the late John 'Shoes' Moshoeu, who played the game of his life that day. The Ghanaian team, with their many superstars, were outplayed. Moshoeu was showcasing not only his general speed, but his skills, and we were just all in awe of how he managed that game and how we played generally as a nation. We were singing and shouting and screaming from the terraces. It was the most memorable game building up towards the final.

The final was a great spectacle because it was a final, but it wasn't the kind of quality of game that we had played against Ghana. Usually, finals are measured. Players don't want to make mistakes. There's very little of that flair you see in earlier games.

But the atmosphere was that of a cup final. This time around we were not sitting at the top. We managed to get tickets behind the goalposts, not ideal in terms of watching an entire game but it was closer to the action because we were five rows from the front. But I was in the stands. No VIPs, no suites. I had no access to any of those things. We were just buying normal general tickets. I didn't know what that VIP experience was about. For me, being able to watch these games that I had visualised as a youngster, listening to the radio and then eventually being able to watch on television, was a luxury.

Just being present at the stadium, regardless of where I sat, was an honour for me. I had no qualms because I had not been exposed to sitting in VIP stands. It was magic being so close to the players.

The magnitude of winning AFCON was enormous. It was the early days of the formation of a national team. The team had gone through a terrible phase before. They called it the 'four-by-four' days where they were being beaten 4-0 by the Nigerians and 4-1 by the Zimbabweans.

To get to the final of the Africa Cup of Nations was special because we were hosting the tournament. We had home-ground advantage and we had very, very good players. It was no surprise that the bulk of the players that played in the '96 squad went and got lucrative contracts to play in Turkey and other overseas countries.

Helman Mkhalele aka Midnight Express, played for several Turkish clubs; so did Fani Madida, Steve Komphela and Teboho Moloi. It was a whole lot of players that left to go play. Turkey was the place where South Africans went and experienced playing abroad so that when they came back they were more complete players. You could see it.

It was incredible being in the stands and watching Shoes Moshoeu, one of the best players ever to don the captain's Bafana Bafana jersey. Then Mark Williams coming off the bench to score the two goals to win the game. (I gave him the nickname of the Nation Builder because it was a moment that really brought the nation together.) The skilful Doctor Khumalo provided the assist for Mark Williams.

It was typical South African football, the way it should be played. There was class in that team under the leadership of Neil Tovey.

Because South Africa was emerging from isolation and

getting the knocks that we got initially, we needed to play our best. We were evolving, still getting used to international exposure. I know people dismiss the whole Rainbow Nation notion, but it worked out that way because that team basically had all nationalities in it. It was not something that was planned. It was just the best players at the time who fitted the criteria to be playing for the national team. Those were players we would have loved to watch on any given day. We saw the emergence of Lucas Radebe and Chippa Masinga, who went on to play for Leeds United. That was significant because Radebe ending up at Elland Road and captaining Leeds United in the English Premier League is massive. We had two of our best players really shining in a foreign country. They took the opportunities and used their talents to come out of poverty. I always say we don't use football enough as a way of poverty alleviation.

Here was a clear example of players who were using their talents to do that. It was a fairy-tale story. Shaun Bartlett went to Charlton. Mark Fish went to Lazio in Italy. All of these men were players of a very high pedigree and regard, and they were getting all of these lucrative contracts to play overseas in highly competitive leagues. It was a special time in South African football.

Being in the stadium watching Bafana win that final, the atmosphere, the victory, things started to evolve for me. I watched the trophy presentation and saw the world leaders who were present there. Nelson Mandela, King Goodwill Zwelithini, the minister of sport Steve Tshwete, who I had read about and seen on television – and there they were, right in front of my eyes.

That victory had so many different layers. It was a critical stage of a country in transition. It had a lot of meaning.

I was absorbing all of this and the celebrations and the trophy and looking at it from a country perspective. Madiba was so loved and, in that photo of them with the trophy, everyone scrambled to be as close to him as possible. In the build-up to that win Madiba had spent a lot of time with the team at their hotel and addressed the players by their names. That meant a lot to them. That was true leadership.

Him being there for the trophy and for the presentation and by wearing the team jersey, as he had done for the Rugby World Cup the year before, he was able to replicate that. He was a consistent leader, a caring leader, but also a leader of winners. You can't help but juxtapose that with what Fikile Mbalula later called 'a bunch of losers'.

Madiba was cultivating a whole legion of winners and leadership was very critical. I also always looked at Steve Tshwete as arguably the best minister of sport that this country has ever had. I think he fought the war well and knew sport. He loved sport. He was part of the vision of what Madiba wanted, and he was physically present as well. All of those things were important in reading what the country's mood was like.

In the stadium, winning the AFCON, we were just celebrating football and a great team and country.

13

Congratulations and welcome to TopSport!

I reached a point where I asked myself what I was doing with my brain. Was I even utilising it? My intellect wasn't being engaged.

I was grateful to Keith Pfeiffer and Celeste for the opportunity to be a continuity presenter but I had to challenge myself.

Continuity became a very easy fallback, a zero-challenge kind of comfort job that gave me exposure and fame and everything else. But it didn't give me that fulfilment of the challenge that I wanted.

It reached a turning point one day when there was a Bafana Bafana game on television and I was watching at home. It was a World Cup qualifier in 1997 and we were playing in Congo-Brazzaville. There was a break in transmission and they had to cut back to studio. The presenter had to pad and keep the conversation going.

It was a big qualifier and the SABC was the sole carrier so there were a lot of people watching. The anchor had to chat to Marks Maponyane who was in studio. The picture kept coming and going so the presenter had to carry it and it was such a difficult conversation. He was a colleague in continuity who was a brilliant presenter, but what they needed was a football person to carry the conversation in a moment of crisis like a prolonged break in transmission.

He needed to be able to talk permutations or different plays or scenarios, to have facts, and that wasn't coming through. In the end, Marks had to carry the conversation because of his knowledge of the game.

I could see that this created an opening and there was a need for a proper anchor at TopSport.

I went about my week as per normal, but I gathered information that there were indeed discussions happening and that TopSport was looking for an anchor. I decided to go and knock on the door. The name of the person I needed to speak to was Rob Rogers and he was the executive producer.

I found out where his office was and decided to pay him a visit. I introduced myself to him and told him about my desire to be a sports presenter. I asked him if there were any opportunities available. Rob said that actually they had just opened up auditions and I should come through on Thursday, which was the following day, at 4.30pm for a tryout. Clearly, my timing was spot on as usual.

I had never been to the TopSport studios before so I arrived early the next day. Again, there was a buzz at reception because people were coming to do auditions and I looked at their faces and there were plenty of famous people. There were all these presenters I had seen who were vying for the job.

I thought to myself that maybe this was the wrong place for

me; it was high-level stuff.

Walking into the TopSport studios was like being at home. I had watched broadcasts so often that it was so familiar to me. I could see where Martin Locke sat and could identify what the studio looked like. It was so much bigger than our little continuity set-up. It was a proper, massive studio, with multiple cameras and bright lights. We just had that one camera that was fixed on us, so this was all much bigger and more wow.

I waited my turn for my audition, I was mic'd up and given a generic earpiece. I was used to having an earpiece doing continuity, but I was about to learn that this was a completely different world. There were multiple cameras and constant talking in my ear. They presented me with a scenario around a game that had to be analysed and they played a little clip that I had to come back from. I had to pick up a few things to talk about and there was a mock person there as an analyst that I had to speak to. It was such a full-on audition.

I was in disbelief, for the most part because I was sitting in the seat that I'd always seen as a kid on that grainy television screen in eNkandla. I had to pinch myself. Was this really me?

This is what I was born to do. I was quietly emotional. I didn't even have an opportunity to evaluate how I had done. I just did my best and there was a bit of chatter in my ear. The producer asked if football was a real passion of mine and I said that's the reason I'm here. It always has been.

What I didn't know at the time was who was in the control room, listening to my audition. None other than Martin Locke.

GQIMM SHELELE

This is how Martin Locke remembers that day:

We liked to hold auditions on a regular basis. We liked to keep ahead of the game and find who's in the market. We had about 60 to 70 people this one morning and it was quite interesting. Everybody thinks they can be a presenter and they come along and most are really not suitable and they just think this is the life. We look for any kind of television presence. I was sitting up at the top in the control room of these huge studios. We looked down on all these people and we've got two side by side. Di, the producer, was doing her lot and I was doing my lot. I was about to do one. Suddenly I heard this voice, this deep voice, and it took me ten seconds and I said, 'Di, who's that kid?' She said, 'Why? Why do you want to know?' I think she wanted to keep him for herself. I said, 'I want that kid.' I said, 'I'm in charge of this. I want that voice. I want to speak to him, whoever it is.' And she told me who it was. And so I waited till I'd finished mine. Quite frankly, I wasn't interested in anybody else. It was just wow, absolute wow. He's got the most stunning voice and appearance-wise ... Well, the girls love him. He's done very, very well wherever he's gone. I just got hold of him and we became great, great buddies because we had a lot in common. We were both mad about soccer and knew the rest of sports as well. But I just knew from the appearance. First of all, the voice is very important, but in television personality is really critical. You don't have to be good-looking, but personality and the character count, and he had the lot. It's a little bit infuriating that he's about six foot two and I'm about five foot seven and a half. So, yes, I was very, very excited. And we became fantastic friends because I believed in him. He believed in me. And we've had this wonderful relationship.

Of course, I wasn't aware that Martin was even in the control room. I was just told they would get back to me the following day or the following week. Cheers.

I went back to res and lay on my bed, replaying in my mind what I had seen and how overwhelmed I felt by just having been in that studio. It was like a kid going to Disneyland. My head was spinning. I was sure I had delivered, but what were my chances? I had that image in my mind of all those famous people there and I thought, clearly, I had wasted my time.

I waited for the phone call. They had told me it would come the next day but it came that night. Rob Rogers was on the other end of the line. He said we have a game on Sunday at FNB Stadium, Orlando Pirates versus Bloemfontein Celtic. They anchor the show from the FNB Stadium. He wanted to know if I wanted to start that Sunday or if I wanted some time to think about it and start the week after.

I wasn't quite sure what was happening in my ear. No, those were the two options that I had because I had got the job. My heart started beating even faster. I asked him to repeat himself.

I was clear in my mind that if I could not do a Pirates versus

Bloem Celtic game then I should not be wanting to do this gig in the first place. So, I told Rob that if those are the two teams playing on Sunday, I would start on Sunday.

He warned me that I may be throwing myself in the deep end, but I was 100% sure. These were two teams that I knew extremely well and had followed through time and I didn't deserve to be there if I couldn't do that game.

That was it. He said he would send me a schedule, and that Saturday I went through to sort out some logistical things. For me, I just kept thinking, oh my God, what is about to begin here?

It might not be happening in the studio that I had been fantasising about all these years; it would be at FNB Stadium, but I had never been this close before. I was about to see my dream manifest itself. I prepared myself as best as I could. They didn't tell me much about what was expected. There was no autocue and no script. I was just given a running order to follow, saying who I should link to and when the breaks were.

I didn't sleep much the night before the game.

On Sunday, I arrived at the stadium and scaffolding had been erected for the makeshift studios. The idea was to bring the viewer closer to the live action. We could show the visuals of the teams warming up and analyse the game right next to the field.

I sat down, and soccer journalist Thomas 'TK' Kwenaite and former player Deshi Bhaktawer were my analysts. These were two guys I had also followed closely; I knew about TK's work as an ace journalist who I had read in the *Sunday Times* clippings my mother had kept for me and I had followed Deshi's career as a goalkeeper from Arcadia Shepherds and Swallows to his retirement. Here they were sitting next to me and this was a moment to cherish. They were both supportive and I was overawed just to be rubbing shoulders with them. I was nervous as hell.

The field reporter was Brian Mulder and I had been watching him for years. Brian was the voice of boxing and football and here I was anchoring with the top dogs in broadcasting.

The cameras were set up on the scaffolding and the backdrop was the field behind us. We went live.

The show started with a sting and then moved into a package of overlays of the previous games. Then they cut to me and I had to welcome everyone. I just remember holding the paper and shaking from the overlay. But I was mindful of the fact that we were live and there were no second chances. I had to try, even with my nervousness, to project and do a good job.

When I look back now, I was nervous, I was shaky, but I got through it. I knew that the minute the overlay finished, the entire world of sport in the country would get a first glimpse of this new kid on the block who now had the responsibility of anchoring football at TopSport.

The nervousness was probably the right level that I needed before they said, 'On camera and cue.' The words came to me and sport allows you the latitude to colour it whichever way you want. I couldn't wait to cross to TK and Deshi and start chatting to them so I could breathe a little. I got through 80 seconds of the opening, which felt like a lifetime.

It all happened so quickly. I had to link to the log table and link to the analysts and Brian. Everything was happening. It was real and it was the manifestation of a dream coming true. I was at FNB Stadium and I was live on television. What a day and what greater joy would I know.

It felt surreal that I was doing it. You have people continuously in your ear. You have a director shouting at different cameras while you're talking. Then you've got a PA who's counting down the studio and somebody else counting down the broadcast and there is a lot of activity happening in your ear. I was used to doing continuity where it was much quieter. There was singing in the stadium, there were vuvuzelas. Plus, I had to talk to my guests and hear what they were saying, make sense of it, formulate a sentence, cross to the field reporter.

There was a lot to divide in my mind and, as a first time, not everything was going to be smooth. I never expected my first experience to be at a venue. I never expected it to be that exposed. I thought it would always be sheltered within a studio where you don't feel as bare. It was a tight environment. The cameras were close, the lights were close, we were literally sitting kneecap to kneecap with the guests.

At the end of the broadcast, I took a deep breath and I could hear in my earpiece that they had opened up the audio and, in the van, Rob Rogers was leading the applause. Everyone was clapping.

Congratulations and welcome to TopSport! The journey had begun and I was overjoyed. That propelled me into a career that became my life.

Deep down inside, I was exhausted. The anticipation, the lack of sleep, the nerves, the butterflies, all of that had been building up inside of me. I had felt the pressure because I loved the game too much for me to stuff it up at this stage. I didn't want to be the cause of my own downfall.

For now, the game was done, it was wrapped, the post-match interviews were over, the credits had rolled and there was a moment to reflect on the reality of what had happened. It was a culmination of so much. It was a day of high emotion.

I can't for the life of me remember what the score was in the game. I have no clue. But I know that Robert won his day. That was the game. That was all that mattered.

14

Yimina uMadluphuthu onibingelelayo

Anchoring the football on TopSport changed everything. My dad was always a big Pirates fan so he was beside himself with happiness. My mother was so proud. It made them more comfortable with my decision to drop out of university and give up the scholarship.

The reality of seeing me anchor on TopSport was a big deal. It was literally the only sporting platform at the time. They couldn't argue against the magnitude of what was happening.

Relatives were phoning my dad and his friends in the football world inundated him with calls about his son. It was all very positive and they were proud and happy about the job that I had done. It was all very humbling too. I had got one episode done, but could I match it in the following broadcasts? That was the big challenge.

The Tuesday after that first broadcast, we had a feedback session and it was immediately very positive. Rob Rogers was full of praise, but I also knew there could be improvements. I had never been on a platform like that and I was nervous.

The main things Rob was focusing on were: Did you carry

the conversation? Did you ask the right questions? Did you utilise all of your guests properly? Did you follow the game? Did you analyse it properly? Did you ask leading questions? Were you attentive and were you engaging? After all, it's a conversation that people at home must relate to. Outside of the rough edges, the overall impression was that it was a job well done.

I was happy.

The minute Rob had said they would sign me up for TopSport, continuity was done. I couldn't straddle the two. I also wanted to create credibility. Simunye was fun and exciting, but that was the end of it.

Rob was the person behind my being employed. He was a very fatherly type of person, very production orientated, very television orientated, somebody who wanted excellence, brilliance and to elevate the product into something new and in a different direction.

He wanted me in the mix and I got a lot of support from other people. It gave me a feeling that I had made the right decision but I was still anxious about what lay ahead.

I was hoping that I would get a chance to work with Martin Locke. He was part of the Tuesday feedback meetings but I had not had an opportunity to actually work together with him.

Talks started about the next production and other people joined the conversation around the table. People I had always admired on my journey towards realising my dream, like Marks Maponyane. He was the famous jersey number seven for Kaizer Chiefs, with the wristband. He tackled like hell and was a superstar. He was such a role model for me because he was a professional footballer but also a businessman. He was thinking about life outside of football too. There were guys like Mike Mangena, and Deshi and some other big names too.

I wasn't intimidated, but they were big names. I also realised that my role was different to that of former footballers. I was a broadcaster. All of these things were working in my mind, that whatever happens I will respect them because these are the people I admired growing up. But I couldn't be walking around feeling as if there was an air of impotence about myself. I am in the mix among South African football superstars. My role was completely different. I started to understand this very early. I think it was also necessary for me to not see myself as that because my journey was only beginning. They had retired, they were former players. This was an opportunity for them to earn an income talking about the game that they love. For me, it was an entry into talking about the game, but also engaging them, trying to get the best out of them as former players. So, I needed to be on my A game.

I had to focus on my journey and how I could improve. I had to focus on what I could learn in those production meetings. I paid attention and brought a little notebook, took down notes of whatever was being planned. I had to think about things like who would be the impact players, pick three players to talk about, choose four in case one is injured or is on a yellow card. I had to get into the swing of how to work, how to structure conversations. I had to gain my independence but also ensure I didn't lose my mind in that process.

I learnt that preparation was essential. How could I carry a conversation without being prepared? I had to know the details and the minutiae, why a player missed training the week before, why a player was playing out of position, why someone was being fast-tracked. Those were the kind of conversations that I had to bring to life on air.

There was no internet, no logging on and searching on Google. It was what I brought to the table. I had to research it and go and talk to the coaches and have access to newspaper publications that were there at the time, that I relied on to gather the bulk of the conversation.

The field reporters were closer to the coaches. As an anchor, I grew those relationships over time as I began to get access to them. I had to do a lot of reading. The reports then in the *Sowetan* and other newspapers were much longer and the reporters were sharp. Nothing was being shown on television so a press conference would be reported in detail. I would read *Sharpshoot Soccer Mirror, Soccer News* and all that helped me to understand and know the detail, such as that Mark Anderson, the goalkeeper for Sundowns, is a very religious person whose favourite meal is pap en vleis.

I had to read all of those things and have a photographic memory. You never knew when there would be a dead moment on field and they would throw back to the studio and I would have to pad. I wanted to avoid a situation where I would be stuck. I knew I might not use this information today, but I might use it the next month or the next. That was crucial for me to just collect as much info as I could to keep a conversation going, to throw it in, to be able to tell a story but not waffle.

If there was a Doc Khumalo who was involved, you need to tie him up with his storyline of having gone to Daliwonga High School in Soweto, his father being Eliakim 'Pro' Khumalo, and there he is now, number 15, coming through, taking over from Jan 'Malombo' Lechaba, stepping into this Kaizer Chiefs fold where he became a superstar. I had to be able to tie in and marry all of these little stories, so the person sitting at home would be fascinated to say, 'Oh, so Pro Khumalo, one of the founder members of Kaizer Chiefs, oh, he's Doc Khumalo's father. Oh, okay.' And then you move on.

The next production, you bring in a Teboho Moloi and then you link him up to the great Chippa Moloi of Orlando Pirates who died under tragic circumstances. But he, being one of the all-time superstars of Orlando Pirates, has a son now who is playing for Orlando Pirates. So, you've got Chiefs and Pirates. Two sets of very famous families, the Khumalos and the Molois, whose fathers, respectively, were superstars of those two teams. And here they are now gaining this fame within these two teams. Can they match what their fathers lived up to? Is there pressure to live up to a Pro Khumalo or a Chippa Moloi?

That's where I brought in the analysts who were older than me because they had first-hand memories of what those two brought to a stadium and what kind of impact they had at the time.

When I joined, Jomo Sono was nearing the end of his career but he was still playing. He had a brother, Julius KK Sono, who he played closely with. The memories would come back to me from the VHS tapes that I'd watched, that my mom had kept for me of previous derbies. Now I was watching them play, sitting in the scaffolding. I had to tie all these stories together.

It was crucial that I tied things together because if I didn't it wouldn't make sense to the viewers. All of those pockets of information were just things that I would get excited about. I wanted to be out there. I couldn't wait to get out there and share information with people watching from home. I wanted to make it exciting to watch.

Every single production I was getting to know the analysts much better. I got to know what their characters were. I had worked out who I could push a bit and who didn't like who and I could use all of those things to the benefit of the production. It created some drama and a better-quality production. We wanted to create a little bit of watchability, not just staid faces talking in monotone about a game. We could throw in a bit of humour, a bit of controversy, put the analysis in. We had the licence to do it.

People were really starting to enjoy the production. I felt like I was starting to own the platform. I began bringing in my character and making people understand who I was. I became a personality in the process. There literally was no other immediate person who was anchoring football, aside from Martin Locke. So the local product, almost single-handedly, had to grow in those formative stages up until other shows like *Mabaleng* and *Laduma* started to grow in stature. I started to feel a sense of more than just belonging. I had arrived.

A producer, Paul du Plessis, had been given a task to start a new show called *SoccerZone*, which would be a flagship show that carried highlights from the weekend. Paul was very honest and called me and Mike Mangena and asked us to help because he didn't know enough about football. It was prime time. Here was a guy saying, I've got a brand-new show, it's a blank piece of paper, the way I love things to be.

So, we sat down and segmented it, worked out what was going to go where; we would play highlights, structure it. We would bring in the interviews, have a voiceover over the edited stuff, cut out the commentary. We decided to put in some fun moments. We were being as creative as possible. This was *SoccerZone*.

I remember suggesting a feature called 'Moemish of the Week', which then became the drawcard of that show. We would take all the funny moments that had happened on the field and edit them cleverly, add some music and it was an absolute hit. We saved it for the very end of the show. First, we did the moment of the day, which was a highlight, a great goal or something like that. Then we would have Moemish.

We had to become clever with this because it became so popular that anyone who tuned in wanted to wait until the end. There was clever editing, clever usage of music and we would string it along. It was magic because people waited right until the end when the credits rolled.

We brought in a former referee, Sylvester Ndaba, and I nicknamed him El Professori. Then I renamed Mike Mangena to his original nickname of Sporo. I was starting to utilise the nicknames that I used to hear when I was growing up. I think having a proper nickname helped endear players to the people.

Sporo hadn't been used in a while and I thought, stuff that, I'm going to bring it back. El Professori was a play on a popular television show, *Mind Your Language*, so there was a bit of comedy too. He was the professor of the show and would teach us the laws of the game. We also hyped that up in such a way that we would throw forward to it after a game. It also gained in popularity and people wanted to see it on a Monday.

I gave myself the name Madluphuthu – one who eats phuthu/pap.

I'd given everybody nicknames but nobody could get a nickname for me. So Madluphuthu was a name that I had been given in primary school when we did a nativity play and there was a character that I played with that name. So, I thought it ideal to just give myself that name. I was a skinny boy so it wasn't a reference to how I looked. Growing up on the farm, there was nothing better than phuthu, milk and sugar or maas, nice and thick and creamy, so it stays at the top, fresh from the cows.

We had an eight-minute segment and we would choose three controversial moments and edit them and encourage debate between Mike and Sylvester.

It really was a coming together of all that I had been learning and watching while growing up. It was like leading an orchestra, directing, pushing the buttons. A bit like the Pied Piper of Hamelin.

It reminded me of *Inside Stuff*, the basketball show that I used to watch hosted by Ahmad Rashad. What I liked about it was that Ahmad brought a lot of his personality and energy to the show.

I didn't want to copy what he was doing, but it was clear that television gave you the licence to be yourself. To add some spice. To bring in some fun moments. To be serious. To go through different emotions. That's what I have always tried to do. There was no footprint to follow for *SoccerZone*. It was a new baby and we had to make it work.

When I started, there was also very little usage of vernac in studio. Everything was done in English. I have no idea why, but it was strange for me because, the way I looked at it, football was being consumed largely by black South Africans. We were often speaking above people's heads. We weren't connecting with them because we were speaking English. This was SABC1, which was supposed to be Nguni. Rob said it was fine and gave us support, so I made a conscious decision to start adding in isiZulu.

I began opening the show with a line that would become a trademark phrase. I would say: 'Sinibingelele emakhaya, ezikoleni, ezibhedlela, naphakathi emajele.'

Hello, everyone at home, at schools, in hospitals and in jails. Welcome to the show.

'Yimina uMadluphuthu onibingelelayo.'

It is me, Madluphuthu, greeting you.

So that is how I started every show.

At the end, I delivered the catchphrase that has come to

define my broadcasting: 'Sesiyayivala sithi gqimm'shelele.'

We are now ending it; we will be back.

That became the catchphrase. Shelele meant 'we will be back'. So, we're not gone forever.

When I thought of the great commentators that came before me, there was always a catchphrase of some sort. Zama Masondo had 'Zimbi izindaba madoda' and I grew up hearing that. Different commentators came up with different things. My mind just races when I'm in a creative space, but one thing I would always say, even among my friends, I would kind of signal streetwise style with my finger and say, 'Hey, ngisathi nje shelele.' In other words, I'm going somewhere but I won't be long.

So, I thought to myself, how could I heighten this to give it some oomph and some life and make it memorable? In my creative space, I thought about it and the sound of Shelele was so sweet and gentle as an ending that I needed something a bit more hyped up to raise the roof a little bit. So I came up with 'Gqimm', pause, pause, 'Shelele'.

It felt like I was conducting a choir from Auckland Park to millions of people at home who would learn it. They waited for the Moemish of the Week, and then they waited for Gqimm Shelele because they wanted to say it together with me.

So, every show the countdown would get to around twelve seconds to go and that would be my signal to go in to have the adequate pause. I would say 'Gqimm' and then pause, pause, pause and when I said 'Shelele', I looked away from the screen. It was a little bit of theatre. Again, I felt that I had the licence to be creative.

It caught on and people latched on to it and went crazy. People gave me feedback in the streets, 'Hey, nangu uGqimm Shelele.' I wouldn't be called Robert. 'Hey, here is Gqimm Shelele' because we had brought something special. It was also a novelty – all of a sudden there were catchphrases and vernac so people started to feel part of the show because we weren't speaking over their heads.

Ed Griffiths, who was in charge of the programme, and Rob Rogers were both happy. The channels thought this thing was great. So, they asked me to start speaking more in isiZulu. There were phrases, there were words, there were sign-offs, there was a greeting, and in between, when I was engaging Sporo and all these nicknames and there is El Professori, people were starting to understand things were different. They had never seen this on television before.

I kept working on what I could improve, but I also didn't want to do too much at once because that could be a little dangerous. We still had to give people the football. They wanted the highlights, the news, the research, the elements that carried the show and I had to give them my personality.

The name Madluphuthu also raised intrigue about what it meant. White people were fascinated by it and tried to pronounce it. People from West Africa, from Nigeria, tried to pronounce it in weird and wonderful ways.

The intrigue factor for me was the bottom line. That was the important thing. So, I wasn't going to go for something simple and basic as a nickname. It seemed difficult enough, but it was also instilling within the Nguni and Zulu language a sense that I actually belonged. I was able to use it on television and that was powerful. I wanted that response from people, that they would say, I don't have to be a Robert or Trevor or John. 'Hey, here is Madluphuthu.' Here's one of us – umfana wasekhaya – a boy from home. There was almost an endearment factor that said, don't be scared. This is your show. We are just sitting around in this rondavel, in this shebeen, we're just talking football. Make sure you come back next time for Moemish, for the greeting or for whatever happens in between.

SoccerZone quickly got sponsorships. MTN latched onto it and pumped millions into the SABC and it was then called MTN *SoccerZone* for many years. Being a telco, it came with the introduction of an SMS line. We had to find a way to incorporate the SMSes into the show.

People enjoyed seeing their messages on screen so we scrolled them at the bottom. I would pick up one or two and read them out, like Thembinkosi in Springs asking, 'How did Jeff Butler play that player, he is so useless?' We gave out the number and people kept watching to see if they could see their message. It was another component that attracted people.

One of the most popular ones that we had was around the controversial topic of Jabu Pule. He was a very wayward player and he would go AWOL at times, so we asked viewers what Kaizer Chiefs should do about him.

We averaged around 5 000 SMSes in an hour on a normal show. That day with the Jabu Pule topic took it to a record 14 000 SMSes in the hour. The overnight spillover took it to about 18 000. The SMSes just rolled through. That's why MTN stuck with the show and renewed their contract.

SoccerZone was a big part of my success in broadcasting. I did it for around eight years, but other opportunities kept knocking on the door.

15

Martin and mentoring

I only found out later in life that when I did my very first audition for TopSport, my idol and mentor Martin Locke was in the control room.

I had no idea. But Martin was watching my audition and he told me that he immediately responded with 'Who's that kid? Get that kid. He's the one.'

It wasn't surprising, because I had been watching him all my life. I grew up admiring him, trying to mould myself on him and that's why the delivery, the voice, all resonated with him. He knew without a doubt. He was Mr TopSport, so for him to react that way was incredible. Here was my television hero, my reference point, saying he wanted me to be a part of what he was doing.

Gradually, I was brought in to work with Martin on *Mabaleng* on Saturdays, where I was asked to be an analyst, which I rejected, having not played the game nor qualified to play the role. But we really had an opportunity to work together on the 1998 World Cup. That experience cemented it for me and it was an ambition come full circle but also the beginning of a new journey.

I was going to have the opportunity to work with somebody who was an elder to me before he retired.

Thank God, South Africa qualified for the World Cup in France and the SABC had all the rights. There were 62 games that were split in half between Martin and me. I wasn't expecting to do many games at all or for it to be as evenly divided as it was. We were the two main drivers of the show, so doing all the live games was a really defining moment for me in my career.

I knew that I couldn't let myself down, but I also couldn't let down an entire nation. I found myself in a position where I was the heir and the hope. There was no other anchor, aside from Martin Locke, in all of these years who had been given a position like this.

I also had to look at the demographics and I realised what this would mean to a black child who was watching.

TopSport hadn't really had a black anchor stand out or be a lead. Martin was my role model and I was going to be a role model for a black child from the township, from the farms, from anywhere else in South Africa. I had relinquished being a lawyer to become a broadcaster. Now I was turning broadcasting into a career option. It was not a weekend side job. So, there was enormous pressure.

I had to demonstrate to any other child who wants to pursue a career in broadcasting that this is indeed what you can pursue if you're serious about it. So, above and beyond the sheer excitement of the World Cup, there were also these other factors.

What role was I playing for the greater community to be

inspired by whatever it is that I was about to do? I was always cognisant of that fact. I knew that this would be a trailblazing moment, but one that also could come crashing down if I didn't execute as expected or even way above my capabilities.

I had to knuckle down. The publicity had been done. Everybody was aware of what was going to happen. I needed to focus on my games. I needed to focus on my presentation, my research, how I carry it through.

There was a great deal of hype because the SABC was proud to have all of these games exclusively. I assumed that Martin would obviously do all the Bafana Bafana games. To my utter surprise, he insisted that I do one of the team's games instead of him.

It afforded me the respect that I have for him to not want to claim a glory moment, because that would have been peak viewing. He was the senior person and the better person for the job, but he said that if the team got knocked out then I wouldn't have had an opportunity to do one of their matches.

It just showed me a different side to the man. Any other person would have hogged all three games that Bafana had to play in the group stages. But he didn't. He shared that and rearranged the schedule and took it on the chin and said I must do it. That was when he earned my lifetime respect.

It also added to my nerves because triple the number of people would be watching a South Africa game as opposed to any other ordinary game. The nerves wore off quickly and I got into the excitement of the World Cup. I started to gain more of a Robert personality on air because, with every game, with every director in your ear, every floor manager on the floor, I started to have a sense of ease because all of those different components actually contribute to how you project yourself.

The success of that '98 World Cup broadcast lay squarely on the shoulders of how magnanimous Martin Locke was and how generous he was with his time and how he guided me through the entire process. There was no greater person to mentor me and I learnt valuable lessons from him.

Martin also realised that, having been on air for as long as he had been, he needed to reinvest his knowledge and his wisdom in this new young kid who had come through and that he had full support for. He never wavered in terms of that. It was like that from day one until day last and even post the time that he was there. So, for me, it all showed that he was more human. This was a true broadcaster who wanted to hand over the reins or the baton at some point to someone he also firmly believed in.

Martin agrees that he felt it was important to mentor me and that he saw my talent:

> *I was looking for somebody who I felt could operate in a way like I do. And you have to be confident and you have to know your sport. My entry into the game was an absolutely amazing one that I wanted him to follow in a similar sort of way. I saw with Robert immediately that he had my sort of talent and yet he was more imposing than I was. We really grew like brothers. I kept thinking that this guy can make it in such a big way. And he's just moved on and on and on and on.*

That went a long way in informing how I mentor today and how I behave towards colleagues. It is because of Martin's example that a lot of the people who I have thrust into the forefront of broadcasting, I have supported with an open, clean heart and with no expectation. Whether they are men or women doesn't really matter, but where I can, I have made a point of supporting women's voices.

Before the 2003 Cricket World Cup, I went knocking on Head of SABC Sport Mvuzo Mbebe's door, literally at about ten minutes to six, just before I went on air and I dragged Kass Naidoo along. I said: 'Hi, Mvuzo, I don't have much time. I just thought before you start with the World Cup cricket broadcast, I want to introduce you to someone I think can actually anchor cricket, who's female, who knows cricket and who would do your product good.'

I introduced them, said thank you very much, and I left. Fast forward. Kass was thrust in, she did a couple of the games in studio and the guy who was supposed to do the broadcast flew back to the UK. Kass got all the publicity, front page of the *Sunday Times* and various magazines. People were just amazed at how brilliant she was and how much she knew about cricket. Kass had the responsibility of doing the World Cup semis and the final. She has gone around the world doing cricket commentary now with Sky and SuperSport.

I'm not claiming credit for her success, but I had no doubt that she knew her cricket and I wanted to get her into a place where we could all recognise and see her great talent. I think that landed her in a position where she was able to do that.

Otherwise, she may never have been given a chance to do it.

Similarly, with Thato Moeng and bringing her on board for *Thursday Night Live*. She came through for an audition and was huffing and puffing and sweating, with no make-up. Every other person there was dolled up, looking like a model. She was lost, she was late, but there was something in there that said to me this is the person we need to look at. We gave her a chance and she now anchors her own show. She's done Africa Cup of Nations. She's travelled throughout Africa. She anchors live football games. All because she was given an opportunity. Now she's thriving.

Other examples are Julia Stuart and Melissa Reddy. Melissa was a journalist for *KickOff* in Cape Town. Julia was a journalist for the *Mirror* in Cape Town. We flew both of them to come to my Thursday-night show. There was a lot of negative energy in my earpiece. I could hear them saying, 'What do these chicks know about football?' But I knew they knew football. Fast forward, Julia becomes a top anchor at SuperSport. Melissa Reddy goes to the UK, becomes a media officer for Liverpool. Now she's currently a Sky Sports News senior anchor. They cross to her live during Sky Sports News and live games.

You have to give people opportunities based on their strengths and it's difficult for women to get higher in their positions, which are male-dominated. For me, it was just a case of how do we strengthen broadcasting? Because I want to cross to somebody who I know is able to be equally as strong and give off the energy on air and show that they actually know something.

It was the same thing that Martin had shown me in being open and giving. He wanted the best. He was never worried that someone was going to overshadow him. There was never any sign of that. Martin also realised that he had to think about his legacy when he did eventually retire.

He had to be proud of the person he leaves behind, that he can actually sit at home in his retirement and point to the television and say, 'That one I am proud of. That's my guy, that's my chap. He's doing well.' For him, it needed to be an even better product. That is where I have the ultimate respect for him because of just how he embraced me from the start up until the end. That FIFA World Cup in '98 was again testimony to how he was willing to hold my hand right up until the end. I was in my early twenties, I was thrust into the deep end and needed to have nerves of steel.

My demeanour is such that I don't really show the highs or lows. I really try to keep the same level. I might be excited inside, but I hardly ever show it on the outside. I think you need to be very guarded in the space and in this industry because it will sweep you away completely. All I wanted to do was just deliver and deliver the best that I could and that provided that opportunity for me.

16

Being a target

Exposure leads to familiarity. Being in the public eye came with a degree of 'celebrity' status, although I still don't see myself as such. The more exposure I got, the more important things I was able to do. It also came with people wanting to interview me, doing shoots for magazines, appearing on covers, doing shows.

That then propelled me into a different space, beyond television. There were more profiles and posters and a greater awareness. People may have seen me in *Drum* magazine and that directed them to watch the show on SABC if they were not sports people. That led to an increase in my fanbase. It did change how I conducted myself publicly because I was more aware that people were noticing what I was doing. I've never been one to thrust myself into the public eye and want to be on red carpets. I would rather use the back door and avoid the lights and cameras. I never wanted to be that person.

I wanted my career as a sportscaster to be what drives me, as opposed to the other way around. I didn't want to be driven by hype. I didn't want to be driven by what people expected. That is why I was never a regular feature on red carpets. I never wanted to be famous. I never wanted to be to be known or seen. That's why I always sit in the background, slap on my baseball cap and sunglasses and be somewhere in the crowd.

I think what I realised from other people's experiences is that when they propel themselves too quickly, that is also the recipe for how long they will stay. The questions I get asked a lot are: 'How do you stay relevant for so long? How do you stay in the forefront for so long? How do you influence people generationally as much as you have?' I always say I try to control what I do and say publicly. There'll be a stage where I will keep away from all media. But then when I do switch that button on again, it will be strategically here and there, and then I will withdraw again. I've always believed in the element of intrigue where people are wondering: who is this person?

You can't afford to be overexposed because people will generally get tired of you. I think you have to give off the genuineness of what you do, be authentic on air, no level of pretence will get you anywhere. That's part of the ethos that I have believed in. I think that is what has been able to carry me right throughout. Because if I wanted to be famous for sport, then I would have gotten famous for sport. But I probably wouldn't be anywhere near sport right now.

As I became more exposed, I don't think there were scandals per se. I just think that there was a time when anything that Robert did would get front-page prominence on these trashbloids, as I call them. Between *Sunday Sun* and *Sunday World*, there would always be something.

And then *City Press* all of a sudden started doing a gossip section in the paper. Maybe they felt they were losing readership or lagging behind *Sunday World* and *Sunday Sun*. *City Press* was a broadsheet, not a tabloid, and had a lot of credibility. But all of a sudden they started writing tabloidy stuff every Sunday within the publication.

I was accused of having assaulted and then punched a girlfriend in the face, and she allegedly came on air having powdered herself up to cover that. It took me by surprise because I don't think violence of any kind is part of my nature, let alone doing that to a female person, and also somebody that I would have been dating. It was strange. I did not know what the source of that story was.

At the time the story came out, we were no longer dating and my former girlfriend was equally taken aback. We had a conversation about it and she told me that if I was going to pursue the matter legally, then she would sign a statement in support of me.

I was relieved because I honestly did not know. Maybe that was also a start of potential smear campaigns against me because of inroads that I was starting to make and probably questions that I was starting to ask within my line of work.

I approached a lawyer friend and asked if he could assist me with suing *City Press*. I had worked hard and they were throwing doubt on my integrity. My former girlfriend provided me with an affidavit and we sued *City Press* and won the case. They had to pay R40 000 in damages and issue an apology, which they did. It wasn't about the money. I was happy that after that episode, that whole tabloid section of the newspaper was closed down.

I was relieved because that was completely out of character and also just a complete lie. The courts did what the courts did and we got justice. From a scandal point of view, I think that was one in the early stages of my career, but there were various others over the years.

Whatever the trashbloids thought was newsworthy, they would carry it on the front pages. Anything from Robert having beef with Pitso, Robert and Lebo M, Robert being taken to court by a baby mama, Robert not paying maintenance for his son. There was a Namibian lady who claimed she was carrying my baby and faked a pregnancy. There was a story about me hugging a bar and being depressed. All of those things were lies.

I had to learn very quickly that as much as you just want to do your work and do it to the best of your ability, it comes with its own baggage. It comes with being a target.

17
Sink or swim

SoccerZone was flying, but what else was out there? What sportscasting taught me in the end was, yes, Robert, you love your football, but do you love your sport? Because that is a different conversation.

The answer was, yes. I was as intrigued with other sport as I was with football. In 1997 the All-Africa games were being held in South Africa at the Joburg Stadium. That was my first step into multi-sport codes. I was asked to report on anything and everything outside of football and it was a good learnership for me because I got to learn certain terminology for various sporting codes. Later on, I covered the Commonwealth Games and I was selected to be part of the team to cover the games in 2002 in Manchester and then 2006 in Melbourne in Australia.

That was the first time I travelled overseas. The main attraction for me was getting onto a plane. It was my first big assignment outside South Africa.

I was covering gymnastics, synchronised swimming, normal swimming, lawn bowls, boxing, everything. It was great. We ran around because Thabiso Sithole and I were the only two television reporters so we had to rush from one venue to the next. We had to adapt quickly to the terminology and make sure we knew what records were broken and what division we were discussing. I had to sound like I had covered lawn bowls for my entire life in order to win the trust of people.

As tiring as that whole exercise was, I got to create closer ties and affinities with people within other sports, especially hockey and boxing. I got to know the players and the trainers. I struck up so many friendships with people. From a professional point of view, I was also rewarded with the SABC Sport Journalist of the Year Award for the best reporting at a sporting event for my coverage of the Commonwealth Games.

From a diversification point of view, I loved it because I never wanted to be pigeonholed and be known as a football person only. Sport is so diverse and I had the opportunity to broaden my coverage.

Other opportunities also presented themselves outside of *SoccerZone* and covering football on television.

There was still a lot of hype around MTN *SoccerZone* and *Laduma* and the shows I was doing. There was quite a bit of buzz and interest. What we were doing was working and we were giving sport a different flavour and feel and energy.

I was riding that television wave when out of the blue one Sunday I got a phone call from Romeo Kumalo, who was the Metro FM station manager at the time. He was also doing a Sunday repertoire show on Metro. I had just finished anchoring a football game and I was in studio. He had also just finished doing his show on Metro.

He was straightforward, congratulated me on the good work that he had been seeing on television and for the different energy I was bringing to sports presentation. He wanted to know if it would be possible for me to transfer what I was doing on television to radio.

Because of my deep love for radio, I obviously knew exactly who Romeo was. I had been an ardent listener of his show because of the genre of music he was playing on a Sunday. It was the same genre that my friend and dearly departed Eddie Zondi would play, it's the same genre that my current friend Wilson B Nkosi plays. Ernest Pillay and all of those guys played it too. So, I had an immense respect for all of those gentlemen because I listened to them all the time. They were people I revered.

I was in awe of Metro. I had grown up listening to it. I knew that Romeo was the station manager and here he was asking me if I can transfer what I'm doing on television to radio.

There was a dead-air moment because I didn't know what to say. I could hear it was his voice. There was no prank being pulled. I finally found the words to thank him, that someone of his stature and calibre was even watching our humble offering. He was a sports fan and loved football. He felt the time was right and the market was right at Metro for me to come over.

We met in person and his idea was that there was an opportunity when he finished his show on a Sunday at 6pm for me to come in and do 30 minutes of sport. It would be a wrap of Saturday and Sunday games and people wanting to talk about what happened. Thirty minutes, that's it.

I still had a massive reverence for radio and the fear was still there. I had also never been to a radio studio before. This was the biggest commercial radio station that was calling me.

That next Sunday I finished my television broadcast and rushed two floors underground to where Metro was. I hadn't been shown around or taught how to use the desk.

I walked in and Romeo was wrapping up his show. He packed his stuff and pointed across to the control room and said: 'That's Andrew.'

He explained that Andrew Botopela was the man who would to be taking my calls and helping me technically with anything. This is the microphone button, here you play your ads and I will listen on the radio in my car. Have a good show. Cheers.

That was my induction to radio. I was shown Andrew. I was shown the microphone button and we have to play the ads and he's going to listen in the car when he's driving home. Good luck. This is Metro FM, for crying out loud!

I looked at him and thought he was crazy. This was prime-time radio. Is this what people call sink or swim? I was so confused. I looked at Andrew. I had never met him and didn't know him. I felt so many different emotions. I tried not to panic. There were butterflies in my tummy and I was nervous. I knew of radio inside out. Everybody would be listening to Metro at that time. It was peak listening time because of the Sunday Repertoire and the music being played.

I had to think on my feet. I had to try to conceptualise and deliver. I gave Andrew whatever numbers I had on me. I didn't have a producer so I had to get Andrew to phone some people. I had a microphone I had to attend to. This gentleman said he's got all the confidence in me to do what I do.

I went on air, thanked Romeo for the opportunity that I had been given. We're going to be doing a live sports show. Welcome to it. We let loose.

That 30 minutes felt like it was hours and hours and hours and hours and hours. All I remember was that those switchboard lights and the phone calls were blazing after about five minutes. Something had been triggered by what I had introduced.

I thought we would get a sense of what it is that people want to chat about initially because I hadn't planned anything. I looked at my phone and thought who could we phone. Let's get a coach who has gravitas. It wasn't just a phone-in. I could see Andrew looking at the lines and trying to juggle them all.

In the end, as nerve-wracking as it was, I think people found a certain outlet on a Sunday after all the lovey-dovey songs had been played. There was a time when spirits could be lifted by talking football and sport and letting rip. We devised a formula and I could come better prepared next time around.

It was the start of something.

I always look back at that moment and say that is where my career could have bombed. I think maybe Romeo knew something that I didn't. Maybe he had more trust in me than I had in myself. But one thing I know is that I never let him down.

We were quickly negotiating a proper sports show and a better time slot. There had been people in the past who had been doing sport in and around Metro, but I just think Romeo wanted something fresh or engaging. That was the beginning of that journey that would later in life become a daily radio sports show.

18
From the extra strongs to the presidential suite

Radio has always been the holy grail for me.
With television, I could visualise a family that I was talking to. But knowing how big Metro FM was, that automatically worked on my mind. I knew I wasn't talking to a family of five people. The magnitude of the station was huge and I was always mindful of that when I got into studio.

But once I settled down, I was comfortable and Andrew, the technical producer, and I struck up a very good friendship. He was great, so we got into editing and preparing clips for the show and things started to improve on air.

From a listener perspective, there started to be regulars that were tuning in to the show. I could tell that the demand was spreading and people were loving it. The timing of the show was also great because, being on a Sunday after the weekend's football, people wanted to talk about the games. They wanted to celebrate or complain about certain players or a coach or a refereeing decision. It was all organic and happening instantaneously.

People had a voice. They didn't need to go to their local

pub or bar or shebeen to moan and groan about the game. I started to enjoy it and really loved it. I started to get used to the immediacy of radio. I had to be sharp. I've spoken about the heroes in radio that I looked up to and it was a mammoth task for me to carry that on and walk in their shoes.

The demand for the show grew so that it was quickly shifted from Sundays to a full-on talk show every day in the week. Morio Sanyane and I would share the duties. After a while, Morio left and I was on my own to carry the daily show. The demand continued to increase and it was extended from 30 minutes to an hour every day.

I didn't want it just to be about football. There were also discussions on rugby, cricket, athletics and other sports. There was always an audience and people responded, but there would be a football bias on certain days. Fridays turned into a preview and legends show and that gained a lot of popularity. It was also important for me to use the platform to recognise a lot of individuals I had admired while I was growing up. These were real legends and heroes of football. I might act tough and not show emotion, but these interviews really moved me. There were moments where I was really starstruck because I was always a football fan. That part I could never hide.

Having a one-on-one with a Pule 'Ace' Ntsoelengoe, for example. There was no greater player while I was at school that could match the name of Ace Ntsoelengoe. He was an icon, the famous jersey number twelve of Kaizer Chiefs, the man who went to play overseas. I'd read up almost anything and everything about him.

I almost pinched myself the very first time he walked into the studio to come and do an interview because, for me, this was like the God of football.

The job was starting to become extremely fulfilling in many ways. I was facilitating debate and it was satisfying from a personal perspective.

I asked myself: How does one make this show special? What do people want to hear?

I had to conceptualise how best to run the show. I had lots of different ideas coming through. I've always looked at myself as a very creative person when it comes to original ideas, but also just doing things differently. A sports talk-radio show being just a sports talk-radio show can be very boring. So how do you colour that? It had to excite. When people ask what kind of people listen to the show or what kind of people watch television or watch your shows, from a radio perspective I always use that analogy of the FNB Stadium. The people sitting in the extra-strong stands are listening. Those sitting in the super suites and the presidential suite are listening. It's the whole spectrum. It's that entire layer of society that is tuned in.

So how do I not speak over people's heads, but also not make it something that a lawyer or doctor or smart human being can't tune into. It must be mentally stimulating but exciting. There must be fun, but there must also be accountability. I had to move through those different layers. How do you achieve it? But how do you keep growing it at that level?

From a creative perspective, I met a gentleman I've now

worked with my entire radio career, Thabo Nkoala. Thabo is brilliant when it comes to imaging and bringing a unique sound and an original look and feel to the show. We had to box clever and we would never have achieved that were it not for Thabo. He was tasked with imaging the entire Metro FM, but he took a particular liking to the sports show because he loves sport – he is a Chelsea fan – so there was extra love and care for the fledgling sports show.

Those were the days of Mini-Discs, so we would have to listen back to the show in full and make notes of time codes so we could put together the intro of the show, which is a sizzle reel of different clips. It took so much work that in the end it was all put together by Thabo.

The intro is hardly about football. It's knitting together pieces of conversation or funny jokes or whatever is happening in society. It's cutting edge, borderline, cheeky. I want it to almost be like, 'Huh, did I actually hear that on radio?' That helped with bringing a different audience who are not really sports people. It had to be cutting edge, catch people off guard, but obviously be respectful. People were hooked by the intro and ended up staying and listening to the show until the end.

There was a lot of preparation for the show, but we also wanted it to sound unique, so we had to work on the imaging. It was pacey. It was sharp. That was teamwork between Thabo and me. I wanted it to have an international sound – radio at a different level.

Production values are extremely important to me because it shows that you care about the show. You want it to evolve.

You want it to sound a certain way. You don't want it to be like any Joe Soap. You don't want it to just be. You want it to cause some form of talkability around it.

We built a completely different audience. People would say, I never used to be a sports lover or listen to sports shows, but somehow you made the experience worthwhile. I started listening to sports or started becoming interested in sport because of how you were doing your radio show.

People needed to be entertained. They wanted to be educated and journey with us.

We also had to ensure that guests were exciting and interesting too. The availability and calibre of people who were coming to the show was crucial. We had access to football players and coaches. Then we started holding people accountable in the management of sport. Club chairmen, league leaders and CEOs and so on also became a major part of what we covered. It became a no-holds-barred show where, for example, if a Trevor Phillips, who was the CEO of the Premier Soccer League, comes through, we would cover everything. What was good? What went right? How did the league grow? What were the shortfalls? What were the shortcomings?

I would press him on certain issues that I had picked up from a listeners' perspective that they were not happy with. Sometimes it was a case of fans not being happy with the price of the tickets or access to the stadium. The gates would be closed while they were on the way and running late. I give credit to the late Trevor Phillips because he came on to the show knowing it was not going to be an easy ride.

He was fair enough to keep coming back because he valued the platform. I respected him for that because he never, ever took it personally. There were times when I'd really push him and he would answer. If I felt that the answer was too diplomatic or evasive, then I would ask the same question differently. I loved that about the show, because then the people got involved. For me, it was always about the listener; the boss.

That was the difference between radio and television in that people could almost immediately really get involved in the show and the issues.

Different publications started quoting what was said on the show. It was growing. Sponsors got involved. It became known as *Discovery Sports Centre* for a few years. Then MTN pushed to be on the radio show too. Then it became *083 Sport at Six with Marawa*.

The highlight for me was seeing the show's explosive growth. From 30 minutes on a Sunday to eventually an hour and a half at the time of the 2010 FIFA World Cup and beyond. It was the growth of the show, the increased demand from the public and still people wanted more.

19

'Ah, Robert, you work too hard'

Madiba leaned on his walking stick, his PA Zelda la Grange alongside him, and carefully made his way towards me. He was wearing a trademark gold Madiba shirt. We were backstage at the President's Cup golf tournament at Fancourt in George in 2003. Security was swarming and the major cable networks were set up all around us. I had been given the illustrious task of MCing the opening and closing ceremonies of the event. More than 102 million households would be tuning in across Africa, Europe and the US on NBC, Turner Cable and ESPN, amongst other channels. I was nervous!

'Ah, Robert, you work too hard,' the former president joked.

My retort was, 'No, Madiba, you are the one that works hard. Who am I to even come close to it?'

'No, no, no, no, no, no. You see, Zelda here keeps telling me that I've been resting for 27 years, and now I work!'

Those words became engraved in my mind immediately. How could somebody who has suffered and been punished and sacrificed so much in prison for years even call it 'rest'?

That was one of the most humbling comments I have

heard from a person of that stature. It also motivated me and encouraged me that the journey I was on and the path I was travelling was meant to happen.

I am a football lover who wanted to do football on television and here I am now being asked to host and MC the Presidents' Cup. That baffled me. It was the kind of tournament that anybody would want to have as a gig and attach their names to.

My father may have been a golf caddy but I didn't know anything about golf. Living on the farm in Fort Louis, I never saw the purpose of his golf clubs. He also didn't spend enough time trying to convince me to learn the sport because he was also just busy trying to make ends meet for the family. But he really loved the sport.

I was scared because I didn't know the terminology or the scoring and I really had no interest in golf. I had to do research and find out what the President's Cup was all about. It was where the world's best get to play against the United States of America, and they were going to be here. The world's elite.

The very best golfers in the world were there, from Tiger Woods to Ernie Els. I could visually identify some of the big-name players. Also, there was former US President George Bush senior. He and President Thabo Mbeki walked in wearing gold blazers.

I couldn't believe this was happening. These guys were metres away from me. It was real. These were the world's best golfers. There were the best US golfers. It was a prestigious event, like the World Cup of Golf. It's a once-off and doesn't happen often. There were world leaders. I had to introduce them all and officially open the event to the world. I was at the helm of this event.

There was no autocue, just a couple of cue cards, and I had to maintain the dignity and prestige of the event. I had to focus on the job.

It was at times like that that I realised that maybe there is a purpose to what I am doing. The initial calling would take different forms but it was really overwhelming. The entire world was watching and I think that's what freaked me out more than anything, trying to not stuff up in front of a global audience.

That was just one of the jobs I did for the presidency during my career. When Nelson Mandela was still president of South Africa, the initial request had come in to host an event called the Premier and Presidential Awards held annually in Pretoria and hosted by the sitting president.

I had thought it was a hoax or somebody was pulling a prank on me when the request first came in.

I'm a sportscaster. I'm living my dream. I'm an admirer of politicians like Madiba, as we all were at the time if freedom and equality were what you were looking for. In terms of my broadcasting space, I was really just knuckling down and doing what I was doing. So, when a call came through from the Office of the President requesting and asking me for an email address so that they can begin a conversation as to whether or not I was able to host that event, I then had to believe that it was happening and I accepted.

It was a black-tie event full of politicians and people in the entertainment industry. I barely even got an opportunity to meet Madiba because introducing him to the podium and shifting aside doesn't actually count as meeting the man.

But it became an annual event and I was asked to host it several more times, both under Mandela and then Thabo Mbeki's presidency. I wasn't sure what earned me the right to be called up, but I took it as another confirmation that I was doing the right thing and to keep going.

I did eventually meet Madiba at one of the awards ceremonies. It was towards the end of his presidency, so he was more relaxed.

In true Madiba style, during soundcheck and rehearsals he came across and congratulated me on the job that I had done at these events over the years. I was grateful that he even knew my name, but Madiba was meticulous in always wanting to greet people by name. Here was the most revered man in the world showering me with praise. It is something that I really cherished.

Through all those events I formed a relationship with his assistant, Zelda. I was always sure to pass on birthday wishes and, with the events that I had done, the relationship was always cordial.

In my mind I was thinking I couldn't let go of this opportunity. I wanted to get an interview with Madiba. I knew so many current-affairs shows had failed to get him onto their programmes, whether it was radio or television. Some big hitters in the world weren't able to get a one-on-one with him.

Who am I to expect to get it right? Plus, I was doing a sports show, so that was even more of a problem.

I put the proposition forward to Zelda and it wasn't rejected straightaway. I was told it could be a possibility. I was very blunt with her and I said I know Madiba is a politician. People want to hear him speak politics. I am not a politician. I do not do current affairs and I don't do a politics show. But I also knew that Madiba was huge in terms of sport. I knew that Madiba was a former boxer and he loved his boxing. I knew that Madiba was the first person Hansie Cronje phoned when he was caught in the match-fixing saga. I knew that SARU president Louis Luyt was the first person after Madiba's release to send Madiba back to court.

I thought, with just those three angles, I could pull it off and get him to agree to come to the show. I bought the book chronicling the court case with Louis Luyt and read that cover to cover to understand the legal issues. I also had to understand what was happening with the cricket case and the match fixing because whatever Hansie had reached out to Mandela for might not have been public knowledge at the time. So, it made sense for me to try and get it firsthand from Madiba. What was it that Hansie was reaching out to him about and why him?

Zelda spoke to Madiba and he agreed, and the interview was set up. They also then decided to grant a few other interview requests on that same day. Gareth Cliff and Noeleen Maholwana-Sangqu were then put into the mix with their own interviews. The beautiful thing was that they accepted doing it live, not a pre-record. It was still a new thing for Metro to broadcast from the reception area and it was like a fishbowl with people gathering around to watch you.

Normally, I was talking to millions of people who I didn't see so it was unnerving with people physically watching. I had to go through protocols. The SABC management all came to be present there, to welcome and meet Madiba. There was a whole spectacle and people gathered all around. They wanted to see this man in the flesh. There was so much buzz that it was more than just a radio show; it became a showstopper in Auckland Park.

Just his arrival was presidential. It was Madiba. They had to bring him in a little bit early because he got distracted by people. He wanted to greet and have a handshake here and there. I got to spend some time with him in the holding room. He was in a good mood. He was wearing a Madiba shirt and I had my own version of one on too.

I didn't write questions or submit questions to him. I think there was enough trust that was built between us before the interview and I wanted it to be a conversation. I then saw the Mandela I had seen on television. The smile was wiped off. The laughing was gone. I could tell now that there was this shield that had developed within a short space of time. And was that going to work for or against me? Was I going to get a Madiba who is going to give me one-word answers and throw it back to you to try to navigate your way? I just told myself I'm going to be confident. There's a once-off opportunity for you to interview the one person the world wants to interview.

Was I going to stuff it up? Absolutely not. Why must I do that? Had I done enough prep? Definitely. This man was an intellectual. This was somebody who, beyond anything of being a politician or what they wanted to call a rabble-rouser back then, was actually a humane and very smart person. So, I needed to bring my A game.

The Interview. Wow. It was 29 minutes' flat go, no ads. I think it got to a stage where he also felt it was the kind of interview that he needed, that wasn't about trade unions or politics. He opened up and I was not wrong in having judged him as a sports-loving person.

He really cared about sportspeople. He cared about the late Baby Jake Matlala. He cared about former boxers. He cared about the role that he had played in shaping and uniting sports in this country. His memory of the details of the Louis Luyt case was incredible because what that triggered within Mandela was his legal background. Then branching off to the Hansie Cronje side, he had a very soft spot for the former captain. I think he had a soft spot for a lot of people.

Although some might even criticise him and say he's an apologist, I think he had been exhausted by divisions in this country. He had been exhausted by seeing people suffer, who were oppressed. So, how do you bring the oppressor and the oppressed together? That was always the conundrum. What role could sport play?

If I look at current presidents and how little they actually care about sport, that is problematic for me because sport is such a unifier and it is no coincidence that they all have different quotes that they attribute to Mandela about sport and it being a unifying factor; it is. A unifier in a country that has been left desolate like South Africa was important.

When the National Sports Council was saying that the Springbok emblem must go, cricket must be Proteas, rugby must be Proteas, and that is it. Mandela made an unpopular decision. He was trying to unify a country. So, if you remove the Springbok from rugby, what was going to happen? He had to tread very, very carefully and make unpopular decisions. He also had to have a bigger picture in mind.

That's also what triggered my being so vociferous when it came to rugby and transformation, because I was also on the side of 'to hell with this thing, it must go'. Being able to have a one-on-one with Mandela and understand his vision and what he wanted from it then gave me more of an impetus to say, 'Let me fight for this transformation.' If there was one thing that Madiba interview helped to shape in me, it was to have enough resolve to continue a fight where ministers of sport after Ngconde Balfour just became ceremonial people. They had to cut ribbons and make a noise on television. As the media, we then had a role to play in keeping them accountable. Unfortunately, that role came with a great deal of sacrifice and unhappiness in certain quarters.

That interview with Nelson Mandela was definitely a highlight of my broadcasting career. Over the years I have interviewed four sitting presidents. Not bad for a sports guy.

After my mother left nursing we stayed in eMondlo township in KwaZulu-Natal. Here she is busy crocheting a jersey for me.

My grandfather in his purple vestments at our house in Fort Louis; he was a bishop of the Anglican Church, based in Eshowe, KwaZulu-Natal.

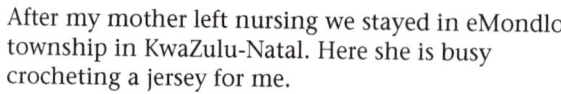

With my sisters, Nomvula (left) and Gugu, in our Sunday best.

My first year at Little Flower; the school motto was 'Success through Toil', words I continue to live by.

Beginning my high-school journey on my first day at Hilton College, accompanied by my mother.

My sleeping area at Falcon House, Hilton College, was a celebration of RnB and hip hop artists.

After a session of rugby training at Hilton College.

With Dumisani Kunene (left) and my late best friend Aubrey Ndlovu; preparing for the matric dance before meeting up with our partners.

My parents hand over a traditional and symbolic key at my twenty-first birthday party.

With Gugu, Nomvula and Vanessa, after a family Christmas lunch at the Holiday Inn in Ulundi, which at that time boasted the tag of being 'the smallest Holiday Inn in the world'.

I finally agreed to do a *Drum* cover shoot in 1997 for the 20 February issue.

Next magazine ran articles about my career as interest in my work grew.

In 2001 there was an even greater demand for me to do cover stories, leading to a further *Drum* cover on 11 October.

The inside story of the *Drum* feature of 11 October 2001.

Brazilian football legend Ronaldo, sporting Madiba's famous prison number, when he was in South Africa in 2005 for the launch of Tokyo Sexwale's A1 Grand Prix series.

Getting to know the great President Nelson Mandela ahead of our historic and groundbreaking in-studio interview at Metro FM.

Born in 2011 on the same day as Nelson Mandela, 18 July, my son Awande Sakhile Marawa loved napping on my chest – what an honour!

I organised a memorable fifth birthday party for Awande; it was also a lovely way to reconnect with him after his time in Australia.

Awande's fifth birthday party was attended by his mom, Zoe Mthiyane.

My dad wanted a simple tombstone, which we visited as a family, including the grandchildren, Awande and Sango.

President Kgalema Motlanthe is a firm football fan who shared many stories about the golden era; I took him around the Orlando Stadium during one of the Soweto clashes.

I love being in the crowd. Talking to me is Musa Sokhulu, then a prominent Pirates fan, who I helped become a cable basher for SuperSport, after which he became a cameraman. He's now also popular on TikTok.

When Sundowns president Patrice Motsepe first brought Barcelona to South Africa in 2007, he asked me to MC the event.

The Nedbank Cup 'Ke Yona' tournament was known for using top female models to hand over the Man of the Match Green Jacket.

With Pearl Thusi presenting one of the Naledi Awards, recognising and rewarding excellence in the performing arts in South Africa, at the Lyric Theatre.

I honoured Wilson B Nkosi with a surprise tribute to mark his thirtieth anniversary in radio on my *083 Sports@6* show on Metro FM.

In a sold-out black-tie affair at the Sandton Convention Centre, I had the honour of hosting and interviewing global boxing icon Floyd Mayweather Jnr for SuperSport in 2014.

With Kobe Bryant in Soweto.

20
Opportunity comes knocking

I was flying at the SABC. It was the height of the *SoccerZone* success at TopSport and it was the most-watched magazine show on television.

For talkability, fan anticipation, live games, controversial moments, the fans were loving it. Everyone would wait for Monday night and it developed something of a cult following. Everyone was talking about *SoccerZone*.

Unbeknown to me, there was a rival broadcasting channel in Randburg, M-Net, that was watching what we were doing and began to show some interest in me. One day, in around 2002, I got a call from a gentleman who was heading up SuperSport, Robin Kempthorne. I had heard of him because he was one of the most successful sports producers in the country.

Robin wanted me to meet with Lazarus Zim, who was then the boss at M-Net. Zim was interested in me joining M-Net and SuperSport.

My awareness of M-Net at the time was that it was that channel you could catch during 'Open Time' if you were lucky.

But if you didn't have a decoder you were in trouble. That's all I knew about M-Net. SuperSport did not yet have rights to local football so that was all still carried by the SABC.

I knew that going to SuperSport would be a big jump. The offer was humbling, but did I want it? I was asked to think about it and my first thought was no. I conveyed that to Robin and he told me that they had already drafted an offer for me. That offer was formally presented and when I looked at what I was earning at the SABC compared to what I could be earning, I thought, oh my goodness! This could have made all of life's problems evaporate.

But even though I needed the cash, I was not motivated by money. I never have been. I told them I couldn't accept the offer. I felt that we were building a really important product with MTN *SoccerZone*. The public loved it. We all loved it. It was just not something that I could drop for an offer of more money. I knew that my number-one love was football, more specifically local football, and that was not on offer at SuperSport. I had a public duty to carry on with my work at the SABC.

I didn't even use the offer as a leverage for more money from my then employer. This wasn't the right time, and we were making history and breaking records on the show. I carried on with my measly salary because I wanted to grow this product that had my fingerprints on it.

I was the anchor and, having been inspired to put my personality on the show, I felt that it would be unfair of me to leave. The more the show grew, the more I understood how important the audience and the viewer were to the entire product working. People loved all the personal touches that we were bringing and all this was new to the viewers. They loved that we were throwing in a bit of tsotsi/kasi-type vibe that people associate with football growing up in townships and locations around the country. We were able to connect the people with that kasi flavour and people could identify with that. We weren't speaking over people's heads and they could relate to it in the same way that they could talk to their next-door neighbours about the game.

The M-Net/SuperSport chapter was closed and I forged ahead. I felt that I had to commit myself to the SABC and I had to give black South Africa what I thought it deserved in terms of on-air presentation, quality of guests, quality of content, humour, conversations, stats, research, and all of those things. I really, really put my everything into it so that it was credible, but also friendly enough for non-football people to tap in and watch. I never regretted the decision not to go to M-Net. And I don't think they held any gripe against me in terms of me rejecting that offer.

One day in 2004, I was on assignment in Cape Town when something I never expected caught me off guard. It was so completely out of my realm of thinking that I had never considered myself doing.

I was in my hotel room when my phone rang. At the other end was businessman Patrice Motsepe, who had recently become the majority shareholder of Sundowns football club.

I had never met Patrice and had never spoken to him, but I obviously knew who he was. Why is he calling me? I wondered.

I could tell from the slight delay on the line that he was phoning from abroad and he told me he was in New York. He said he just couldn't wait to share a proposition that he had for me and that he expected I would accept.

I asked him what the proposition was. He said he would love for me to be the CEO of Mamelodi Sundowns. Motsepe had taken over the running of the team from the Tsichlas family and he was looking to make changes. We chatted for 45 minutes – I asked one question and for the rest of the time he spoke about how excited he was about me potentially coming on board.

He told me I shouldn't worry about not having any experience with administration because he would guide me through everything that needed to happen and it wouldn't be a problem. He was willing and eager for me to shadow him and speak to him on a daily basis and learn from him as he was running his mining companies too.

He could tell that I was a bit hesitant and that it was all very unexpected for me. I was so taken aback. This was Patrice Motsepe, mining magnate, billionaire businessman.

I knew that money wasn't the beginning and end of everything in life. It's always great to earn money but you must also earn where you know you can deliver and be productive and bring change.

I seriously considered the offer. It was something different.

Sundowns was under new management and there was a new culture. Here was a very ambitious young businessman who was in charge and maybe I could be part of that new culture.

But I had a gazillion reservations about the offer. I remembered my dream. I remembered what I wanted to do in life. I wasn't willing to bring that to an end for something completely unknown and for a new entity. I would be stepping into a dark room. I was willing to learn but learning on the job had its own problems.

At the end of the day, Sundowns was a football club and I would have to be accountable for it. I was the same person who was holding other people in the administration of football accountable to their fans.

After three-quarters of an hour, he promised that he would set up a face-to-face meeting with me when he was back in the country and, true to his word, he did. At the time, his day job was at the Sandton law firm Bowman Gilfillan. I arrived for our scheduled meeting at the offices, but he said we would be having the meeting out at a restaurant.

We took a gentle walk to the Brazilian coffee shop in Sandton City, which used to be next to the Edgars. It was a popular outlet and it was always busy at lunchtime. I was intrigued by his choice of location because we were both well known and recognisable. We weren't going somewhere private. The chairs and tables were all set out in front and it wasn't like we could hide out in the shadows inside. We were in the full glare of everybody and people were walking past greeting us and shaking our hands.

He still insisted that he wanted me to join the team. I had to emphasise to him that I was pursuing my long-standing dream of being a broadcaster. I wanted to be a better broadcaster.

I told him I was humbled and taken aback by his generous offer. We had not discussed money but I was sure that, working for him, I would be able to see money that I had never experienced in my life.

I had to make a big call and I chose to remain being a broadcaster.

Part of me did begin to wonder if this wasn't the start of attempts to get me out of the industry and if it wasn't the early stages of moves to push me off radio and television platforms.

If I ventured off and became the CEO of Sundowns, would I be guaranteed to stay in that position? If there was a backlash from Sundowns fans who thought I was useless, I would get chucked out.

I turned down the offer. I had heard unsubstantiated rumours that there were plans to offer me lots of money to do other work that was not broadcasting related to get me off air. When I look at this kind of offer, it fitted right in with that suggestion.

I was not willing to have my dream derailed. I was enjoying myself and challenging myself on a daily basis, and being a sports administrator was not in my future plans.

The SABC was my home, but I can't deny that after that first approach, there were various attempts to lure me to SuperSport. There were informal conversations that happened over drinks and a chat. But then it came to a point in 2006 when Imtiaz Patel, head of SuperSport, reached out to me. He didn't beat about the bush.

SuperSport had been expanding and he tried to entice me by asking if I wanted to grow and expand in terms of my own broadcasting career. By that stage, SuperSport had all the major rights except for those to local football, although they had a smattering of domestic games that they covered on *AmaTuesdays*.

Imtiaz told me they had been watching; they knew I had been approached in the past but this time they were really serious.

Not long after that, the World Cup in Germany rolled around. I was part of the SABC team assigned to cover the tournament for television. At the time Gordon Templeton was my producer and he thought it would be a good opportunity to do my radio show on Metro FM from the World Cup too.

I explained to Gordon that it would not be logistically possible. I would be travelling to various locations for TV and would be crossing in to the breakfast show regularly. Doing a daily radio show was impossible. But he went ahead and continued with plans for the radio show to happen from Germany. In the end, those plans got approval from management at the SABC.

We got to Germany and I did the breakfast show on television as planned. Later on, I walked into the broadcast centre and I saw Gordon setting up for radio. I asked him who was going to be doing the show and he told me I was. It was my show and I had to present it. I reminded him that I had already told him I couldn't do radio. I was there to focus on what had brought me to Germany, which was television.

Everything had been approved, obviously, on the premise that I was going to do it, despite the fact I had put it on record I wouldn't be able to do both. We wouldn't be staying in the same places. There were games that I was chasing in my Opel Kadett on the autobahn as fast as I could. It was impossible to do a radio show from a fixed position if I was moving from city to city.

I wasn't saying no because I was trying to be funny or belligerent. I was saying no because it was impossible. At that stage we weren't technologically that advanced. I would also be giving my audience back home a really crappy product.

There were also problems on the television side. The World Cup was at the peak of the European summer in June/July and FIFA was trying out fan parks for the first time. The SABC had not got accreditation for any of the games, so I couldn't actually get inside the stadiums to report on the football. We didn't have any tickets. They had not been arranged.

So, what now? We had to cover the stories behind the stories, doing packages from fan parks, going to the broadcast centres. It wasn't a problem because we brought the vibe and the colour and the fans, and made it look like we were at the stadiums. There were big screens and the beer was flowing and it was fun. But I was a football person. I wanted to do the football and not colour pieces. We spent 42 days in Germany and the SABC spent millions for a below-par product.

It was great to have a presence in Germany. I understood that from an SABC perspective. South Africa wasn't there, because we didn't qualify for the tournament, but there were five African countries participating and the coverage wasn't good enough. In my mind and in terms of my own growth, I had to ask myself if this is what I wanted. I returned to South Africa disappointed.

Shortly after returning home from the World Cup, I was asked to anchor a game from the FNB Stadium. It was a packed-out match and I was looking forward to it after the Germany experience. It was just what I needed to get my enthusiasm back. I was on the scaffolding next to the field, hosting the broadcast.

Everything that could go wrong went wrong. The comms didn't work properly. The leg of my chair kept getting stuck in the scaffolding because the mat was missing. There was so much noise in my earpiece. I could hear the guys in Auckland Park speaking through to the outside broadcast van and nothing was making sense.

It was probably the beginning of the wheels coming off at the SABC. I don't even know or remember who was producing or directing that day. All I know is there was chaos. Obviously, for the sake of the integrity of the broadcast, I had to try to keep everything in order, although at times it was difficult. I felt like the world was watching how bad things were. We were trying to do a crossing to Brian Mulder but he couldn't hear me. Then he would try to speak but his microphone would be off.

It was a combination of so many different things. We wanted to improve, not regress. It was disappointing to see things falling apart.

I thought to myself, what am I doing here?

In the back of my mind was the conversation that I had had with Imtiaz Patel shortly before the World Cup. I signed off that day with a very unconvincing 'Gqimm Shelele' at the end of the show.

I went straight home from the stadium that Saturday, sat down at my desk and began to write my resignation letter from the SABC.

I didn't end up sending that letter for a few weeks. But I knew my glorious stay at the SABC had probably come to an end. I was prepared to go and sell hot dogs in Braamfontein if necessary.

I needed a new sense of motivation, a new challenge, a new platform, a new arena. I'd seen what SuperSport were doing with *AmaTuesdays* and their productions were good. There was something they were cooking. They had one or two magazine shows they were trying to get going. I would have been happy to cover pigeon racing or bowls, to be honest. I was just keen to get out of an environment that was slowly but surely starting to suck the excitement out of what I thought was a really great platform.

It was very difficult for me to leave the SABC. I had always had a love and respect for it. It was my first platform and one that I had desired as a kid. But things were starting to unravel.

I was not experiencing the standards I had become accustomed to. Half the time I was rescuing a broadcast as opposed to being part of a broadcast that I enjoyed and put everything into. I was dreading going into a production knowing something would go wrong. Someone would not pull their weight and I would be left exposed. I was having to save broadcasts and give them the integrity they deserved.

This was not what I had signed up for. It had nothing to do with anything or anyone else. I needed to test myself. Maybe I had also become complacent. It was many things, but it was a jump that was necessary at the time.

Before I had the opportunity to announce that I was resigning, other forces intervened. This was the beginning of a wave of similar experiences that involved me being fired or not having my contract renewed at various jobs over the next few years.

I submitted my resignation on a Friday to Mvuzo Mbebe, who was then the head of sport at the SABC, and that weekend, the *Sunday World* newspaper broke the news that I was leaving the SABC for SuperSport. It was the front-page headline.

Like so many things that happened within the SABC, it was probably a leak from within the broadcaster to the newspaper. *Sunday World* was always the default tabloid that knew things I had privately spoken to the SABC about. There was obviously a line of people who had got wind of what was going on after I resigned.

Once I saw the headline, I knew there was no denying it. I could also tell that an internal person from my employer had leaked the story. SuperSport wasn't commenting on the story; I wasn't commenting on the story. *Sunday World* was confident enough to run it on their front page because they knew it to be true and could live and die by the headline.

That Monday I went and did my radio show on Metro FM as per normal. At that stage I had two separate contracts for radio and television. It was something I always insisted on.

I had resigned from television but not from radio. Once the radio show was done for the day, I headed off to do *SoccerZone* on television.

Before that could happen I received a message from Mvuzo's PA telling me not to bother doing my show on television that Monday. Clearly they didn't want me to be on a live broadcast.

I think what triggered them was that they didn't have the time to deal with the resignation letter and to decide what to do. *Sunday World* had got the story before they could act. I had not leaked it. I didn't even know anyone at *Sunday World*. Why would I leak anything? I could only assume it came from within the SABC.

I didn't see the front-page headline coming. I didn't see me being barred from saying goodbye on air. I couldn't say goodbye to the *SoccerZone* audience nor to the *Laduma* audience for the live games on Sunday the following weekend.

We had built this beautiful thing and I couldn't say goodbye to the audience. That first one hurt. It was the beginning of a pattern, but that first one really hurt. I had built this rapport, I had built this audience, I had built this loyalty. I had literally built all the different foundations that were there. I wasn't even afforded a five-minute segment, just to say a dignified thank-you for the support. Thank you for the love that you've shown. Thank you for being part of my journey. Let's meet again soon.

There was no finality or closure. It was a gaping hole. I won't lie. It was designed to hurt and it did hurt because I didn't see it coming. Anything to do with SABC television was done just like that.

I had to roll with the punches, take them on the chin, regroup and start to think ahead. This was my first lesson in the world of broadcasting that was not pleasant and I had to learn from it because it happened many times again in the future.

21
Soaring at SuperSport

It's difficult to gauge what the backlash to my leaving the SABC was like from the public because social media wasn't present then like it is today.

Internally, people who I had worked with for many years weren't happy. Cameramen, lighting, sound people, floor managers, you name it.

There was no mistaking that we had changed the landscape of how sport broadcasting should be done. *SoccerZone* was by far the biggest product that was affected by my departure. People came in and tried to emulate what I was doing rather than being original and carving their own niche. They copied what I had been saying, my mannerisms, the little things, but there was nothing in terms of originality.

My focus shifted to what I looked at as being the Sky Sports of African sports broadcasting. That's how I had looked at SuperSport and its growth and how they covered things.

They had professionalism. Left, right and centre. They covered things thoroughly. Where the SABC had started lacking in terms of professionalism, SuperSport was developing at an international level.

My concern now was facing a new audience. In the past I had been broadcasting to a non-subscriber base that was mostly black. I knew that SuperSport was more of a niche market with a predominantly stronger economic hold. I wondered whether I would get the same reception at SuperSport that I had received at the SABC.

There were undertones of people feeling that I had sold out. Some thought it was my decision to leave but I don't think they appreciated the fact that in putting in a lot of work, you then get recognised outside of your space. People get to appreciate what you do. It's part of growth. It's part of not being pigeonholed into doing one thing over and over again. People see the potential for growth. People see what you can bring onto their different platforms.

I understand that people thought I ditched SABC Sport and went to SuperSport, but I couldn't employ myself. They wouldn't have known that Lazarus Zim had approached me years prior and I had turned him down.

I have had to develop a crocodile skin over the years because I have had to expect and accept criticism at every stage of my journey. In the main, people have been happy, but there are always individuals who are going to take potshots at you for whatever decision you make.

I looked at it differently. I looked at it as, 'Those of you who were with me at SABC Sport are going to journey with me to SuperSport one way or another. That's going to be our journey.'

SuperSport made a big deal of my move. They went on a

huge marketing campaign and put up Robert posters all over the country. Taking the face of SABC Sport and making it their own was a big acquisition. It almost seemed like the transfer of a major football player to another team and I was highly visible at stadiums while doing touchline presentations

I didn't know it at the time, but the main driver for SuperSport was a bigger push to try to get the rights to broadcast local football, although they didn't share this information with me.

Stepping into SuperSport was very daunting because of what I had seen of their product. I felt that I had not dropped my standards at the SABC because my desire was always there, but there was a level of complacency.

The English Premier League (EPL) was one of the first products I had to concentrate on, which was a change for me. I needed to follow the league even more closely than I had before. They put together a panel including ex-Manchester United goalkeeper Gary Bailey and former Southampton and 1966 World Cup winner Terry Paine. That was huge for me. How would I deal with that? I had to be at a level where I could sit and converse with these two legends, never mind anybody else who would come in and rotate as panelists. These were two standout individuals in world football.

I had to drive the conversation because I was the anchor and I was mindful of the fact that these were some of the most revered superstars.

When I initially got there and I got into a studio set-up, there was friendliness, but I also sensed an underlying tone of doubt. I felt people were thinking, who the hell does he think he is to come from the SABC to front an EPL production? Was I good enough to hold this thing together? I came from a local football background at the national broadcaster so people assumed I didn't know anything about English football.

It wasn't verbalised, but I'm wise enough to get a sense of how a person reacts or how they respond to a question. I wasn't coming in without any experience of anchoring or knowledge of football, but this was an already moving train with well-established ex-football players who had obviously set a standard for themselves in a premium product at SuperSport.

Anchoring EPL was a whole-day affair on a Saturday, starting from 11am, doing three or four games back to back. It was a lot of preparation, research, note taking and watching football.

I told myself that it was the same round-ball game that was played by the local superstars. I just needed to sharpen everything else that had to do with the sport.

The first couple of weeks were tough. I could pull off the broadcast and the feedback wasn't overly negative, but I think I was too worried about the people sitting with me in studio.

I had also watched them from a distance, even before I joined SuperSport. I had seen their body language and it informed what I thought about them. I had watched when former Nigerian footballer Idah Peterside was brought in as an analyst on a panel discussion with someone like Terry Paine. They would be in the same studio discussing football and Idah was an ardent Arsenal supporter, but he was dismissed. There was negative body language from Terry; he would look away and not engage Idah while he was making his point. In terms of television language, you should grant the person the respect of actually looking at them while they make their point. Idah would be talking and Terry would look away from him.

The studio was difficult initially because of what was already planted in my mind having witnessed this negative body language. Whether you see that as classist, or racist, or what, I don't know. It was just weird to see. In studio, as the anchor, the interaction initially felt strange. I had never experienced anything like it. It seemed disengaged and I felt like I was talking to myself. We should all accord each other an opportunity to talk; look at the person, engage, seem interested, retort if there is a retort. That was my perception.

But the more hard work I put in, the more I was able to earn respect from everybody in studio. It took about four months at SuperSport to win everyone over and then the situation literally flipped.

It changed to such an extent that when we got the team sheets and we were making quick notes, Terry Paine would be the first one to say, 'Hey, Robbie, listen, man, that guy who has just signed up for Wolves. You know, jersey number seven, which club did he come from?'

All of a sudden there was this trust that had developed. There was this energy when we were discussing things just before we went on air. There was a complete change in the dynamic within the studio with the same people who had doubted me. That level of trust became so ingrained that these legends were able to ask me questions if they were in doubt about anything.

This initiation into SuperSport actually turned out to be the kind of introduction I needed into a new workspace. I needed to know there was no room for complacency and no room for short cuts. This was pure hard work and I needed to bring my A game each and every day. It was humbling for me.

It was also a sign that it was the kind of move that I needed because my hunger and desire to do sports broadcasting were back again. There was a desire to do more research than I actually needed to and to delve into all sorts of things.

In the end I became trusted because I came with information that was not just superficial about football. I would bring in content about a player that was more than about simply his contribution to the game.

I formed really good relationships with Terry and Gary, to the extent that I had them both on my Legends slot on radio. I don't think they would have granted that if they felt I was not worthy of hosting them on a platform outside SuperSport.

Later on in my time at SuperSport, former Premier Soccer League striker Marc Batchelor also joined as an analyst and I got to do more games with him. I had a very good relationship with Marc from his playing days. He was genuinely a good guy. We would exchange voice notes or messages and he would insist we meet at the infamous Tashas restaurant in Melrose Arch. I would find him there with all of these big, bulky heavyweight men. I really appreciated the human being that he was. I never passed any judgement about any decisions he made in life. His coming on board and being part of the panel alternating with Terry and Gary was great.

Marc used to hate it when the aircon wasn't on in the studio. Studios usually have very high air conditioning because of the lights and the equipment. You've got to keep it cool and Marc loved that. The minute the aircon was off, he would cause a scene in the studio and you would see a cameraman or floor manager nervously scurrying to switch on the aircon. Marc would come from the gym with beads of sweat all over his body and shout about the aircon. And then you would be sitting in the freezing cold. I was thinking, oh my God, what the hell is this guy taking? Is he on steroids or something? That was Marc.

He brought an energy to the show but he was not a popular guy with the management at SuperSport. The discipline factor counted against him. The negative publicity in the newspapers also counted against him. So SuperSport inevitably had to make a decision to part ways and end his contract.

Around the time of mining magnate Brett Kebble's murder trial, you could tell there was a lot happening in Marc's head. He would come into the studio and his focus was all over the place and he was on the phone a lot of the time. He would leave the studio and not even watch the game. I could tell there was something amiss; it wasn't the same Marc.

It was sad losing him at SuperSport. And it was a sad loss when Marc was killed. When the unfortunate picture started circulating of him being shot in the car, I was not even in the country. A colleague showed me the picture. What a sad way to check out of this world. His life choices were against him at the time. But we missed his presence, especially his joyful, playful nature around the SuperSport building. I think even the cameramen who were scared of him missed his rants and raves.

Once I had settled at SuperSport, the head of production Tex Teixeira was keen on starting something on a Monday that was about local football and similar to *SoccerZone*. Tex was always very open with me; he wanted to build the local product. He knew that *SoccerZone* was the flagship show at SABC and had the highest ratings of any show in the country, but he was also scared. *SoccerZone* was on from 9pm to 10pm and he wanted to start the SuperSport show at 10pm. He had conceded there was nothing that could beat *SoccerZone*.

Once I left SABC television, I never watched *SoccerZone* again. I didn't even know who was hosting it. I kept moving forward and focused on what I needed to do. Because I knew how much work I had put into those institutions, I didn't want to be in a space where I felt disappointed. I focused on my next move.

So I said to Tex, we should start our new show at 8.30pm. We would go on 30 minutes before the start of *SoccerZone* and then we would load the hot stuff for the day at around 8.50pm or 8.55pm. We would take our first break at 9.10pm.

Viewers who had latched on to watch from 8.30pm would forget that there was *SoccerZone* at 9pm. We would keep them on until 9.10pm. By that time, they would be so hooked that there would be no turning back for them.

Tex looked at me and asked, 'Are you sure?'

I said, 'Tex, Listen, I'm not telling you nonsense. Don't do 10pm. By 10pm people are sleeping. We hit it prime time, but we go on at 8.30pm.' He gave me that stern look and I said, 'Tex, trust me.'

We were starting a new project and I had a blank slate, which was the hallmark of what I had done since I started broadcasting. Tex respected my view, so he said, 'Let's do it.' When Tex says he is going to do something, he does it. That is one thing I grew to respect about SuperSport: the level of application. You didn't have to go through different layers and ask for permission, wait for so-and-so to approve and all kinds of red tape. There was a decision-maker. That decision-maker was Tex, and after that it was about implementation.

That first show was called *Extra Time*.

SuperSport did not have the football rights at that stage but Tex knew they were heading in that direction. That's why he wanted to have a show that would be strong enough by the time SuperSport got the rights to football to have a platform for a review show.

We secured guys like Farouk Khan and Neil Tovey for the show. One of the things that had worked on *SoccerZone* was that we had two very strong analysts and a former referee, because in every game there's going to be a controversial moment that needs a former referee to come in and analyse. That was a no-brainer. I knew there was one guy who was very articulate and smart, who would work on the platform. Ace Ncobo, a former referee, had worked within the PSL structures; he was also very ambitious and very opinionated. I reached out to Ace; he agreed and came on board.

The show started taking off. There was a lot of marketing around it and viewers began to get engaged. That started translating to audience ratings. One of the main drivers of viewer interaction was emails. People would almost instantaneously email their opinions to us. A lady called Prudence, who was the PA, would come through to the studio with a wad of printed emails during every ad break. I would quickly read through the comments to find ones that were relevant that I could read out on air. The more I read people's emails, the more they would send. People loved hearing their views and their names being read out on the show. The level of viewer engagement became unprecedented.

Then there was the addition of former Kaizer Chief midfielder Isaac 'Shakes' Kungwane to the team. Shakes had been at SuperSport previously, but he went to SABC and now he was desperate to come back because he was not happy there.

He reached out to me and said he had made a big mistake and he wanted to come back. He believed he could fit in at *Extra Time* but the only problem, he joked, was that we spoke 'too much big English'. I knew Shakes's qualities – he was a character and a funny guy. He would bring an element of kasi flavour. I told him not to worry about the big English and I would make his case to management.

We had a full component of analysts and a proper structure but we needed him to bring himself, the guy everybody could relate to and who would be vocal. He could come in and shut down Ace or Neil and tell them they were talking nonsense and disagree with them.

I went to speak to Happy Ntshingila, the CEO at SuperSport. I told him Shakes wanted to return, that he was apologetic, that he had made a mistake, and Happy got it. Happy is a football lover who understands local football along with advertising and marketing. He told me to bring Shakes to see him. One meeting and Shakes had signed up and was back.

Shakes became one of the drawcards of the show. We did 'Kasi Flavour Moment' with him. We would put together clips of somebody putting a shibobo through, doing what they call a tsamaya, or a show me your number. All of those things were put into a package that we called Kasi Flavour Moment. It was another unique component to the show that people looked forward to.

Viewers really enjoyed Shakes. Here was a relatable guy who came in and mixed isiZulu, Sesotho, isiXhosa, whatever. He also was not trying to sound like Tovey or Farouk Khan. He was himself and it worked. It was a beautiful thing to watch. He had the antics and the theatrics, but he understood the vision. Shakes really elevated the show. He became Mr Extra Time. I will always miss him and his contribution.

Everything was coming together. Former Kaizer Chiefs goalkeeping great William Shongwe also joined us on the show. He was the guy who was competing for the Chiefs keeper position when Gary Bailey moved from Manchester United to come and end his career at Kaizer Chiefs.

William Shongwe's fingers pointed all over the place because he never wore gloves and goalkeeping takes its toll on your hands. I would tease him on air. I would get the cameraman to zoom in on his fingers and we would joke about them. He was always scruffy, so we would tease him about his crumpled clothes or his torn shoes or we would get someone to bring him a freshly dry-cleaned jacket on air. It was all part of the theatrics and drama around the show. But according to William, his wife hated me because I was always making fun of her husband on air. I told him to tell her we were making television. It was nothing personal. We always walked out of there laughing and chatting and being good friends.

One of the key things to drive and grow shows is to do unique stuff and to do things that appeal to people at home. Strictly football discussions can be boring for the viewers. If you're a purist that's fine, but you want to engage everybody in the family and have everyone watching the show.

People would be looking forward to what William was going to falter on. Would he have combed his hair? Would he have shaved? What would I pick on him about? He was undeniably my target. People would watch just for that. They would watch for whatever theatrics Shakes was going to come up with.

Those were the add-ons to the show that the entire family could be entertained by. People who never gave a damn about sport would watch and tell me how much they had learnt about sport through the show.

Similarly to when I arrived at the SABC, everything at

SuperSport was in English and we had to change that. The one thing Tex stressed when I got there was that I must never throw away my 'Gqimm Shelele' at the end of the show. That was a direct instruction. The Gqimm Shelele must go nowhere. I had to keep it on this new platform.

I thought I would drop this sign-off once I moved to Randburg. It was done. But Tex was the first one to say in our initial meeting that I must never drop it as it would resonate well with the audience. So I kept doing it.

That Monday-night show, *Extra Time*, became the most-watched show and it beat *SoccerZone* on audience ratings. It got to a point where the SABC felt that *SoccerZone* wasn't bringing in any value any more – no audience, no money, no revenue; the compromise, ironically, was that it was moved to 10pm.

Tex had another vision for me to do a preview show on a Thursday night. It was an existing show called *Engen Premium Soccer*, which was on at 8.30pm. It was a pretty staid format and I didn't really enjoy it. So after a while I approached Tex and told him it wasn't working and asked him to give me a blank piece of paper to create a new show.

Tex asked what I had in mind and I explained it was something very different. Before I could tell him, Tex said he wanted me to do a show with sport and music mixed. He thought it would get people excited. I said, exactly! Sport and music have always combined and especially with local football. For example, in the days of Abdul Bhamjee, he would make sure if there was a big occasion, a cup final or a charity spectacular, superstars would be brought in to perform. Rebecca Malope or Lucky Dube would perform and people would pack the stadiums.

That thought came to mind and I agreed 100% with Tex. We would do interviews, keep it informal, look at other sports and preview the games. We would include boxing or Formula One or cricket or rugby.

That was the birth of *Thursday Night Live with Marawa*. I was intentional about attaching my name to it. Having come from the SABC, the name was important for association.

We held auditions for somebody who would be a buffer to me on the show, a foil for me to bounce off. We wanted to bring in a woman, so we put out a call to the industry. People came through all dolled up; some were models, people who looked great on television with make-up, but most of them were found wanting and didn't work.

They had tried everybody, except one last person, and that was Thato Moeng, who rocked up late, sweaty as hell with no make-up, and we just engaged. That was the beginning of the journey and Thato became the regular for *Thursday Night Live*. We worked extremely well together. There was no rehearsal, but I could converse with her about any topic and she would respond.

Again we had to find a way to innovate on the show. I visualised *Thursday Night Live* to be a talk show like Larry King or David Letterman, with the host behind the desk and guests on the couch. That was the beauty of SuperSport – they were able to listen and trust me with the journey; if I asked for something,

I got a positive response. They built the set, there were good directors, good lighting. Everybody worked together.

Over time, that couch became known as the 'magic couch'. Everybody we brought in to sit on that couch went on to score a hat-trick or win Man of the Match. It became the notorious magic couch. Coaches and players would come through and rub it, and it grew in fame.

But the glory of the show was the musical element, because every artist in South Africa wanted to be on the show. We provided the instruments. It was like a show at Wembley Arena. Artists took the performance seriously.

We had a great director in Ibrahim Badat; he cut that show as if the artist had gone on to do a music video. He experimented and did things differently. It was an opportunity for anyone on production to show their A game. Nightclubs wanted to partner with us in getting the artists to come through to their venues after appearing on the show.

We also had proper calibre guests coming through across all sporting codes. We would get international stars in. Real top hitters. It was flying. People were watching. It was just growing and growing and growing. In my mind, moving to SuperSport was probably the best career move I had ever made.

There were many positive stories while I was at SuperSport. There was a lot of trust in terms of my ability, particularly from Tex Teixeira. He also always tried to challenge me and make me grow.

Ahead of the Rugby World Cup in France in 2007, Tex

offered me an opportunity to anchor the tournament for SuperSport. He knew that I knew rugby and that I had played the sport. He knew that even on the radio show we were starting to profile a lot about rugby. He felt that, given I was part and parcel of SuperSport, it made sense that I become part of the rugby offering.

For the first time, I turned Tex down.

I gave it some careful thought. I had been propelled as the face of football. Sure, I had done the Commonwealth Games and the Olympic Games and the All-Africa Games. But I was also Mr Football. Remember at SuperSport, rugby and cricket were the main drivers. Football, and especially local football, was a lesser priority at the time. I was committed to upping its profile.

I didn't think I had the energy to drive rugby properly. As much as I knew my rugby, there was a lot of anger in the country at the time, especially within the white Afrikaner community, towards the transformation project that was going on. They were blaming players of colour for coming in and weakening the team. Jake White was at the helm of rugby at the time. Some of his comments also didn't inspire me much. So I don't think I was buying the South African Springbok story at the time personally or what their intentions were as a team. That would have made life very difficult for me to be at the helm of their broadcast. It would have been a challenge for me and my principles.

I had already carried too many other struggles on my shoulders to want to go into another battle. I was very aware of the dominance of media and the views that I had, and the transformation element that I had started to preach even at that time. It wasn't going to be pleasant.

There were a lot of new rugby rules that had been introduced and I was okay with them. I could have carried it as an anchor. I had to make a hard decision and I said no. Tex was supportive of my decision and understood why I chose not to do it.

I could have anchored every game of that World Cup that the Springboks went on to win, but I felt it wasn't the right move for me at the time.

22
Cooling off

It was the middle of June 2007 and I was sitting in a meeting at SuperSport in Randburg when someone burst into the room with an urgent message to relay to me. The CEO Imtiaz Patel needed to see me immediately at the Premier Soccer League offices in Parktown. I had to get there ASAP.

There was zero indication what this urgent meeting was about. I arrived at the PSL offices and I could immediately tell there was a buzz about the place. There were cameramen and something was going on.

I walked into the boardroom to the sight of celebration. There was a cohort of board members of the league and all the big bosses from Multichoice and SuperSport. At the head of the table was PSL chairman Irvin Khoza. Kaizer Motaung, John Comitis, Mato Madlala, Imtiaz Patel and Tex Teixeira were all there.

I could see balloons and champagne and cake. Khoza announced that they could begin the celebrations because the one person they had been waiting for had arrived! Still I had no clue what was happening. But it didn't take long for it to dawn on me.

Multichoice had secured the rights to the PSL games. It was a five-year deal worth a billion rand. SuperSport would be the official broadcaster of PSL matches.

There was clapping and champagne corks popping. The cake was cut. There was a photo opportunity. There I was in the photo smiling alongside the SuperSport and PSL execs and that photo started circulating. I was dragged into the celebrations but there I was in the image. It was big news.

While the celebration was underway in Parktown, at the SABC the CEO at the time, Dali Mpofu, was furious. My colleague, sports reporter Mahlomola Morake, went to interview Mpofu and he denied that the rights had been sold. He insisted the SABC still had the rights to the games. He described them as delusional and crazy.

I had seen the PSL leadership in Parktown so I knew there was nothing fake about the announcement. It had happened. The standoff was starting to brew. I began to find myself in a corner because that photo of me was becoming problematic.

I was still doing a radio show on Metro FM but I was doing television on SuperSport at the time. Technically, there was no direct conflict. But the bosses at the SABC saw that photograph as being triumphant and celebratory.

That day I had to do my radio show and this was obviously the big sports story of the day. Morake reached out to me and told me what Mpofu had said to him in the interview – that there was no deal, it was a lie and they were misleading the public.

The SABC was saying there was no way there could be such

a deal because a public broadcaster had to broadcast football. Football is the people's game.

We had to sort this out on the show and get answers for the listeners. I asked my producer, Beverly Maphangwa, to phone Dali Mpofu and ask him if we could speak to him on the show. I asked her to phone Imtiaz Patel from SuperSport. Then I asked her to phone Irvin Khoza, the chairman of the PSL, because we needed to speak to him. Those were the three people – he who had lost, he who had gained and he who owned the rights.

As a broadcaster, I needed answers for football fans. There was shock, disbelief, confusion and we had to clear it up. People knew the only place to get the real story was on my show. At 6pm we went on air.

We started with Dali Mpofu. He denied there was a deal. Government would never allow a private entity to take football away from the people. He was adamant. They were fooling themselves.

Next on the line was the chairman Irvin Khoza. He spoke about what a happy day it was for football. More games would be broadcast on television. There would no longer be delayed-live broadcasts as SABC had been doing. There would be magazine shows, preview shows, review shows. The SABC would get a percentage of games to broadcast. Clubs would receive monthly grants as part of the deal that would keep them afloat and players would benefit from that too. There would be financial viability and clubs would not have to rely only on gate takings. It was record breaking. History making.

There was excitement about the deal, but people were still concerned that if they didn't have a decoder they would be in trouble and miss out on the broadcasts. At the same time, there was a growing black middle class, a lot of people had dishes and DStv decoders by then, and more games would be accessible.

The final interview to balance the story was Imtiaz Patel. He came on the line and told us how the deal would change the footballing landscape. They had been in talks for some time to change the production of football. SuperSport would be able to show midweek games and more games live on weekends. The winner would be the viewer.

Mid-stream through the conversation with Imtiaz, Beverly started waving her hands around, telling me to cut the interview. Cut, cut. She tells me Dali wants us to cut the interview. I could see she was on the phone, stressing, panicking. I was still busy with the interview and I couldn't drop it halfway through. The listener needed to have a balanced view. It was a crucial time in our football and broadcasting history. It was the first time the SABC was losing the rights to local football and it had to be documented. We had to get every single role player on air to tell their story and the listener deserved that.

I was not going to cut the interview while Imtiaz was talking. I refused.

Beverly told me she had been instructed to drop the call from the control booth. I was busy fighting this war while trying to do the interview. I told her not to drop the call and she was caught in the middle. She thought she was going to be fired.

A whole CEO is telling her to can the interview. I continued up until its logical conclusion and ended the conversation.

But then I said on air, because I believed the listeners should know, that there had been pressure off air to end the interview. I had to let the audience know, in the event that I got fired after that, what the reason was.

Lo and behold, it didn't take long before I got a message telling me I was suspended. The interview coupled with the photograph of me at the celebratory event were used against me. There was this front-page photograph of everyone charging champagne glasses and here I was using an SABC platform to undermine them, so they tried to twist the story because the SABC had lost the rights. I had nothing to do with that. I was just carrying the news for the people as objectively as I could because that was my duty.

How do you run a credible show if you are going to misinform people in the process? The credibility around the sports show was such that people relied on it for objectivity, honesty and engagement. I was not going to change that approach because this story was against the SABC. It was of their doing, not mine. Otherwise there wouldn't be a story.

I was told not to bother coming in to do the show the next day and that I needed a 'cooling-off period', so I made the most of it. Barcelona were in town playing against Sundowns and I had not planned to go to the game because I was supposed to be on air doing the radio show. This meant I now had an opportunity to go to the stadium. I had already hosted their welcome at the Sandton Convention Centre and I had the opportunity to shake hands with the likes of Ronaldinho. Now I could go to watch them play.

I drove through to Loftus Versfeld Stadium in Pretoria and just as I passed the Shell Ultra City in Midrand, I switched on the radio. Although I didn't usually want to listen to my shows after I had left them, I tuned in that day. My colleague Romy Titus was at the helm and she was carrying on the show as if nothing had happened. But it was an interactive show and she had to open the lines to the callers. It was a disaster.

The first caller was scathing. He wanted to know where Robert was. Why is the SABC acting like a bully? Romy tried to explain that I would be back. Then the call was cut. The second caller came through asking why the first caller had been cut. Same story. They wanted to know, as the nation, why this was happening after the events of the day before that they all knew about.

As a fellow broadcaster and as somebody who knew Romy personally as a good friend, I felt sorry for her because she had been thrust into a position that was not fair. Not enough was done to protect her and guard her in that transition. Not enough thought was put into production so that they didn't have to take calls.

They opened the lines when the nation was angry, knowing now officially that the PSL product is lost to the SABC and knowing that the interview I had had the night before was the cause of me not being on air. People were raging. This was the biggest sports show in the country. The ANC Youth League also released a statement and so did the UDM's Bantu Holomisa condemning my suspension. Romy really took uppercuts. She didn't deserve it. I switched off the radio and drove to Loftus.

As I walked into the stadium there was such a buzz. I never really got to see any mid-week games, so I was really excited. I went through to the suite and one of the first people I saw was Mam' Winnie Madikizela-Mandela. She said to me, 'My son, what are they doing to you? Is everything okay?' Obviously she had heard what had happened and wanted to know if there was anything she could do to help.

I told her that I did what I was supposed to do and explained what had happened. She was so kind and sweet and full of praise and concern. She was maternal and comforting. With all the negativity that was happening, I always tried to look for the positives and this was definitely a positive.

One of the world's greatest female leaders, who had endured so much pain and suffering in her own right, felt the need to reach out to me and reassure me and remind me that I should never think these setbacks had anything to do with my abilities. As it would turn out, my suspension only turned out to be temporary and I went back to do my radio show at the SABC.

But in that moment, I was able to sit back, relax and watch Barcelona and Ronaldinho play beautiful football.

23

Twenty-three minutes from death

It was 2008 and the stock market was crashing. I was living in a freestanding house in Northcliff in northern Johannesburg and I had to get out of it. I had bought the house as an investment for the long term. It had everything I could need, including space in a granny flat for when my mom came to visit from Durban. My biggest desire was to get Mom to be comfortable to come and visit more often and to have her independence and space in the house. There was also space for a potential family, if marriage and children were in my future. It was not just a move but it was a move for the long term.

I hadn't banked on the fact that moving to Northcliff was probably the worst decision I had ever made.

Before living in the house I had been in a complex where I could lock up and go. Now I was literally on the street and I could be monitored by people I didn't even know were monitoring me. There were strange occurrences, like a random woman knocking on the door looking for an imaginary person who didn't work there. She was clearly scoping the joint for a syndicate.

There was a lot of crime in the area and there were more and more stories of well-known people's homes being broken into. The house neighbouring mine to the left was broken into. There was a spate of robberies in the area.

At the time I was driving a car with a personalised number plate, GQIMMM GP. I would stop at the traffic lights in Northcliff and people would say, 'Ah Gqimm, that's Robert.' It really made me feel very uncomfortable. I was also making controversial statements on radio and it was bringing unnecessary attention to me. I was worried I could be targeted.

One morning at around 10am I was at a meeting at SuperSport in Randburg and I got a call to say my house had been broken into. They had hit it in broad daylight. The security company had got there in time and thwarted the attack. The robbers had taken the plasma TV screen from the wall. There was literally a shoot-out outside the house. They had dropped the screen on the couch and run.

I had only been in the property for two months so a lot of my possessions were still in boxes but some electronic equipment had been stolen.

I started to question living there.

A week later I arrived home from work to find the entire street cordoned off and littered with police cars and an ambulance. It was chaos. The attention was focused on a house three down from mine.

That afternoon, there had been a buzz at the door of the house and the lady working there had opened. There were men claiming to be from a garden service. They forced their way into the house and shot and killed the owner.

That made the decision for me. I was out. There was no way I was going to carry on staying there. I phoned the estate agent who had sold me the house and told her that we needed to get it back on the market.

The economy was caving in and it was a terrible time to sell property but I was desperate. I needed to breathe. I needed to sleep at night. I needed to get back into complex-style living. I took all my stuff and put it into storage and phoned a friend who was running Emperors Palace. He helped me with a deal and I went to live in Emperors Palace for months. I sold the house at a massive loss and I landed up paying it off for years to come.

But staying at Emperors wasn't conducive for me. There was lot of travelling up and down to the SABC in Auckland Park to do my radio show and it became a strain on a daily basis. Thankfully, my childhood friend S'thembiso had an apartment in Rivonia and he had just received a job offer in Durban. He offered for me to stay at his place while I was in the process of looking for a home.

While I stayed there I had to reevaluate a lot of things in my life. My stress levels were high. I was disappointed. I was overweight. I was working too hard. I was losing my mind. I decided to go back to gym to deal with my frustrations and my health.

There was a Virgin Active down the road in Rivonia so I signed up. Part of the induction at the gym was an opportunity for a staff member to explain the equipment and the basics.

Halfway through my assessment, I was feeling exhausted. I was sweating and my heart rate was high. I had barely exerted myself. I knew I was unfit but this was off the charts. I asked the guy doing the assessment for a bottle of water and told him I had to stop.

All I wanted to do was leave the gym. I needed to get into my car and leave.

I had played sports and exercised all my life but what I was feeling was very unusual. I was struggling to breathe and I was in pain. I got into the car and put the aircon on full blast. I reclined my seat and tried to cool down. I was sweating profusely. The car guard was trying to get me to reverse. I pulled myself together and thought I should go back to the apartment. I also had an appointment with representatives from Absa so I had to get to SuperSport.

Once I made it to the apartment, things got even worse. I knew I needed help. That's when I called S'thembiso and told him I needed an ambulance. He knew the address so he made the call and within a few minutes, the paramedics arrived.

They checked my vitals and loaded me onto a stretcher and took me to the ambulance. S'the had sent one of his friends to check up on me too. The paramedics needed my medical-aid card and I had left it in my car in the middle console. I explained to S'the's friend where it was, but he struggled to find it.

There I was, lying in the back of the ambulance, dying, in pain, and the hunt for this medical-aid card was going on. It didn't dawn on me how important it was. The decision for the paramedics was would they take me to Sunninghill Hospital five minutes away or would they hit the highway and take me to Baragwanath, which was 40 kilometres away.

Fortunately, I remembered that my ENT was at Sunninghill and I told them to call him. He had all my details on record. Once they had everything they needed, the driver threw the car into gear and screamed out of the complex.

At the hospital there was suddenly a level of urgency. I had lost valuable time with the ambulance delay. The nurses hooked me up to the monitors and I could tell from the doctor's reaction that something bad had been detected. He looked at me and told me that I was having a heart attack right at that moment.

It didn't make any sense to me. I was 35 and had no history of cardiovascular disease. I was shocked. Did I only have a few minutes left to live? I tried to stay calm. I hadn't phoned my mother or my sisters. The doctors needed to roll me into theatre. It was like the drama you see on television as they wheeled me down the corridor into theatre to insert a stent into my artery.

The following day in the recovery ward the doctor, Eric Klug, came to speak to me. He is a big Arsenal supporter. He told me I was so bad that he didn't even recognise it was me that he was operating on. They had to rush to save my life. I was 23 minutes way from death's door.

I couldn't help but think of the time we had wasted in the ambulance looking for my medical-aid card. If they had taken me to Baragwanath I would have died on the highway.

Dr Klug will always feature top of the list of people who have played a major, major role in my life, because he literally was that person who saved my life. He taught me to change from a lifestyle perspective so that I could try to improve my health.

My mother came up to Johannesburg to stay with me and look after me. Having her at the apartment, physically present, looking after me, really helped me to recover. I needed her presence around me and she offered her time and we got to bond a lot and talk about life and what I wanted to do. She was looking after me like I was a child again and I was so thankful for that.

That entire experience made me reflect on where I was at that time in my life and the different stresses I was going through. There was the stress of moving houses, of living in a hotel. I hadn't been eating well. I hadn't been sleeping well. There was a lot on my mind and I was experiencing disappointment at different levels.

In retrospect, I was glad that I had gone to gym. I was grateful that the workout I did had triggered the heart attack because if I had left it, I could have suffered a massive attack that would have killed me on the spot.

Having had a near-death experience, I realised that I had a second chance in life. What would have happened if I had passed away? I began to think about my legacy and about my desire to start a family and have children. I loved kids and always wanted to have a family of my own, but obviously at the right moment and with the right person. All of those conversations started creeping into my mind.

I was obsessed with doing my work and doing it as well as I could but I was also thinking about what legacy I would leave behind. Having a heart attack made me want to approach things differently, to start working less and to start focusing on a family. I also needed to find a safe home and an environment to live in.

24

Beyond my wildest dreams

The football world descended on Soweto in June 2010 and I found myself at the very centre of it all. As a sportscaster, it was the stuff of dreams to have the FIFA World Cup in our own back yard.

SuperSport had constructed a cutting-edge, R60-million, multifaceted studio for the event. It had various set-ups and we could do multiple shows from different areas of the same set. It was really world class. The channel was the driver of the international broadcast and the content was second to none. The construction of the studio was an indicator of intent. The question then was who would be hosting this top-class broadcasting product. There was a South African, an African and a global component to consider.

It was humbling to see the schedule when it was released. I had been given the responsibility of hosting the opening and the final at Soccer City, as it was known for the tournament.

The story of that opening match was crazy. Bafana Bafana were playing Mexico as the first game of the tournament. From all of my history, I knew the FNB Stadium and its terrain and its fans well. I knew there would be people with no tickets wanting to take a chance and there would be people with no parking tickets trying their luck. There was a huge bottleneck of traffic with people trying to get to the front of the queue. It was a World Cup and not a Telkom Cup final so there would be no bribery, no talking your way through if you didn't have accreditation or a ticket. That meant people were forced to turn back and that caused massive traffic problems.

As the anchor of the broadcast, I had to be at the stadium at least an hour or two ahead of the time the production started. We set off from SuperSport well ahead of time. I was with Liverpool legend John Barnes and a technical assistant.

It was taking ages to get anywhere and traffic was crawling towards Soweto. Time was ticking and it was getting closer to kick-off. We had to start the build-up to this World Cup broadcast and the entire world would be watching, but we were still stuck on the road. There was no police escort for us. We just assumed everything would work perfectly because it was a World Cup and it would be properly run and it would work like clockwork.

Chevani, who did all the coordinating, was on the phone with us constantly. 'Robert, how far are you guys?' We had 45 minutes to on-air. Chevani was panicking. Could we see the stadium? We were close but we weren't that close to really see it. People were walking, cars were stationary, there was nothing the driver could do, and the team in the stadium was freaking out.

John Barnes and I made the call to walk the rest of the way.

We dumped the car and went on foot, in our suits and ties, iPads tucked under our arms, and moved as fast as we could.

John, of course, is a great football legend. I was also pretty recognisable. So walking through the crowd was not as simple as it seemed in theory. There was an added problem of everyone stopping us to say hello and asking us for photographs.

People were festive and this was the first game of a World Cup! Fans had been waiting for this moment. It was a carnival and people had been drinking all day. We were in a hurry and it was like running the gauntlet. We were in a rush and guys were adamant they wanted to chat to us.

John had bought himself a new pair of shoes for the occasion and he was starting to struggle. They were pinching him and he was getting blisters so he took his shoes off and started walking barefoot to the stadium. There he was in his suit and tie, barefoot, with his new shoes in his hand, stopping for photographs with fans and the clock ticking down. It was madness. Chevani was still calling us like crazy so eventually we were running. We made it to the gate of the stadium and she came down to meet us and it was confusion trying to find the right gate and accreditation and everything was chaos. John was complaining about his feet. Our adrenaline was pumping; we were sweating.

With five minutes to go, we made it into the suite and the support team descended to mic us up and put make-up on us, using a towel to wipe our faces. Fortunately, there were a few minutes while they played a snippet to build up to the broadcast so we could get it together.

Then in my ear, 'Five, four, three, two, one' and 'Good afternoon and welcome to the 2010 FIFA World Cup opening match'. We made it seem like we had been there since the morning.

In reality, it had been madness. For the rest of that week John came into the studio wearing slip-slops because of the blisters on his feet!

The World Cup was without a doubt a highlight of my broadcasting career. Being in a packed stadium with people singing was amazing, and seeing that unexpected goal from Siphiwe 'Shabba' Tshabalala was phenomenal. Our studio was on the side where Shabba scored and we witnessed the ball flying into the back of the net.

I saw him kick the ball. I saw the flight of the ball. I thought it was going to end up in row 56 somewhere because he really took a punt at that shot and the ball just sailed in and I saw the net bulge. I couldn't believe it. It was like I was living in a dream. I had seen some of the best football games locally and internationally, but there was so much hope in the stadium that day.

We had a World Cup-winning coach in Carlos Alberto Parreira sitting on the bench. He knew the art of winning tournaments. I couldn't help but wonder if this was the start of the Madiba magic happening for us again.

Part of my excitement was that my nephew Sango was one of the kids who walked the players onto the field. McDonald's had a lucky draw and his name had been pulled out so he made the cut. I was excited for him. Sango was big on football and he knew these superstars and he was a little tiny tot walking onto the field. I don't think he even knew how huge it was. Every corner of the world was viewing this match. Seeing that spectacle through his eyes was also incredible. In a way, it reminded me of my dream as a young boy his age.

For me, hosting the opening of the World Cup was obviously the culmination of a dream. I had been to Zurich as part of the broadcasting team from the SABC when we had lost the bid to Germany to host the 2006 tournament. I had witnessed the disappointment of that loss.

I had also been at the Union Buildings the day that the announcement was made that we would be hosting the 2010 FIFA World Cup. President Thabo Mbeki had been to Zurich and had made a presentation. Former President Nelson Mandela had also played a role. Our bid was strong and everything had been done like clockwork. The day after the presentation, Mbeki had flown back to South Africa to wait for the announcement.

I thought we had a very good chance. I had been posted to the Union Buildings to be with President Mbeki so I could interview him straight after the news broke. Mbeki was nervous and kept asking me, 'Rawbaart,' as he liked to pronounce my name, 'who do you think is going to win, Rawbaart?'

As South Africa's name was called out, all hell broke loose with celebrations countrywide. I had the task on behalf of the nation to speak to the president and find out his reaction. He gave a very celebratory but dignified acceptance speech and an assurance that we would be able to pull it off as hosts.

I was cognisant of the role I was playing and the journey I had travelled. A lot of responsibility was being bestowed on my shoulders.

Now here I was at the stadium at the opening match of the first World Cup to be hosted on African soil; it was a full-circle moment. I was also standing next to John Barnes, who was my personal legend, a guy whose posters I had had up on my wall as a kid growing up. We were beamed into the homes of football fans across the country, the continent and the world.

Thinking back to that football-crazy kid at Little Flower listening to the radio with his friends, this was never part of my dream. I just wanted to watch a football game live. My dream didn't extend to South Africa getting to host the World Cup. My dream never expanded towards knowing there would be a SuperSport that would be interested in my talent. It never got to a stage where I ever thought I would rub shoulders with John Barnes or with so many other greats who had come through our studio. So many of the major names I had watched on television as a kid came through our studio during that World Cup. They were listening to me asking them questions. I was the conductor of their world as analysts.

That is why I have never taken anything for granted on my journey. I think a lot of it has been very humbling because it was just a dream. And dreams don't usually come amplified in the manner that they have been in my world.

Nothing made sense. The people who I was with in the studio didn't make sense. The fact that I was anchoring the show didn't make sense. But I needed to make sense of it all for it to make sense to the people who were watching at home.

When you knit all of those things together, that is why I say a little silent prayer on a daily basis that whatever God was trying to engineer via me and my journey, I was seeing it being fulfilled each and every day.

When I was a young boy and my grandfather was battling with prostate cancer, he would say to me I needed to keep my focus, that I was the pride and joy of the family, and that I needed to make my mother proud whatever I decided to do when I grew up. He had silent faith in me because he knew I was a quiet child and a deep thinker. He knew there was a lot happening in my mind that I did not need to verbalise. He wanted me to know that and to carry it with me.

After watching me host the World Cup, my mother said to me that she wished my grandfather had been alive to see how I turned out and what I had achieved.

25
The cycle of life

After my heart attack and my near-death experience, I was ready to settle down and build a family. I didn't actively go out and seek someone to have a child with, but I certainly began thinking more seriously about who I was dating and who my life partner might be.

In the industry I was in, it was difficult to find a genuine person who saw me as an individual who deserved love and attention, as opposed to Robert, the person on television who they could walk down red carpets with.

I had to question what a potential partner saw when they entered into a relationship with me. Did they see flashing lights and glitzy events? Or did they see a person they could look at building a family with. Unfortunately, the profile I had established through my work brought with it that level of uncertainty in how genuine a person was. I had to know that this was the right person, a friend who knew my journey and appreciated that there was more to me than the public saw.

Zoe Mthiyane had been at Little Flower a few years behind me. We only overlapped for about a year. Our paths crossed again around my thirtieth birthday when a mutual friend invited her to a big birthday party I was throwing. Zoe was involved with Coca-Cola *Pop Stars* at the time. We met and realised that we had a shared experience of coming from the same place and going to the same school.

We developed a strong friendship that was entirely platonic. We travelled to KZN together and enjoyed the same music. I love driving on the N3 so we would road trip to Durban and then she would go to Richards Bay to her family. There was no girlfriend-boyfriend story; we just struck up a good friendship and we were comfortable with one another. She was not entirely in the industry but she did understand what the industry was about.

We had conversations about her family. Her father was a polygamist and she was very close to her mother, which resonated with me because I'm so close to my mother. We shared a lot along similar lines.

Our relationship got to the stage where we liked each other a lot and we moved to the next level.

It was still very difficult for me to find a relationship that I could be comfortable in and trust because the industry makes it so difficult for that to happen. But in the end, I never ever took my eye off the belief that I had a strong love for children. My parents had been married for 52 years and we grew up as four kids. Family is everything to me.

Being an uncle was part of that for me and I took on the role of a father figure to my nephew Sango. I always took him to school on the first day of term. In a way, it was like having the experience of a brother because I only had sisters growing up. I missed the feeling of what it feels like to have a brother. But the fascination with having a son of my own was there. I always wondered if I had to have a child, would it be a boy or a girl? I always secretly loved the fact that if I had a boy, that would be God's blessing to me. That would be God giving me a brother that I never had. As a young boy on the farm I had no one to play with and I would be kicking a ball by myself. I craved having another close male relative. That was my dream, my desire, my prayer, to have a son.

Zoe and I didn't get engaged or married, but we had discussed the possibility of having kids. I don't think I was ready for marriage. I'd always said that I was married to my work. I was doing daily radio and television shows and travelling and I had to go overseas regularly. It wasn't the most conducive situation for marriage but I felt that I had enough scope to be able to have a child. I was confident that I would have the kind of support team and structure around me to see it through.

When Zoe fell pregnant, she almost immediately stopped working. I was excited and we went for regular checkups and scans together. Everything was healthy and the baby was progressing well, but I really wanted to know if it was a boy or a girl.

At one of the final scans, the doctor finally pointed out on the screen that it was definitely going to be a boy.

Even before he had made his presence known, there was a sense of joy and elation within me. God had answered my prayers. All I could hope and pray for was that he would be in good health when he arrived. I kept the image from the scan with me for a long time because it was something that I had really prayed for.

By that stage, Zoe and I had drifted apart romantically. Many things took their toll in the build-up to the birth. It got to a stage where it would have been unfair to try to carry on. We were no longer in a romantic relationship, but we were committed to being parents and raising our child together.

Zoe stayed in Richards Bay and the idea was that when she went into labour or close to the due date, I would get there because I wanted to be present at the birth. Zoe was staying at home with her mother, preparing for our boy to arrive.

Just a few weeks before Zoe was due to give birth, her mother went with a group of ladies from her church to a funeral and, tragically, the Avanza they were travelling in was involved in a terrible accident. Zoe's mother passed away. She was never able to meet our child.

Heavily pregnant, Zoe had lost her support system. Her mother had been ready to help her and guide her through raising her child and now she had been killed. It was a tragic time on many different fronts because we were also worried about Zoe's state of mind, given that she was carrying at an advanced stage. We didn't want there to be a further tragedy.

I went down to Richards Bay to lend support on the day of the funeral and then I had to rush back to Joburg to do a massive broadcast. I was worried about how Zoe would fare with the trauma that she was going through. Thank God the checkups continued to show great growth and everything was on track with the baby.

The due date was 18 July; early that morning we arrived at the hospital in Richards Bay together. It was 5am in the middle of winter and it was dark. We had already been told it would be an induced labour. I was anxious that everyone would be healthy and my nerves were shot. This was my first experience of having a child. I was on the brink of being a father. I was about to realise my dream of another human being brought onto this earth who was attached to me. It was a big deal for me and I was also thinking about Zoe and what a big deal it was for her. I am an overthinker and my mother had warned me to be patient. Zoe was doing exercises on a yoga ball and the nurses were constantly monitoring her.

By 6pm she was exhausted, mentally and physically. I kept thinking about all the scary stories I had heard. The staff were so supportive and maternal and understanding.

I was secretly hoping he would be born that day because it was Mandela's birthday, Mandela Day. It would have been incredible to have that association with the great man. Maybe he might end up being as great as Madiba was. Would he be as good a leader? Would he be as inspiring a person? Would he have the charm? Would he have the intellect? All the various things that were associated with Madiba.

The clock ticked past 9pm. Finally, there was movement and it all started to happen. Just after 10pm on 18 July 2011, Awande arrived.

It was a moment to really savour. When you see this body coming to life and you're studying every detail of its structure, hoping and praying everything is healthy, there is a sense of shock and disbelief. The scary part was having to cut the umbilical cord. I remember him opening his eyes and running them around the room and then closing them again. I will never forget that moment. That and how hairy he was!

The responsibility of having a child happens almost immediately because you become aware that you are a human yourself. It's the cycle of life. Once I too had to be nursed and looked after. Now I am responsible for another human being who will be receiving the same kind of treatment and care. It changed my world in many ways because there was an appreciation that one day this little person would be able to call me 'Daddy' and ask for guidance and advice from me. I would be able to run around and play with him, kick a ball, punch a bag, play sports.

In the past, when I went to work, I was working for myself. Now I had to double my efforts to make sure that this little human being would be provided for. That was the main driving force for me as I celebrated his coming to life.

After Awande was born, I asked four of my friends to assist me in putting together the purchase of sheep and goats and groceries to go and pay damages at Zoe's family's house. We had alerted the family that we would be coming through to make the payment.

I went with two longtime friends from Little Flower, S'the Mhlongo, Khulile Mhlongo, who was also the godfather to Awande, Fortune Mvezi and an older friend of his, Xolani Dubazana, who was wiser and knew better so he could guide us. Once we were allowed in to the house we had to ensure that we had the right amount of money. We had brought the goat in the back of the car. It was all a very fascinating journey. It was an acknowledgment on my part, accepting that I am the father of Awande and I was officially presenting myself to the family. The damages were an acceptance that there would not be a wedding but I was taking responsibility for Awande. I was comfortable to share the responsibility of parenting with his mother.

From then on I was involved in Awande's life although he lived with Zoe. I paid monthly maintenance for him. I regularly visited the Baby City near Gateway and stocked up on nappies and clothes and toys. And then Granny and Aunty Gugu and I would go to Richard's Bay to visit.

There was never a moment where I shied away from responsibility. This was something I had always wanted – to have a child.

When Awande was around two years old, his mother got an offer to be part of the production of *The Lion King* in Australia. She was going to take Awande overseas with her. Obviously, I didn't want him to go. I knew she would be busy with the production and rehearsals would be day and night. It would be a demanding, hectic schedule. *The Lion King* is a massive production. I was willing to look after him and be the primary caregiver so that he could stay in South Africa. I consulted a child psychologist and she told me that Awande still needed his mother as he was still so young so I couldn't fight that.

Had they gone to the United Kingdom or Europe, that would have been more practical. I could have jumped on a flight on a Friday night and spent the weekend there and then travelled back home. Going to Australia is like going to the other side of the world and it's really impossible with the time zones and travel. It just didn't make any sense.

I reluctantly accepted the facts because that was the recommendation of the professionals. It meant that I did not see Awande for two long years.

We tried to communicate with him via Skype but it didn't work very well because he was so young and he didn't fully understand what was going on.

I continued to pay maintenance throughout. I went to the FNB ATM every month and transferred money. No amount had been agreed on but I put through what I believed was needed, which was more than adequate for him to survive and go to daycare and for clothes and food. I also put him on my medical aid as a dependant.

Being separated for two years definitely affected our relationship. There is a lot of development that happens in a child in those early years. I didn't have that bond with him that I could nurture because he was away for so long. His welfare remained my primary concern.

They returned to Johannesburg and this meant Awande was physically closer to me, but my relationship with Zoe was strained so I wasn't able to have continued direct access to him. There was a lull in getting to see him and I struggled with it.

I would juxtapose that with my relationship with my nephew Sango. He had a mother and a father and there was equal love and he was excited about being around them. I wanted to forge that kind of relationship with Awande.

Things improved and when his fifth birthday rolled around, it was really special. We had a great party with both his mother and father present and he was extremely happy, having the time of his life.

During that entire period I would see things in the media. There were articles in the *You* magazine or the *Sunday Sun* or *The World* or wherever. Zoe wrote open letters that I would keep and give to my lawyer, but I didn't want to counter anything she said about me in the media.

A lot of the lies and the hurt that was being driven through all of those reports were playing out in the public space. They were an attempt to undermine me as a person. The aim was always to try to showcase me as something that the public does not know. To always try to bring a person down. I'm not about that. That meant trying to bring your child down too. If my career is destroyed then I can't support him. I honestly never paid any attention to it.

Zoe took me to court for maintenance and so I had to attend the proceedings in Atteridgeville in Pretoria. I had never been in court in my life and now I had to go to court. She was asking for R35 000 maintenance per month. What kind of baby gets maintained on R35 000 a month? Who are we maintaining here?

Her new partner, Lebo M, was also there and even took the stand to give evidence about what share of the DStv Awande was using and the cost of the garden service and the nanny. They were trying to justify getting to R35 000. I also wanted to counter the perception in the public that I was not paying maintenance every month.

Of course, I had a paper trail of all the monthly payments. The bank simply produces a printout of all the transfers that had been done and all the contributions made to the medical aid. I could prove it all.

After all the negative headlines that had been written about me not taking responsibility for my own child, not one journalist came back and reported on the outcome of that case. They lost the case with costs. It was proven that maintenance was always paid and on time.

That entire experience was a bitter pill to swallow because some of the top journalists were sucked into it and decided to take a position on it. They were being vindictive and unfair on something they knew nothing about. But it was easier to sell the newspapers using my name or for people to get mileage by using my name. I did not go on a revenge attack because I know that in future, when Awande is old enough, he'll have access to all of this back and forth in the media. It won't be good for him to have to read that there was all of these things going on.

So I've not said anything. I don't think it's worthy of me to say anything. What has happened has happened. I've taken the bullet for it and it's okay.

I continue to look after Awande and I continue to pay for everything for him. I just hope that one day we get to see the best of him because he is a really, really good boy.

Awande was at a day school in Joburg but because of

inconsistency around his homework, I decided to send him to boarding school. From my own experience, I knew what boarding school was about. It wasn't about abandoning anybody. It was about what was practical. We were two parents who are in the industry who spend a lot of time away from home, so we had to find a way to bring consistency to his life. The answer was boarding school.

Initially, the idea was rejected by Zoe but then two years later she accepted it. Awande would have benefited more if he had gone earlier because there was a lot that needed to be bridged that he had lost out on in his formative years. From the perspective of instilling values, including family values, but also his own values as an individual.

He took to boarding school like a duck to water. He loves it. Everyone thought he would be freaked out and constantly homesick. But he has developed his own form of resilience and a certain level of strength within him. He's happy to stay in at boarding school even though he has the option to come home.

He values people. He values friends. He is shy and quiet, but he also understands the world is about other people.

He plays basketball and rugby and I try to surprise him and go watch him. Rugby isn't his first love; the irony is that from when he was tiny he would be kicking a ball around and he has the leg control to play soccer, but it's not an option for him at school, as it wasn't for me when I was a boy.

I do hope that wherever he goes for high school there will be football available for him to play so that he can express himself in that way.

We have really renewed our bond and he has developed a deep, profound emotional sensitivity. Our bond has meaning and there is a recognition of my attempts to improve him as a person. We have deep chats and there is a lot going through his mind.

I'm now his primary caregiver and we recently spent a solid two years together. I would never stop him from seeing Zoe. She has equal access to him. We are a phone call away. We are a message away. We are an email away. We are an anything away.

Being Awande's father is a beautiful challenge, especially given the scope of the work that I do. I'm blessed. I'm lucky that I can broadcast in Durban to be closer to him during half-term or during the school holidays. I get assistance from Granny, from Nomvula and from his friends' parents too.

I would have loved to have more children and to have had the experience of being in my child's life consistently from day one as they grow older. I've also consciously taken the decision that that is not going to be possible. My unfortunate experience has also soured the prospect of having further children for me. But if God believes that it is still a possibility, I would not frown upon it because I genuinely love kids and would have loved to have had more.

My own father died in November 2016. He had suffered for a long time with pain in his stomach. He had been to see several doctors but they couldn't work out what was wrong with him. At one point he collapsed and my mom grew very concerned.

She said there must be something wrong with him. It wasn't just a stomach ache. He went to see a physician and he was diagnosed with stomach cancer and it was stage four. Dad was hospitalised and he deteriorated. You could see he was visibly ill.

I remember when there was a Chiefs and Pirates games and Dad was a big Pirates fan so I had a jersey made for him with his name at the back. I asked SuperSport not to schedule me for that Soweto derby because I wanted to spend the time with him and enjoy the derby together at the hospital. I knew that chances were we wouldn't have much longer together. So I took the Pirates jersey and went to the hospital to watch with him, but when I arrived there, he didn't really understand what was going on or what the jersey was for. For someone who would literally live his life on a Saturday and Sunday watching UK football and local football and every Arsenal game and Pirates game, that to me was an early indicator that we were at a stage that Dad had turned the corner.

He remained bedridden for a very long time. Several times the doctors called us to the hospital to say our final goodbyes and I would travel down to Durban from Joburg. He fought a lot, but then it got to a stage where the doctors said he needed palliative care and they couldn't do anything more for him. We put him into a facility just outside Umhlanga where they cared for him. He always asked if he could go back home but it just wasn't possible.

We were at his side when he died. The nurses had told us that Dad was very talkative and upbeat on the Sunday and he was chatting to some of them in his fluent Afrikaans. We went to see him the next day and got the total opposite. He didn't react at all; he was quiet and didn't say a word. At around 4.30pm, I was supposed to go and do my radio show at the SABC in Durban. I called my manager at Metro and asked him if he could find a replacement to do the show. I felt I needed to be with my mom and my sister Vanessa, who was there. I phoned our priest to come through to the hospital and he did. My mom could see my father was slipping away and we all stood and went to hold his hands. At 6.47pm, my mom told us he was gone. I would have been on air at the time but fortunately I had chosen to stay.

I had never been in a space where I had seen a life disappear before my eyes. You're holding somebody's hand and then all of a sudden there's just dead weight. My mom closed his eyelids and said a prayer. I was very emotional.

He was Dad. He was always supportive of everything that I did. There were never any major flare-ups between us. Even when he was getting older. I understood how not being physically present around both parents felt and what it meant having grown up away from both my parents. I wasn't able to openly ask questions. He couldn't give the advice that I often sought at different stages of my life when I was growing up. Maybe that is why I make it a point now that I am present as often as possible with Awande. I never had a parent or a father on the side of the pitch when I was playing rugby. That is why I try to be pitchside and cheer Awande on, tell him what I know and how he can improve and it's something I will do in the future. I know how important it is.

26

Silencing an independent voice

After being suspended at Metro FM over the PSL rights drama, it wasn't long before I went back to doing a daily sports radio show. For a long stretch of time, I did both Metro FM and anchoring on SuperSport. I know people tried to make it seem like I needed to choose one or the other, but at the end of the day, there was never a conflict.

At times the balancing act became tricky and it also became difficult to juggle the politics of the two broadcasters and the sporting administrations. Invariably, I would find myself in situations where somebody was infuriated with something I had said on air.

At SuperSport everything had been positive and it had been a good ride. The numbers were showing positive growth and I was at the helm of several strong shows. But one of the first times I was hauled over the coals at SuperSport was with the Carling Black Label Cup. The event was introduced in 2011 as a pre-season game between traditional rivals Kaizer Chiefs and Orlando Pirates – the fans would become managers and they could select the teams and decide on formations and captains.

One day I was called into a meeting with management. I had no idea what it was about, but I arrived and all the top brass were there, including head of regulatory affairs Graham Abrahams, head of legal Brandon Foot, and my mentor Tex Teixeira. It was a serious meeting, with all three of them seated at one side of the table like judges on the bench about to deliver a verdict. It was intimidating.

Tex got straight to it and told me that 'The Chairman' was unhappy.

'Which chairman?' I asked.

Of course I knew that colloquially they called Irvin Khoza 'The Chairman' because he was the chairman of the Premier Soccer League. But I also wanted clarity, so I didn't just assume.

I asked why The Chairman was unhappy and Tex explained that I had made comments about the Carling Black Label Cup that apparently did not sit well with Khoza.

I remembered the comments but I had not made them on a SuperSport platform. It had been on radio on Metro FM. I explained this to the panel in front of me and they conceded that the comments weren't made on SuperSport.

So I asked an obvious question: 'Why am I here to answer questions about what I have said on radio? Because, as far as I know, there is no SuperSport FM?'

Their argument was that I was the face of football at SuperSport and whatever comments I made, regardless of the platform, would reflect on them as a broadcaster. Whatever comments I made on other platforms still mattered because SuperSport was in partnership with the PSL – there was that relationship and they had to nurture that relationship and ensure there were no negative comments made about any of the PSL offerings.

At that point I had a good relationship with The Chairman of the league. He had personally asked me to MC events for himself, for Pirates and for the PSL awards. On Metro FM we started a popular feature called 'The Chairman's Chair' and he was always the first chairman who volunteered to come onto the show. When I called him to be on the television show, he would be there. There'd be no problem. He asked me to MC the Orlando Pirates Anniversary Dinner at the Sandton Convention Centre. And I suggested that we host Kaizer Motaung, Jomo Sono and Screamer Tshabalala in a talkshow format rather than have them give speeches at the podium. Our relationship was never a problem, at least not directly from him personally. But there would be comments made to me that he was displeased. 'The Chairman said' ... and it would always be via other people.

They would tell me that he was unhappy with comments I had made, but I was accountable to the listener, to the viewer, to the audience. I carried on doing what I did. If he had a disagreement with me, he has always had my phone number and I have always had his. If there was a problem, he should call me.

Ironically, I have also always been an Orlando Pirates supporter. It's one of the things I've never really spoken about in my whole career as I never wanted to be seen as biased. People are very finicky about these things. I've always insisted publicly that I don't support a local team, only Bafana Bafana. That was my line. People would say I was clearly a Chiefs supporter, or a Sundowns supporter or a Pirates supporter, depending on my comments. Then I knew I must be doing a good job in not being overly biased in leaning towards any one team at a particular time. The Sundowns fans would give me hell because they thought I hated them or the Chiefs fans would do the same.

I could tell this encounter with SuperSport was problematic otherwise I would not be having this high-level meeting with them. I needed to know exactly why Khoza was unhappy.

On radio I had been very dismissive about the Carling Black Label Cup. I thought the inclusion of this cup was very unfair because there had been a 26-year history of the Iwisa Spectacular. That was then transformed into the Telkom Spectacular. That had been a charity spectacular and there were various charities that received money from the gate takings. The public would vote by phoning in and voting for their favourite teams and the four clubs with the most votes qualified to play.

But then the two most popular clubs decided to have a tournament of their own, still getting fans to vote for who they should have in their teams, but it wasn't for charity; it was for a commercial entity and it was great for business for the brewery. People had to buy Carling products to vote. It was a gimmick and I said so.

I had made the comments on my radio show as a talk-show host. It was my opinion and if anyone wanted to counter it, they could come on the show and talk about it. That's what talk radio is about, getting people to speak about issues. Many fans were upset that the Spectacular had disappeared in its traditional form and I had to hold the administrators accountable. I was doing my job as a talk-show host but the bosses at SuperSport saw this as a clash with my position there and they wanted me to apologise to The Chairman.

I accepted what they were saying but their demand that I had to apologise was not going to be met. There were a couple of minutes of dead air, as we would call it on radio, because they were digesting the fact that I was refusing to go and apologise. I was emphatic that it would not be happening. I was not going to apologise to anybody.

While waiting for them to respond I proposed a solution. 'Hey, gentleman, with all due respect, I think we've reached the part of the meeting where we are in disagreement about what needs to happen next. But what I can suggest, so that we can all live happily ever after, is that you should never, ever schedule me for any of the Carling Black Label Cup games that you're going to be showing live. So you live happily and I live happily. I don't have to apologise. And you don't have to have me trying to front up something I don't believe in.'

I wasn't going to be presenting on air sounding enthusiastic about an 'amazing tournament' when I had already stated my opinions publicly about it. My credibility was also at stake because I couldn't say something on a public platform on a national radio station and the next Saturday have people see me at the stadium trumping up the same concept I didn't believe in.

The apology wasn't going to happen so I told them not to schedule me for the tournament. I thought it was the right solution. There was a nodding of heads and I politely left the room. And thankfully I was not scheduled for seven years for that Beer Cup.

There was one problem, though. On *Extra Time*, the review show we had built into a real success, I arrived one day, rushing in to the studio from my radio show, to find a gentleman in a suit and tie, mic'd up and made up, ready to go on air. I asked the producer on *Extra Time*, Ben, who this man was. I was confused because we had already discussed the running order and we were ready for production, but there was a guy present who was obviously going to be going on air but I knew nothing about him. I didn't know who the hell he was.

Ben looked very uncomfortable as he said he knew my views on the Carling Black Label Cup but this person was someone from South African Breweries, the company that distributed Carling, who had been sent to be on the show. It was a 'directive from above'.

I told Ben that I respected him a lot, but this gentleman was not going to be interviewed by me. I offered Ben two options. He could put this gentleman on set and he could interview himself. Or Ben could ask my colleague Kamza Mbatha, who was filling in on the show before mine called *Back Pages*, if he would do the interview instead of me. I would do a link to an ad break and say to the viewer that coming up after the break would be Kamza Mbatha with an exclusive interview, and then Kamza would come in, interview him, and then throw back to me and they could use an insert as a bridge until I came back. But on principle, and what we had agreed on regarding the Beer Cup, was that I was not interviewing this gentleman. That was the bottom line.

A very ashen-faced Ben looked at me and asked if I was being serious. I had never been more serious in my life. I was willing to risk my job. An agreement was made that I would have nothing to do with the Carling Black Label Cup and now I was being ambushed with this interview.

I was so principled about it because the Spectacular was a success in terms of South African football. That's why it lasted 26 years and that's what the fans wanted. It involved two other teams outside of Chiefs and Pirates and I had made a pronouncement on it. How could I then do an interview promoting this other competition?

Ben didn't choose the option of their guest interviewing himself, so he went and spoke to Kamza, who, being the gentleman that he is, was okay with it. We followed the plan I had proposed and it worked well with Kamza doing the interview.

In a way, it felt like a test – will he or won't he? It didn't make sense to me at the time but it was the beginning of SuperSport feeling pressure from their partner, the PSL. I think it was also the beginning of what would become major scrutiny in terms of what I was saying on radio vis-à-vis what was happening on television. I was always mindful and professional enough to know my duties on radio and on television. If I was doing a live game, I was there for the live game. If I was there for Champions League, I was there for Champions League. If I was there for the magazine shows, that's all I was there for.

My role on radio was different because we were trying to help shape a new path for sport. We helped shape a transformational one for cricket and rugby, but also we had to hold football authorities accountable for what they were doing. It was difficult because after the SuperSport sponsorship, you found that there was less recognition of the supporters and the fans of the game and more recognition in terms of the administrators and what they could get out of football.

I felt myself move from being a football fan to being more aware of the administrative blunders. I wasn't just promoting the game, I was more aware of the complete disregard of the people who make football happen: the fans, the spectators of the game, the lovers of football. My role had evolved from being a fan to creating enemies within the different pockets of administration and leadership within football, whether it was SAFA or the PSL. It was starting to become extremely tense.

Meanwhile, at the public broadcaster, as much as there were continuous run-ins with management, there was also success and awards. I was hosting the benchmark radio sports show and there was no doubt about it. Whether it was what people within the industry were saying or whether it was the SAB Sports Journalist Awards or the Liberty Radio Awards, as they were called then, whatever awards and various guises that came through, invariably we would be on the winning side.

Advertisers were happy. Listeners were extremely happy. But we kept on trying to improve the product. The team I worked with – Beverly Maphangwa and Thabo Nkoala – were consistent and we knew what the audience wanted. Despite all this, we did not get full support from management because maybe they wanted us to fail. It was as if they were waiting for us to slip up so they could get rid of us.

In mid-2017, they found their opportunity and again it had to do with the relationship between the SABC and SuperSport.

On a Monday on the show, we did a feature called 'Reaction Monday'. I would ask for various clips of radio commentary in various languages and we would put them all together and play them. SABC was the only platform that had every language available in commentary, so we would take snippets in isiXhosa, isiZulu, Tshivenda and English and make an eight- to ten-minute compilation. Often it would be the less high-profile games because the top games would be broadcast on SuperSport.

It was fantastic from an audience perspective because many radio listeners watched football on SuperSport and had forgotten that the SABC had excellent commentators in other languages. Everybody would reminisce about how they listened to radio as a source of commentary before the advent of television. It was good for radio. It was powerful.

But then management started sending funny vibes about how we weren't allowed to play any SuperSport commentators in that package. There were deliberate traps that were being set. Never mind that the SABC was actually in partnership with SuperSport because, as the main broadcaster, SuperSport would give the SABC games to play and clips to play on the news channels. There was no problem there and there had never been one. They were clearly setting a trap.

There was one day when we needed to play a clip from Baba Mthethwa. Baba had moved from the SABC and had joined SuperSport and was quite successful there. It had become a crime for that audio to be played on my show and we soon heard about it.

At the time, the Group Executive of Sport at the SABC was Sully Motsweni. As I understood it, Sully had instructed a senior person to call Beverly, as the producer of the show, and reprimand her. One thing I feel strongly about is that I will always defend the people that I work with. This was not Beverly's fault. I was the one who made the call and it was my decision to play the audio.

Beverly was suspended and so I took the decision to remove myself from the show until they reinstated Beverly to her position.

Sully was obviously following instructions from her superiors to get rid of me. I felt like that trap had been set because they knew I would not allow them to do that to my producer, so I took a bullet for her and I was put on ice.

There was a back and forth of who did what and where and how and meetings with bosses. All I said was that I had made the decision to play the audio because it made no sense that we couldn't utilise a SuperSport commentator when we had people like Baba coming on the Legends show regularly, and I mean physically coming into studio. We had Zama Masondo, Hugh Bladen, Naas Botha and all sorts of other legends come in who were employed by SuperSport.

How do we then change the dynamic and say no more voices? Clearly this was something designed to catch us out because it was working. One thing I started to realise at the SABC was that anything that works, that people love, then they would want to do something to stop it. Not because it adds value to the listener, but because people internally have the power to do whatever they feel like they can do to upset the apple cart.

It's why the SABC in its totality ended up the way that it is. People working inside have no idea about broadcasting, its nuances, what the dynamic is, what the people want to hear, who they want to hear from. But because they find themselves in a position where they can enforce any stupid idea, failure to do so then has its repercussions.

Sully was almost triumphant about the whole thing. She put out a statement saying that the SABC had 'parted ways' with me:

> *SABC Sport has accepted his decision to repudiate his contract with the SABC, which he entered into with SABC Sport on June 6 2017. The SABC engaged Mr Marawa several times to try to remedy the situation. It was hard for us to accept but we concede his decision.*

She went as far as going to her Facebook page and putting out the communique that the SABC had sent internally to the staff. This lady seemed very happy that she had done what she had been sent to do. I was getting used to the strange behaviour at the public broadcaster and I was sure they were slaughtering a sheep in celebration somewhere.

In the end, people analysed the situation and suggested that I had been caught out – they had wanted me to come out in defence of Beverly and, once I had done that, it would be the end of me. The truth is, I would always do that. Beverly was never going to get fired, but I also don't regret coming to her defence. I never regretted standing up so that she was not wrongfully suspended because ultimately it was my decision. Sometimes people believe the power of the producer is everything that goes on air and it isn't. A decision that is taken is a decision that I take, whether or not the producer approves it or not is immaterial.

I was not going to let somebody go down because they believed that a producer is the person who controls what goes on air. This was a Robert decision and if that meant the end of me as a result, then it meant the end of me.

I don't believe it warranted a suspension or a firing. It was all made-up stuff and they couldn't decide mid-stream that certain voices couldn't be played on air. It was madness. There was no sense or logic in decisions that were taken around me.

It was a success for Sully because ultimately she achieved her goal. But none of them could ever pinpoint anything from an on-air perspective that was wrong. There were always those who were out to set traps and see if you fall into them. Those are the struggles people never got to know. The public would just hear that I was fired. I never made the detail public because I didn't want to talk too much about the internal politics within the SABC.

I believed that there was a 'cabal' within the SABC and its main aim was never about the restoration or resurrection of the broadcaster. Their mission was to rubber stamp their own authority and to gain control and get rid of certain individuals. For some reason, I was always at the forefront of that and a prime target for this cabal.

The real underlying problem at the SABC was that an independent voice did not suit them. It was not something they had banked on. It was all very good and well when Robert was doing shows and praising this one and highlighting that one. But the minute I started to question decisions taken or question authority as to why they were taking those decisions, then it was a case of 'How dare you?', 'Who are you to question what we are putting out there?'

An outspoken, independent voice that challenged authority on behalf of the public simply did not suit the public broadcaster, so I had to go.

27

Pearl

Pearl Thusi and I always disagree about where we first met. My recollection is that it was at the polo at the Inanda Country Club in 2016. It was early evening at the end of the event and I was taking a walk with three of my friends to my car that was parked some distance away. She was driving a VW Golf and pulled up alongside us, rolled down her window and offered us a lift in her characteristically humorous way.

I thought I could do with a bit of exercise so I continued walking but she drove alongside me and we continued to walk and talk. Of course I knew who Pearl Thusi, the actress, was but I had never met her before. She was friendly, laughing and warm. I found her intriguing and I wanted to know more about her.

We arranged to meet and got to know each other better over dinner. We connected and began to see more of each another. She was so much fun. Being with Pearl was fulfilling. She was a fully rounded person because what I experienced with her was a depth of knowledge, a level of intellect and fun. There was a level of responsibility in how she cared for her daughter. Of course she was also beautiful. But you find beautiful people who don't have those other qualities. There was also compassion. She was highly religious. Those are all elements that the public didn't get to see that I was able to experience.

We spent hours together just talking, oblivious of how time was passing. We were so in each other's space that nothing else mattered. I have one standout memory of us being together on a beach in Durban, just us, Pearl sitting on my lap and running back and forth to the ocean and the metro police interrupting us because they thought we were up to no good but we really weren't!

You can get so boxed into the work that we do and become so serious and Pearl brought out a more fun and entertaining side of me. She would host big corporate events with various artists performing and I would go along to support her. I would speak to the organisers and arrange to surprise her by booking into the same hotel she was staying at. It was a side of life that I hadn't experienced before. I was keen to live that life with her because she was a major source of that energy in the loving person that she was. I enjoyed the different things that we were able to do, which pushed me out of my comfort zone. I was able to live a little.

We also shared a work ethic and I could give insights into her work.

She was doing a talk show with Lerato Kganyago and I always encouraged her because I knew she would be extremely good as a talk-show host. She was an opinionated human being. Pearl and Phat Joe were blowing up the airwaves on a

Saturday morning on Metro FM. They were cutting edge and people loved it.

There was also a sensitive side to Pearl in how she spoke about her family. I knew about her family and she introduced me to her father when he was still alive. She ticked all the right boxes and I took her to meet my family. It's not a space that I opened up to just anybody.

What I liked about it was that we were so vastly different and that's why people didn't even believe or understand how we could even be together. But when you get to live within each other's space, then you get to see the human side of that person.

It all just happened naturally and you couldn't ask for much more than that.

There came a time when she was joking around about being engaged. She took a friend's ring and posted it on social media. I took the hint and it also gave me an idea of what kind of ring she wanted. I went to a jeweller in Sandton and asked them to make up something similar.

I had resolved that I didn't want to live a life of regret. The man above had brought someone into my life and I couldn't blindly ignore the signs. I was comfortable enough to make such a big leap.

I kept the proposal very simple. We went for dinner at a French restaurant near the Beverly Hills Hotel in Durban. It was small and quaint and I knew the owner. We popped the ring into the dessert at the end of the dinner and of course I went down on one knee. She reacted very emotionally and the staff and the patrons at the neighbouring tables all cheered. There were tears and thankfully the ring fitted perfectly.

We were truly aligned on what we wanted and that was a life together. We wanted to spend our time together forever.

But life happens.

Pearl was always clear that she wanted to do a movie that would win her an Oscar one day. I supported her in this dream. Just a couple of months after we got engaged, she got an offer to go to New York to appear in *Quantico* on Netflix. It was a massive break. She would be starring alongside famous names like Priyanka Chopra, Blair Underwood and Aaron Diaz, and there were big dollars being thrown at it to be a success. Of course I supported her decision to take it on.

We put together a farewell dinner for her along with some of her friends. There was a lot of noise made around her move and deservedly so. There was excitement, but I had mixed emotions too because I was unsure what would happen next. I had been through a similar experience when Awande went to live in Australia and there was part of me that was anxious about the future.

But I understood what she wanted and in my speech at her farewell I said that if this was part of her journey to getting closer to her Oscar, then we would all be there to support the journey. We wouldn't make it difficult and stand in her way.

I took her to the airport and just before she was about to leave on her business-class flight to New York, she grabbed me around the shoulders and told me I wasn't the only one who would be dishing out rings. As the crazy, fun person that she was, she had gone and bought a ring for me and engraved both our names on the inside. She joked that I had to wear it all the time to keep the women away from me. And I wore it all time. It was the only piece of jewellery that I wore. It wasn't marriage but it was a commitment.

We maintained our relationship while she was in New York. When my father fell ill in 2016 and was diagnosed with cancer, she flew back to South Africa. She had met him before and they had clicked, so she asked for leave from the set to come home for a few days. That meant a lot and it really cemented our relationship.

Although we were physically far apart, it never stopped either of us from supporting each other. There were always gestures between us. Another time she came to visit from New York and brought gifts for the entire family. When I had some time off work I went to visit her and I helped her to move apartments in Manhattan.

Long distance was difficult but we kept it up for a few years. We looked at options for me to find a network to work in New York and do sport there. There were many variables to consider. What if she finished up at *Quantico* and went back to South Africa but I had to stay on in my job? The intention was there but it wasn't necessarily practical. In the end, she did end up coming back to Johannesburg. We were both committed to making it work but perhaps it was inevitable it would end with the stresses of where we both were on our journeys and what our intentions were. Nothing untoward happened that made us split. Our circumstances had changed drastically over time and we decided we couldn't continue.

Ending a relationship that had potential marriage written all over it was extremely difficult. We spoke about it at length. One day she came back from boxing and lay down on my couch; we were both so comfortable in each other's presence even though we had technically broken up. We spoke for hours. We didn't speak like two people who were breaking up with each other. We had a real, intense conversation and spoke about everything. She grew tired and only left the following morning.

There was no bitter taste left between us. It was a sad ending, but I was satisfied and encouraged that there was a great sense of maturity in how we both ended it and to this day I still have great respect and admiration for Pearl.

Amusingly, my mother, to whom Pearl introduced her hair range, often asks me to to replenish her products when they run out. Picture me in Clicks carrying Pearl's hair products with her face plastered all over them and the cashiers probably wondering whether it's the products I miss or Pearl I can't let go of, while ringing up my purchase.

28

Lightning strikes twice

The last time I went to the gym, I landed up being rushed to hospital because I was having a heart attack. Surely lightning couldn't strike twice in the same spot?

In 2017, I decided to try to get back into shape. I had been fired from radio so I had time to work out. I was still a little apprehensive about gym because of what had happened the previous time. Pearl had taken up boxing and she was working out at the Bryanston Fight Club. She would come back all sweaty and tired, but I could also tell that it was doing a lot for her physically and mentally.

I had nearly lost my life in a gym environment once before so of course I was nervous about returning. Fortunately, the boxing gym was well controlled and well managed. I've always loved and enjoyed exercise and I was enthusiastic about boxing. But watching boxing and training are two very different things.

Boxing is extremely intense. It literally works every bit of your body without having to go and lift weights. You walk out of a session feeling like you've been in a boxing ring with Sugar Ray Leonard or Evander Holyfield. It is a different kind of beast.

I felt great after a boxing session because of the resistance that it brings and the weight loss that accompanies it. Once I got over the exhaustion of the initial sessions, I started to get into shape, my stride was more confident and I was walking with my head held high. I really got into it and I trained regularly with Gold, a professional boxer, who was doing one-on-one sessions with me.

One day, we were just doing a boxing session and concluding the rope exercise, whipping it up and down and around in sequence, which is an intense challenge. A couple of seconds into the exercise I felt a sudden sharp pain in my right chest and I dropped the rope.

I immediately knew what was happening. I looked at Gold and told him I had to leave. I would see him tomorrow. Gold looked perplexed. I was just near the end of the session but I told him it was urgent and I had to rush.

I knew that it was another heart attack and I couldn't believe it was happening again.

I rushed to my car, climbed in and started the engine. From where I was, Sandton Medi-Clinic was a hop, skip and jump away. Because of my previous experience I wasn't willing to take a chance with an ambulance again and time was of the essence.

I didn't know if I would have the latitude of time with this experience so while I was driving I called Sunninghill Hospital where my cardiologist Dr Eric Klug had his rooms. Sunninghill was too far in that moment but they told me that he had partners at Medi-Clinic so I decided to take my chances by going there.

This time the pain was sharper and more present. I sensed that I needed help urgently. My vision was beginning to deteriorate. When I pulled up at a traffic light I couldn't tell if the light was red, amber or green. Everything was blurry. I watched the other cars to see which moved so I would know when to pull off.

I began to feel a wave of exhaustion come over me as I pulled into the parking of the Medi-Clinic. The pain was sharper and the blurriness of vision was worse. I pulled up right outside the entrance where the ambulances park and thought, what the hell, I'm stopping here.

The security guard jumped up, ready to accost me, and as he saw my face I heard him say, 'Robert, are you okay?' I apologised for parking there but I had to get inside. I wasn't okay. He could tell I was in distress. I walked up to the front desk and placed my driver's licence on the desk so that the man behind the counter could pull up my profile.

I told him I needed to see a cardiologist immediately but he was taking his time, asking a thousand questions and filling in forms. We could deal with the paperwork later but I needed urgent intervention. Fortunately, someone else appeared behind him, saw what state I was in and called me through to go and lie down on a bed so that the cardiologist, Dr Sender, could come and check me.

I was lying on a bed in the middle of the corridor in the emergency section but I didn't care. I was in so much pain.

With the first heart attack I had made the mistake of not contacting my family immediately so I took my phone and called Nomvula who was in Pretoria. I gave the phone to one of the nurses and asked them to brief my sister. I couldn't speak, the pain was just too much. Compared to the first one, this felt brutal. I could hear myself screaming.

I'm not a very expressive person when it comes to pain but I could hear the noise of my screams echoing down the corridor it was so loud. The doctors busied around me and gave me some medication and it didn't take long before the pain turned into a heat around my chest. They wheeled me into theatre and did an angiogram. Fortunately, Dr Sender was a big football fan and he was warm and was bantering with me about the game while all of this was going on.

The doctors were able to do whatever interventions were necessary to save me. This heart attack felt more severe and more intense than the first one. I felt that I didn't have the luxury of time with this one, but they acted quickly.

The one thing I kept asking was why was God sparing me again.

I was not complaining. I was grateful and thankful, but wow, two heart attacks. How possible is that? I knew of people who had experienced just one heart attack and had died.

It made me wonder if God was saving me for a purpose. Was there something I was being primed to do or that he still wanted me to do? I had all of these questions swirling around my mind. I don't go to church every week but I do pray a lot within my own private space. I do have a connection with God and believe there is a greater purpose and I saw that more after my heart attacks.

I reflected on what could have happened and how severe the outcome could have been. It could have been fatal. But I was able to drive myself to hospital while I was suffering a heart attack. Thank God there was a cardiologist on duty who was able to assist me.

I have always wondered if that heart attack wasn't some kind of precursor, or a prevention of a more fatal heart attack than would potentially have hit me later on. Going to Fight Club may have triggered something that would have lain dormant for a while and would have been much bigger.

Something had to give. I had suffered another heart attack. I had experienced it. I had to change my lifestyle. I tried to sleep more. I tried to be healthier. But it made no sense to me that every time I tried to improve my health and go back to gym, I would have a heart attack. It was counter-intuitive really. I was pushing myself to have a healthier lifestyle, to get my heart rate up and drop my calories and lose weight and this was the outcome.

But fortunately, I had survived, not just once but twice.

29
Making radio history

I was fired from SABC radio, the first time, in early July 2017. A year later, in July 2018, the SABC announced my return to the broadcaster. I would be presenting a new sports show to be simulcast on Metro FM from 6pm to 7pm and on Radio 2000 from 6pm to 8pm, Mondays to Fridays.

While I had been away from radio for a year five different hosts had tried to fill the gap. Thomas Mlambo, Mpho Maboi, Udo Carlese, Joe Mann and Owen Hannie had all passed through that hot seat.

Beverly was still the producer and she was behind the scenes for all five of them. None of them was able to make a real go of it and the SABC was not happy with the situation.

Meanwhile there was a new CEO who had come in to the job – Madoda Mxakwe.

I got a call from Madoda in February 2018. He introduced himself as the new boss and he asked for a one-on-one meeting with me. I told him chances were very, very slim that I would accept heading back to the SABC. He respected that but he also presented me with reasons why he believed I should return.

We met at the Melrose Arch Hotel, in the library cigar lounge.

Madoda introduced himself and set out the daunting task that he faced at the SABC and his desire to turn the organisation around. Since he had arrived and he had looked at the numbers, he was struggling to understand why I was no longer at Metro FM. Given the success of the show, the awards and the listeners and everything else, it made no sense to him how someone who was generating so much money for the public broadcaster was no longer there. Outside of personal reasons, what broadcasting reasons were there? Nobody could provide him with an answer.

That gave him the ammunition to approach me, to sit down with me and see if I was keen to return. He also told me that he believed in my talent and that my return would be beneficial to the SABC and for listeners at large.

Importantly, the radio show on Metro was contracted under SABC Sport and not directly to the radio station.

I had to be honest with him and tell him my concerns. In my view, there were people like Sully Motsweni, Sibongile Mtyali who was the Metro FM station manager at the time, Tony Soglo who was Metro FM's programming manager at the time; these were all people who were still at the SABC who would push back against me returning. They were 100% part of the cabal.

Those were the same people who were working with Sully and under Sully and who got rid of me the year before. I explained to him that it made no sense that the people I knew wanted me out of the SABC at all costs were still there. How would he ensure that my return would be safeguarded and independent enough that they don't have a say in anything to do with my return?

They were all part of the cabal that was running things, whether to the benefit of the SABC or to the benefit of whoever is behind giving them the instruction to get rid of some of us.

I was as open and straightforward as I could be with him regarding the situation.

Madoda reassured me and said he understood my reservations. But he had been given the powers by the board to make huge strides within the SABC, to turn it around and make it profitable once again.

He believed that the sports show, hosted by me, could provide that. How then would we manage it given my concerns about the cabal still being in place? I also wanted to know who I would be working with, not just at management level but also the individuals on my show. I didn't want to work with producers or individuals who would be sabotaging the show.

I had experienced incidents of sabotage towards the end of my previous contract. There were occasions when I was doing an outside broadcast and lines had been booked; I would think we were on air, then all of a sudden we had been zapped off air. Those things shouldn't happen. People do OBs for three hours with no problems. I would be doing a live show from the Durban studio and then there would be dead air, I couldn't hear the caller, or some problem. There would always be something creeping in to all of these productions.

I told him that we had always been a team of three people – Thabo, Beverly and myself. I wanted that to continue. I didn't want to start with a new producer or a new anybody. If we were the same three people, then maybe I could hear him out.

He said he would prioritise that. He also made a proposal that would be a game changer as far as broadcasting was concerned. He suggested that we simulcast the show so it would not only be on Metro FM but on Radio 2000 too. Radio 2000 was always this underachieving station, but with the biggest reach in the country. There's no station that has a reach as big as Radio 2000. Metro FM covers major metropolitan areas but wherever you go in the country, you will find Radio 2000 crystal clear. They had just never quite got the formula right for content.

I've always been keen on new innovations and this sounded quite exciting. It would be one hour on Metro and two hours on Radio 2000.

I had emphasised my worries about the cabal and their problematic ways and he gave me the assurance that all I had to do was focus on the show. He would be there to protect me and make sure that I would be able to do my work.

That was the reassurance. Cut off the noise. Focus on the job. Fine. No problem.

There was a big hooha announcement. Chris Maroleng had come in as chief operating officer and he made the presentation. I was coming back on my own terms. There were headlines about how much I was being paid. There was a report in *Sunday World* by Aubrey Mothombeni that the SABC had to bend over backwards to bring back the 'radio darling' in a three-year deal worth more than R5 million and I would be earning R7000 a shift and a monthly salary of R154 000. Let's be real. There was no such thing. That was fantasy and really stretching it. They wanted to cause a scene with the unions or with the public to say this was wasteful expenditure.

There were obviously those who were directing a narrative around the big payment. Again, it was all being orchestrated and people were taking internal conversations and would then phone this Aubrey character from *Sunday World* and leak everything to him.

Every story that was carried by the tabloid was always Aubrey from *Sunday World*. Sometimes the minute I walked out of the building and got into my car, a phone call from Aubrey would come. I had literally just concluded the conversation and Aubrey had been given enough detail to be able to ask me a question. Every time I finished a conversation with HR or with legal, by the time I got to the parking lot my phone would be ringing. It made no sense.

Obviously I was glad to be returning to radio and to the listeners. The success of the radio show was prolific and, coming back, there was an expectation that there would be the same level of interrogation and of independence and that I would continue tackling issues in a resolute manner. There had been an outcry because that had been lacking while I was gone and it added to the CEO's case for me to come back. I always respected that and have always said that the listener is my boss. The listener comes first. I have always stuck to that in any way, shape or form.

One of my conditions for returning was that the name of the show had to be Marawa Sports Worldwide. I was deliberate about including my name because I had been stuffed around by the SABC so many times. In the past, my show had been sponsored by big corporates like MTN and Discovery and these were major sponsors that the SABC benefited from. In the 2018 contract, I tried to negotiate that a percentage of any major sponsorship that was signed, I as the anchor should get 10% of that.

The CEO was initially open to it. It was refreshing in terms of his approach and he agreed, but that then became a stumbling block. When the contract came back to me that clause had not been approved. There were murmurings that if they allow me that clause, then they will have to allow everybody else too. I didn't understand that because we all had individual contracts and we don't have mass contractual negotiations. People must fight their own wars and fight for what they believe is right.

My insistence that the show was called what it was called was because I knew that the same role players were still at the SABC and those who had outside influence also knew when my contract would come to an end.

Remember this was now July/August 2018. My SuperSport contract would be coming to an end early in 2019. The intention was always to try to get me out of radio and television at the same time so I would have no platform. They had not anticipated that a new CEO would come to the SABC and bring me back on board.

The plan, in my opinion, was always from football leadership although it is difficult to pinpoint who exactly. It depends how you look at it. I always felt that the biggest disquiet about what I was doing on radio and what I was achieving was from the local football authority. I was questioning many things to do with the PSL. I had run-ins with SAFA a lot. I think the SAFA leadership got to a stage where they were mature enough to take being questioned on the chin.

I don't think that was the case with the PSL. When football authorities were not happy with what was being said on radio, they would use their partnership with the SABC as an excuse to put pressure on me. They would ask how they could formulate a partnership if management was allowing me to say negative things about their product.

The question was what the definition of 'negative' was. Is questioning authority negative? Is asking questions negative? Are we supposed to be public relations officers or spin doctors or marketers of the PSL? No, we are broadcasters and we are supposed to ask questions and, as football fans, we are supposed to ask questions as well.

Going back to radio was critical in the fightback against my voice being muted altogether. The CEO had seen things differently and had asked me to come back. There was an assurance that I would have independence and that there would be no interference. We were starting a new chapter and making radio history with a new simulcast proposition on the biggest commercial radio stations in the country.

For me Pirates was the obvious team to support and I got to know the individuals, the coaches, the players, the history. All of it. Jomo Sono became a cult figure. I got to know the mixture, the culture, the team. Born in 1937, there was so much that made them special. The heroes that were there, the cult figures, how they filled up Orlando Stadium and then later on when Chiefs was formed and the rivalry between them. Football really started taking shape for me at that stage of my life. It all gripped me.

My father definitely played a role in that for me because I would not have known about Orlando Pirates if it wasn't for him. I wouldn't even have known about the existence of football. I was on the farm and there were no structures, no football teams, nothing. Here I was getting introduced to this world of fanatical sport and I began to know individuals. I was starting to realise their brilliance, their athleticism and all of the things that made the sport what it was.

I also learnt what it meant to just give of myself emotionally. If somebody missed a penalty, then I would take it personally and felt that that person should be dealt with. How dare they miss a penalty? Because now we are going to be losing! So, then I started to learn about teamwork and loyalty.

Later on, when there was Chiefs and then Moroka Swallows, nothing mattered for me except for Orlando Pirates.

When a new player came in, I would know about it. If I had to look at a photo of the starting eleven from back in the day, I would know all the names. I always did my homework. It was my curiosity at the time but I was able to name all of and at home. He was strict but he was a loving father and proud of his kids. He tried to be as involved as he could be, and paid special attention to me and motivated me because I was the only boy with three sisters.

I first got to love football through my father. But over time my love grew far beyond his love of the game.

Dad was an Orlando Pirates and Arsenal fan. We knew of English football on the farm. In 1963, Tottenham Hotspur had come on a tour to South Africa. But Arsenal was his team; it was in his DNA.

I was a Liverpool supporter from day one. I think it was because of the influence of John Barnes. He was brilliant and stuck out like a sore thumb as the only black player. It was the power of representation. He also experienced hardships as a player; fans rocking up carrying billboards saying Niggerpool, and other insults.

It was good for rivalry in our house. When Arsenal played against Liverpool, I would stick it in his face, knowing there could be backlash.

Locally, he was an Orlando Pirates fan.

Throughout my career people have asked which soccer team I support locally. I always say I support Liverpool internationally and locally I support Bafana Bafana!

My dad supported Orlando Pirates and I supported Orlando Pirates. It was the one time when there was a unity between my dad and myself. My mum supported Kaizer Chiefs, so it was always the boys against her. At a later stage, my sister Gugu got involved too, although she didn't support a particular team.

30
Near death

I felt the hand grasp my neck and begin to throttle me. I began to run out of breath. I tried to muster the energy to fight back but I felt completely drained. Everything had been sapped out of me. It was like a supernatural force I couldn't explain. The room was pitch black, the curtains were drawn and the lights were off. I felt the hand tighten its grip around my throat. The images flashing through my mind were what I imagined walking to heaven would be like. A long dusty road lined with trees. It was tranquil and inviting. I had to fight back against this force that was pinning me down. I thought about my mother and about my son Awande. There was no way I was going to leave either of them behind. They were my priority and I had to fight for them. The grip on my throat was tightening. It was choking me. But I knew I had to do something. From deep within me I found the resolve and let out a scream. 'Awande!'

The Russian World Cup kicked off in June 2018 and I was anchoring the broadcast for SuperSport. We had brought the best guests into our studio and we were showcasing the event to the world. It always felt special to be at the forefront of such a big tournament. Management had shown great faith and trust in me and my abilities in front of the camera. This was the biggest sporting spectacle and I was leading it. We were also just having so much fun and I was loving every minute of it.

A few days in I began to feel uncomfortable, physically. Studios are always cold spaces and the aircon always has to be on but I was really struggling with it. It felt like the aircon was blowing directly on me in the presenter's chair.

Usually I would choose to stay in my seat and concentrate on watching the game while some of the guests would go through to the VIP room and grab some snacks and watch the game there. I had to be present and make sure I wasn't missing a minute of action.

But this aircon thing was bugging me and they couldn't do anything about it because it was all centralised, so I was up and walking around. I thought maybe I was getting sick but I just felt a general sense of discomfort.

I had spent a few days in hospital at the Folateng ward of the Charlotte Maxeke Johannesburg Academic Hospital before the start of the World Cup and the doctors had cleared me to go home and go back to work. I could tell that I wasn't 100% well.

I then started struggling with my sleep too. I would wake up in the middle of the night. I've always had trouble sleeping but this felt different. It was like I was being woken up. Something was forcing me awake. I had a sense of a presence in the room, like someone was there.

I would ignore it and try my best to go back to sleep. So it would continue – I would come back from work exhausted, fall asleep and then be woken up in the middle of the night again by this overwhelming force that seemed to have some kind of power over me in my sleep.

It felt like my brain was semifunctional as I was half-awake. There was a level of distress because I thought somebody was there. I would try to flip my duvet over me and it felt almost impossible to do, like there was some kind of resistance against it.

It was then that I felt it. Until today, I swear it felt like a hand that was coming to throttle me. It was as if my breath was running out. The images that kept running through my head were those that we were taught at school when you were going to heaven. It was so intense.

I thought to myself, what the hell is going on here?

I've never been a person who has ever encountered witchcraft or any other supernatural force. I was raised in a Christian family, in the Roman Catholic Church at school, in the Anglican Church as a family. It was just something that I had never encountered in my life before.

I had experienced two heart attacks before and thought this was not a heart attack. This was not that. I am convinced it had nothing to do with my heart.

It felt like a force trying to strangle me. I am the biggest disbeliever in all that I am describing in this incident and yet I am sure of what it was. Even in my mind today, I don't believe it myself because people think I'm telling a fairy-tale story. But I remember it like hell.

It felt like this thing was going to suffocate me to death. I was screaming. I was all alone in the room, all alone in the house, and I was screaming the names of my mother and my son. There was no way I was going to leave either of them behind. My son was my biggest priority. My mother has always been my priority and I was her support structure. I was trying whatever I could to fight back but whatever resistance I tried was not enough. It had the upper hand and it was weakening me minute by minute. The ordeal felt like a lifetime. I could feel that I had been punctured somehow.

I think my one and only saving grace was me shouting at the top of my voice for Awande and for my mother over and over again.

All of a sudden I saw my phone next to my bed start ringing. It must have been around 4.30 in the morning and I had left my phone on silent. I saw it flashing and I could see that it was Nomvula calling. Her contacts are saved under her English name, Ingrid, which kept flashing on the screen. Why was she phoning so early in the morning?

I tried to reach across to answer the phone but I was a mess. That's when I realised I had a big problem. All I needed to do was to stretch my left arm across and swipe the screen. I couldn't do it. I couldn't move my arm. I had zero capability to move.

The phone stopped ringing. Deep down I hoped she would call again. She did. Nomvula was being persistent. Somehow she knew something was wrong.

She would later tell my mom that she had woken up in the early hours of the morning and had a vision of me walking up a hill and I was struggling. She immediately phoned me. When I didn't answer the first time she called back again.

I mustered the energy to pick up my right arm, move across and swipe in one motion so that the green icon lit up. I had managed to put the phone on speaker.

'Themba, are you okay?' she asked urgently. Because Nomvula is medically trained as a nurse, she could tell immediately that I was in distress. I didn't sound myself. She told me she would call an ambulance for me and I had no argument for that. I was so defeated. Nomvula told the ambulance to hurry and to bring oxygen.

The security at the gate of the complex let the ambulance in. Fortunately, I still had my bag packed from my previous hospital admission so we grabbed that on the way out. Because of my previous experience with an ambulance, I was urging the paramedics to hurry up and get going. But they were insistent on finding out what medication I was on and my medical history.

I knew that time was of the essence. I didn't think it was a heart attack but I wanted to get medical help ASAP. I'm eternally grateful to those paramedics because they put foot and got me to hospital. They took me to the Folateng ward at Charlotte Maxeke Hospital again because that is where I had been a few days prior and my doctor, Dr Nqoba Tsabedze, was there. He is the Academic Head of Cardiology at Wits University and the

Clinical Head of Cardiology at Charlotte Maxeke.

The nurses took one look at me and I could see the horror etched on their faces. I had been discharged just a couple of days before and I could see their concern. They immediately rushed me to ICU, there was no messing around. They were trying to stabilise me, giving me oxygen, trying to keep me alive. I could hear an argument between some of the nurses and my sister who was trying to get into the ward.

The staff were trying to prevent her from coming in. She assured them that she was a nurse and she wouldn't be disturbed by whatever she saw, but the nurses told her that what I looked like would be frightening to her. She insisted she wanted to see me.

Nomvula walked in, drew the curtain open and I saw her whole face collapse. I didn't know what I looked like but her reaction said it all. She would later describe me as being 'ashen grey'. In medical terms, when you are ashen grey, your time on earth is basically over. I will never forget the expression on her face. She had never seen me like that before, in all of my health scares in the past.

Nomvula is a very emotional person so she had to fight off the tears but I could see them building up inside her and her eyes welled up.

My mom struggles when she recalls that episode because she thought she had lost me forever. Nomvula had called her and told her that I was ashen grey and they were both nurses so they knew what that meant:

This side I was praying like there was no tomorrow. Sometimes I wouldn't even know what to say to God. But I just wanted my son to live. I was drained. I love my son. He's the only one and he cares. He has got a good heart. I was just asking God, I can't imagine life without him. He was gone. It was God. Or maybe his will to live. Since my dad was a Christian and a bishop and all that, we were born and bred in Christianity. I believe there is a God. Because when things are bad and I pray, things do get better. Maybe God listened. In the mornings, I prayed with the priest. I asked for extra prayers because it was bad, bad, bad.

I still felt weak. My ears were buzzing. It felt like there was a choir singing in my ears. At one point I even asked one of the nurses to ask the patient next door to switch off the music. There was the sound of choral music in my ears. I do wonder whether it was linked to the images of heaven that I had been conjuring up in my mind. But that sound of choral music lingered for days.

I spent days in ICU and you can't sleep in that environment. There are constantly machines beeping and they are poking and prodding you incessantly. Every morning at 4.30am the sister would come in and draw blood. Then the next day, more blood. We were going for CT scans. I was blue and black. My veins were messed up where they were giving me injections to the stomach. This was a medical journey I'd never been on before. And that sound of choral music just wouldn't go away.

It was like this speaker had been on since I got to this damn hospital.

The doctors were in and out. Then a group of specialists would come through. They would discuss and look puzzled. I was always fascinated by the specialists who always came in the morning and would literally open up the blankets and just feel my toes to see if they were getting colder or see if they were getting bluer. The nurses took more blood and more blood as the medical team tried to work out what was wrong with me. It felt like I was there forever.

Dr Tsabedze was the doctor primarily responsible for my care. He had initially looked after me the first time when I was admitted.

> *His older sister called me and she was concerned that Robert wasn't well and that his lifestyle wasn't good. I arranged for an admission for him and that lasted around a week. His cardiac biomarkers were negative. He was short of breath, very lethargic, but not in heart failure. I had to basically treat him empirically with antibiotic therapy. He responded to the antibiotic therapy. I then put him on more cardioprotective therapy to prevent him from having future heart attacks. We did a lot of tests and fortunately he recovered very well.*

After that first episode, Dr Tsabedze was very concerned about my lifestyle, which was high pressure, mostly nocturnal, and I wasn't eating very well. I was under a lot of stress, constantly travelling and broadcasting.

He was taking care of me again this time around and describes from a medical perspective what they were dealing with:

> *Robert presented with shortness of breath, and he was having chest pains. Again, I thought it was another heart attack. Cardiac bio enzymes and troponins were negative; he was not in heart failure; the cardiac echocardiogram showed good functioning. This time around, what was unique was that the septic markers were high. I thought he had another infection. I treated it with broad spectrum antibiotics and we had to escalate to really broad spectrum intravenous antibiotics. He initially responded for a few days. When we stopped those antibiotics, he immediately relapsed again. He was having pain and it wasn't clear what was going on. We did CT scan tests, which picked up an effusion, and I also performed the D-DIMER test, which is a test we use to exclude pulmonary embolism and which came back positive. We then decided to do a pleural tap, placing a needle into his lungs, which came back as straw-coloured fluid. In South Africa, if you have a pleural effusion and it's straw-coloured, the diagnosis is TB – tuberculosis, until proven otherwise. That's the last thing I would have thought someone like him would have. After tapping that fluid, he felt much better. We then started treating him with TB treatment, and he was planned to be on TB treatment*

for a total of nine months. Therefore, TB with superimposed bacterial pneumonia and pulmonary embolism was the working diagnosis.

When they drained my lungs it was the most painful thing I had ever experienced. Every time I would take a deep breath, there would be something in my nostril that indicated that there was fluid in the lungs. They would prick at the back and extract the fluid and you would see it. I had to go in on high-intensity tuberculosis medication. Dr Tsabedze explains what they found:

We were treating him for TB with superimposed bacterial pneumonia and pulmonary embolism. I explained to him this issue of TB being in the environment, and if you are immune-compromised, you are at a very high risk and he is HIV negative. Lack of good diet with lack of sleep, overworking, your immunity does get weak. That's what I believe had predisposed him to this. I'm a scientist and I must answer things with medical rationale. If you have water in your lung and your lung is not expanding, it makes perfect sense that you will not be able to breathe well; you will struggle, and especially when you lie on that side. I could explain a lot of the symptoms from what we found. The only challenge was I would have never thought someone like Robert could complicate with TB, but that's something that can happen to anyone. It was just an unexpected presentation.

> *But the symptomatology of the effusion, the severe pneumonia, etc. can easily explain those things in terms of why he was feeling unwell. I'm certain there were a lot of things that compounded this with work and stress. Everything seemed very frustrating and overwhelming and I understand why he could easily feel that way. This was now also déjà vu because he had a similar incident about a year ago or two years ago and now it comes back again and this time even worse.*

Everything was just so hazy. I was in a state of shock because I had never, ever in my entire life thought I would have to explain to my mother that I had this experience of a supernatural force that presented itself to me at night.

I am convinced I was under attack. By who or what, I don't know. Who sends the supernatural forces? How do you trace them back? How do you know what the motive is?

There was a lot of speculation around certain people within the SABC. People would always say I should try not go into the building too early. Most of the time I would sit in my car until three minutes before 6pm and then, when I heard the news jingle on the radio, I would walk in just in time to go on air. I had already prepared before of course so I didn't need to get there hours earlier.

There was speculation that people were jealous or envious or just downright didn't want to see me succeed. Outside of those I had fallen out of favour with among the rugby, football and cricket administrators were those within the building who did not like me for their own reasons or purposes.

But why would they go as far as trying to eliminate a person from existence is another question. Why would they feel so strongly that I don't deserve to live? Because that is how close it got. It took something extremely, extremely powerful to get there.

To this day I can't shake the feeling that somebody wanted me dead; that I believe I was a target for immediate death.

Who knows what they had tried before that had just not worked. Maybe they had considered trying to poison me or shooting me and they were unsuccessful. I know the people that I regard as so-called enemies, but this felt extreme.

My personal goal was to get better in time to anchor the World Cup final. I had done the opening and I was on the schedule for the final. I had spent the majority of the tournament in ICU and I wasn't able to watch the bulk of the tournament.

SuperSport were supportive enough to keep the slot for the final open as I was recovering. It was motivation for me to recover. I do think part of it was that whoever didn't want me to play a part or be visible during the World Cup wanted to eliminate me.

When I was discharged from hospital I went to do my recovery at my sister's home in Pretoria. I was so exhausted that I slept like a baby because you don't get to sleep in ICU. I had to give my lungs time to recover. But my sister looked after me. Nomvula went out of her way to make sure that I was back on my feet. She was preparing healthy meals every single day and caring for me.

The date was getting closer to the World Cup final. I was resolute that I wanted to host the final. While I was in hospital, I had found a gentleman on Instagram who makes designer suits. I wanted to get a suit made to wear for the final. Yeah, I'm going to go get a suit made, because I am hosting the World Cup final! That was my motivation as much as I was still trying to recover.

One of the first things I did was to go to Randburg to meet him so he could take my measurements. I came out of hospital a slimmer version of myself.

Now I was chasing time. I was still exhausted. My sister didn't think I was showing signs of recovering in time to be ready and the recovery was difficult. It was bad. It was long. It was arduous. I couldn't talk for 30 seconds without being out of breath. My lung was injured and needed to recover.

The final was on a Sunday. On the Saturday, SuperSport called. They needed to make a decision. How was I feeling? Could I make the final?

I consulted with my sister and we talked and talked and talked. I had a level of difficulty with speaking but we both felt like I was good enough to take it on.

I walked into studio that Sunday to present the World Cup final, dressed in my brand-new tailor-made suit. It felt so good.

I was still in recovery, but I felt like I had achieved success when it had been set up for me to fail. A lot of people were in complete disbelief that I was actually fronting up a World Cup final.

It's a memory for me that sticks out because it brought me

even closer to God. It's a reminder that we are fighting all of these battles together and we are overcoming them.

I wouldn't have made it without my faith in God. Playing that gospel song over and over and over again in my head, I never would have made it without that. Now I play Marvin Sapp's 'Never Would Have Made It Without You' in my car, not in my head.

Never mind the heart attacks, this episode seemed like it was finality. Having been this close to death on several occasions, surviving is ultimately the greatest feeling when I think about how close I was to not living any longer.

I have been spared a few times and I don't even know if I deserve it, but I always pray and say, God, whatever the purpose is that you're keeping me here for, please present it to me so that I can action it and do as you wish for me to do. That is always my prayer. I just can't believe that I am still here.

31
Backlash

My time at SuperSport was full of more highs than lows. I began doing pitchside reporting, which was exciting for me because it got me out of the studio. It was also good value for SuperSport because it allowed fans who maybe did not have a decoder to see me with a SuperSport microphone. So they knew I hadn't completely disappeared from the football space.

From a growth perspective, I also needed to do something different to what I had been doing. I enjoyed the interaction with the coaches, asking questions, watching the game from a different perspective. I gained a lot in terms of that, but I was also aware that, with the success of the magazine shows I was presenting, people would be unhappy. People would also be displeased with the views that I was sharing on radio.

As I mentioned, I felt strongly about advocating for women, growing female talent and pushing the talented women I came across to advance in a male-dominated environment. I wanted to see them grow and flourish. Based on relationships that I had with various women working behind the scenes, I would hear regular stories of how a person in a director's seat or a person in a managerial position would take advantage of the fact that there were women in their environment.

I had heard stories about what was happening at outside broadcasts or even in studio with women being put in positions that amounted to sexual-harassment scenarios, such as being forced into spending time with a director in exchange for regular appearances on the schedule or to be given more shifts.

There was a consistent conversation that they felt like they were being treated as pieces of flesh because that is how certain directors behaved. If you were an on-air personality and you wanted more regular shifts, then you had to have a physical relationship with a director. Or there was an expectation that, if you were doing games away on an outside broadcast, there would be some sort of contact conversation with a director.

When I heard about a few of the cases, I asked someone I have an open relationship with workwise if it was true and they said they had experienced it. That jolted me and I thought, how widespread is the problem if some of the more popular and influential members of the SuperSport team are also being sexually harassed in the workplace? How far does it go? Some of the women were scared for their jobs. Then one of the women decided to be open about it. Fellow sportscaster Mmaphuti Mashamaite wrote about it on social media and she said she had laid an official complaint against her superior, who she described as a sexual predator.

Most didn't rely on favours and were just brilliant at what they did and didn't relent to the pressure. So they would share these stories of what had happened to them.

At the time, the CEO of SuperSport was Gideon Khobane and he and I had not clicked. I did not understand him or his vision or his anything really. It reminded me of the personal duels that I had experienced with people at the SABC. I was fortunate to have had bosses like Tex and Robin Kempthorne and Happy Ntshingila and Imtiaz Patel who were progressive, and now I was faced with this chap.

I had a meeting with him and raised the issue of sexual harassment that I had heard about. I told him there was a problem that I had picked up and I was being very open and honest with him. I asked him if he was aware that a lot of our female staffers were experiencing episodes of sexual harassment from people he employed.

His reaction was very strange. He was shocked and said that they had sent out circulars to all staff and if there were incidents of sexual harassment then people must report them. But you know that if somebody sends an email back to you with their names on it and naming the people who are sexually harassing them, that's going to be a problem because immediately they're going to be left out in the cold because now they've outed whoever the person is and you'll go confront that person. There was no anonymity.

Gideon wanted to know what I expected him to do and I told him as the CEO he should understand what to do. He picked up the phone and called the head of production and head of football to his office. He wanted to know if they knew anything about what I was telling him. He lost his mind. I don't know what I did wrong or said, I was just bringing it to his attention. It wasn't even the primary purpose of our meeting – I just raised it in passing.

That is why I was taken aback by his reaction and him calling extra people to be witness to this mad guy that just walked into his office to tell him about sexual harassment. I wasn't mad because I knew I had firsthand experience of the encounters relayed to me by the female staff.

There were other issues with SuperSport that were bubbling under and my lawyers had sent a letter of complaint. There was an incident during the time when there was a lot of public chatter about my relationship with coach Pitso Mosimane and a director had broadcast a shot of a banner with derogatory words, essentially saying I hated Pitso. That was a problem because the director would have seen the monitor in the OB van before cutting to it. He was supposed to protect all talent at SuperSport. That had potential backlash because it gave the impression that I had an agenda and that I hated Pitso.

Things were getting tense and there were a lot of issues that were piling up. People believe the hype they have been fed.

Gideon promised he would follow up on the sexual-harassment claims. But I could tell from his anger levels that he was just saying that to walk away from it all.

I carried on with my work.

As with everything else that happened on my journey, people would wait for the right time to strike. They wouldn't do an immediate firing. They would check when my contract was coming to an end and then they would use that as an excuse

– that the contract had not been renewed. It happened on radio and on TV. The same thing happened this time around.

In May 2019, my run at SuperSport came to an end. My contract had already expired three months earlier and a new contract was being delayed. I had continued doing work but it was falling outside of any signed agreement. We decided to have a meeting with Gideon to discuss my contract and my lawyer, Cedric Ramabulana, was present as well as another lawyer at SuperSport.

The meeting took place on a Tuesday and lasted 9 minutes and 17 seconds. Gideon thanked me for the work that I had done at SuperSport and told me that unfortunately my contract would not be renewed. A decision had been taken and thank you for your service and we wish you all the best.

This was a Tuesday and I had a show to do that Thursday night and it would be the last *Thursday Night Live*. A couple of days later, on 1 June, it was the UEFA Champions League final between Liverpool and Tottenham Hotspurs and that would be my last and final assignment for SuperSport, which was the agreement between us.

That Thursday I had finished doing my radio show and was ready to rush through to SuperSport to present my final *Thursday Night Live*. I was already half dressed for TV. I got an SMS informing me that I was not required to do the show.

So my time at SuperSport was done. Just like that, with immediate effect. It was exactly what had happened at the SABC. Just before my final show I got a message to say don't come in. You can't say goodbye to anybody, you can't say goodbye to the audience that's watched you bring up this formidable *Thursday Night Live*. You can't say goodbye to the people who have religiously watched UEFA Champions League. You can't say goodbye to anybody. It's done. They're not going to let you in.

Thato Moeng had to awkwardly present the show by herself and repeatedly told viewers that it was suddenly 'the last show'.

SuperSport put out a statement about me leaving.

'SuperSport is in the process of an exciting refresh of its local presenter line-up, which will be unveiled as part of our new football season campaign. This restructure includes us not pursuing our contractual relationship with Robert Marawa. Robert was personally advised of our decision earlier this week. We are grateful for his contribution over the years and wish him great success in his future endeavours.'

I had tweeted hinting at what had happened.

'Imagine paying for a service where people who are guilty of sexual harassment are employed and encouraged to work.'

'One day u will ALL know. It will cost me my life but you will know' adding that *'The Mafia! Incorporated with lackeys. An amazing story.'*

They were scared of what might be said on the final show because of the honesty that I am committed to. They were also avoiding firing me and waited for my contract to come to an end. It didn't make sense, though, because I was excelling at SuperSport. I was about to host the UEFA Champions League final and that was the singular biggest property that

SuperSport had on the African continent. I had been doing it for years and then all of a sudden they zapped it right at the end.

I ended up watching the Champions League final in the reception at the Fire & Ice Hotel in Cape Town with a couple of friends.

On record, I had never said that the sexual-harassment claims or what I had said to the CEO led to my being fired from SuperSport. That was what the media alluded to because that's what was circulating on social media at the time. It wasn't something I had put forward as a reason. It could have been a contributing factor. Only the people responsible would know. Maybe I touched a raw nerve at the wrong time. They just said that my contract was coming to an end, although I was still scheduled to do games. They said they were renewing the line-up, but it showed it was a whole cooked-up story.

Multichoice CEO Calvo Mawela was reported as saying that there were no reports of sexual harassment against senior managers that were brought to his attention.

I think there were several reasons why I was sacked by SuperSport. I think a lot of them had to do with what had happened already. It was not just my utterances about local football. I had also been outspoken about transformation in rugby and cricket too. Remember, SuperSport had agreements with other sporting code bodies too.

On Metro FM, we had set up a platform called 'The Room Dividers' within Marawa Sports Worldwide. It was driving a very serious transformation journey and it became the talk of the town.

There were very vocal former players such as the late Kaunda Ntunja, a commentator at SuperSport, Lawrence Sephaka, former Springbok coach in the women's national team at the time and Thando Manana, the author of the book *Being a Black Springbok*, who was doing commentary for Radio 2000. They were all brutally honest.

When we started this journey with them they told their stories, spoke about how they were treated as black rugby players and the ascent to Springbok level, their treatment as black Springbok players and others who fell by the wayside and others who were ignored. All of this started to build up into a formidable Tuesday offering on radio because these were very powerful voices.

The most important thing was that it grew organically and became about the plight of players at a top level and how the coaches treated the players of colour. The stories just became crazier and crazier. The Room Dividers became a movement on radio.

We were fighting a cause, challenging the sitting Minister of Sport Fikile Mbalula. He had been presenting transformation documents and the Eminent Persons Report and everything else that they were doing as government. But at the end of the day, transformation was not happening in the most visible area, which is the Springbok national team. You couldn't talk transformation and tell people that there are a couple of black kids who are playing rugby at a certain level, but it's not the level that the whole nation sits up and watches because, like Bafana Bafana, if you're not winning games, don't tell me that Banyana Banyana are winning or the under-23s are winning. We want to see excellence and brilliance at the highest level, which is your senior national team.

Mbalula came on the show but I didn't think he understood the magnitude and the seriousness of how all the members of The Room Dividers felt about transformation. He was being held accountable publicly and the sway of the argument was so strong in favour of The Room Dividers that the minister never really had the right answers to give us. That then exposed him for not delivering on the transformation deliverables that they had promised the country.

The SABC would say I was being too harsh on the minister because they were very beholden to people in government. That is why Mbalula requested that I be fired. He denies it now but I also received a legal letter from him.

But what are you hiding? Why aren't you as a government official doing the right thing? Would previous sports ministers like Steve Tshwete or Ngconde Balfour have accepted something like this. That is when I realised that all of these comrades who find themselves in positions are not necessarily capable of holding those titles because they know nothing about sport. It was all about creating the noise. Yes, Mr Razzmatazz brought a lot of fun and energy into the sports ministry but he also had his flaws. Instead of trying to listen to what we were saying, he was trying to fight.

I've always been outspoken about sports administrators

and sports ministers and that is because I believe that I have a responsibility to hold them accountable on behalf of the fans.

Fikile Mbalula is somebody that I've always been close to and we always had open communication lines. Mbalula and I have always been close. He made sure he was at my father's funeral when he passed away in 2016. We travelled together to Senzo Meyiwa's funeral.

He is somebody who occupies public office but is also human and has friendships. I just think the miscommunication that people don't get is they don't understand that friendship ends the minute you sit across the table or the desk in the studio because now you're a sports minister. Sure, we are friends but that doesn't extend into studio. I'm not working for myself. I'm working for the people who have tuned in to the show who need certain questions to be asked. I would do exactly that when I was on air.

We are still friends. I just think that through time, maybe he might not have understood that my work is my work and there is absolutely nothing personal. That spilt over into social media and people spoke about the 'twars' that we had and whether they were warranted or not. We do still talk but maybe not as frequently as before.

We held him highly accountable on The Room Dividers. Under his tenure, the issue of transformation was massive and we were fighting that he was not doing enough to ensure that transformation is a reality, especially within rugby and cricket. He always referred back to the Eminent Persons Group Report on transformation and what they had done in terms of their studies to show that transformation was on the go and succeeding. But any transformation results are seen via your main national team, which is the Springboks and the Proteas. We were not seeing enough of that.

Ngconde Balfour never took it personally when we challenged him. If we were duelling on air, then he would come with his big belly laugh and say 'you and your bloody tough questions'. We could laugh about it and I appreciate that. Ministers should never personalise these things. Unfortunately, you don't find that these days.

We became enemy number one. We became the people who were stirring up trouble. Kaunda was also being called on the side and being asked why he was part of The Room Dividers. SuperSport didn't look kindly upon his participation. There would be days where he couldn't come through.

I fought for The Room Dividers to get a stipend of some sort from SABC up until we left. None of those members ever got paid a cent from the SABC and yet they were regular contributors. I fought all the time when I had meetings or contract renewal to include The Room Dividers. It was just not gaining traction.

There were formal complaints that had come through from the minister to the SABC about us. It became a sticky topic for anyone at the SABC to then contract The Room Dividers and actually pay them. I remained eternally indebted to them because they gave their time on air, transport and value proposition.

As much as we were getting the backlash from the

authorities, we knew that we couldn't stop. We tried to ask the president of SARU to come on. Negative. We tried to bring on the CEO of SARU. Negative. They never had anything positive to say about us and the show, but it didn't deter us because we were still going to talk about the topic whether they came on or not. We were going to carry on. In actual fact, it will give us more motivation to talk about it because you don't want to step forward and become accountable. So we carried on.

There was pressure being put on Hlaudi Motsoeneng, the then COO of SABC, to get rid of us. Despite all his faults, if there's one human being who stood in support of #MSW and The Room Dividers, it was Hlaudi Motsoeneng. He had been approached several times, not only from rugby people, to get rid of me. And on all of those occasions, he said no.

SuperSport was also a contracted partner of rugby, through SARU, the professional wing. When looking at who would have wanted me gone from the platform, I knew that there were different franchises and associations that had a problem with me. They did not feel comfortable having the rot in the game exposed to the public.

They were just happy to say we were a Rainbow Nation, stronger together, united and whatever. Yet there were deeper underlying factors that came to the fore. All the people who did not want to come onto the show, whether it was the president of SARU or the CEO, would then go and complain in Randburg about me. Whatever I was saying outside of SuperSport was coming back to me and my job on television. In my mind, the conspirators were the administrators from football, rugby and cricket.

I couldn't put my finger on one specific thing that led to the end of the relationship with SuperSport. I went into that final meeting with Gideon knowing what was coming my way. I had also just come back to radio after being off air for a whole year. I believed that the plan that had been brewed was to get me out of radio and TV at the same time to ensure that I had no platform at all. It had not been anticipated that I would be brought back into the fold at the SABC, so I remained on air with that platform.

Television was one thing I wanted to always do in my life, and I never imagined that in my forties, which in TV age is extremely young, I would not be on mainstream TV for the next four to five years. I knew it had nothing to do with my ability on camera. But it's got everything to do with the politics around my presence thereon. As misguided as I think it was, I had to understand that my comments on radio clearly, in the end, had a direct bearing on my future in television. Which is weird because radio was never part of my journey. I wanted to do television. Radio became a default inclusion of my journey and, ironically, it was radio that affected and put an end to my television career.

I also learnt that what I had witnessed as a kid growing up – pure football and love of the game – was also steeped in a lot of behind-the-scenes shenanigans that I might not have been aware of. I used to be able to enjoy football as a purist but then I realised that South Africans were being duped.

I made it my duty to balance the reporting on football with

the darker side of the game, exposing the politics and holding the administrators to account for all of the happenings that were going on.

But because of the power that the different associations had with the broadcasting houses, people chose what made financial sense to them above the quality of what was being broadcast on air. I had to learn to live with that and be okay with it, but still be able to sleep peacefully at night because I had not offended anybody except the people who refused to come and account to the fans.

32

I live by everything I've said

By now I was an old hand at surviving the politics, the cabal and the forces that were working against me. I had all the experience of 'contracts not being renewed' as an excuse for getting rid of me. I knew exactly what I would be up against at the SABC and it wasn't long before the old modus operandi began to rear its ugly head again.

Despite having an assurance from the CEO that I would be insulated and wouldn't have to deal with the cabal, all the signs began to show themselves.

One thing that I was trying to bring to the show was consistency because that is what advertisers look for. But with the show being simulcast on Radio 2000, we were regularly being bumped off air for live cricket commentary. It made no sense at all. There was a fight that happened around what would happen to the cricket commentary now that this new show was on air.

At least we were able to be live on Metro while the cricket was happening on Radio 2000 but you really wanted both platforms to be strong and consistent. Management was also pushing for the online option but that just wasn't a possibility because a normal person who has no privilege of affording data can't go online.

There were little compromises in that they tried to have us cross live to the cricket a couple of times in the show to get an update but then we would find ourselves breaking away from a Chairman's Chair interview to go to the cricket. What if a brand wanted to sponsor Chairman's Chair? That just didn't work out. In the end it was agreed that cricket would go online and that was a victory for the listener who wanted a proper talk show.

I was starting to face increased resistance from within the organisation.

The Metro FM station manager, Sibongile Mtyali, made it clear from the outset that I would not be allowed to do my simulcast show from the Metro studios. I had been on Metro platforms from day one of the radio show and it made sense that we broadcast from Metro because they had a bigger studio and, with the profile of guests that were coming in, it would make sense to go to that studio. The Radio 2000 studio was a minute little space.

There was a directive – not officially on paper – that was put out by Sibongile that the sports show will not be done at Metro. They would just take the audio from the Radio 2000 studio but physically we must not set foot in the Metro studios.

She did that because she could. Of course she was part of the cabal whose initial decision to get me out was being turned on its head. She had to play her part in ensuring that we were not comfortable.

Metro would have two spacious studios sitting empty while we had to squeeze ourselves into a tiny studio when on air. We could have a Sundowns winning coach and four players jammed in there at once.

But we made it happen because that's what they wanted. I'd become very used to those underhand tactics and I always said to the team, 'Let's focus on the bigger picture.' We were going out on air, let's utilise the Radio 2000 platform. They were sitting on 280 000 listeners when I joined and we could grow that. Metro was already declining from six million. We could capitalise on the platform and let it thrive and grow. We weren't wanted at Metro so we wanted to focus on really getting Radio 2000 going.

Unfortunately, we were faced with a programmes manager at Radio 2000, Christopher Choane, who was constantly causing problems for us. There was an issue over the simulcast being Radio 2000 and Metro and it is quite a technical thing to get right. If we took a break on one station, we had to take a break on the other and the ads had to be the same length.

They have got to have somebody sitting in there to make sure that everything runs smoothly. If the ads don't match up then you have to play a promo until one station catches up with the other. But talk is not like music. You can't stop someone mid-sentence. At times you'll overrun a minute because people don't have any sense of time.

Chris would send emails, copying all the SABC sports operations people, complaining that I had skipped station promos and had moved ads. He said that I didn't adhere to the show clock.

Now if Metro's ads are about to end and the show promo is not generating money, it's just an advert; the show promo has to go. It might be scheduled but I must also be able to make an informed decision to say, I only have an hour and a half and I'm not going to play a two-minute promo. I couldn't afford the time so I would chuck it out.

It would be a different story if I was throwing out an advert that had a dollar sign attached to it.

I think Chris was just overly obsessed and he didn't like the idea that the show was on Radio 2000. It was just backward and forward meetings, with him finding fault with everything that we did.

Thank God there was a station manager at Radio 2000, Puleng Thulo, who was supportive. She knew the struggle. She sent an email congratulating us on growing the listenership from 93 000 to 465 000 and what a pleasure it was to work with such a good team. Almost immediately after we came on board, the numbers started shifting upwards and people were recognising it. Regardless of what Chris and others were trying to do, the numbers were saying something completely different.

Resistance was building and I would share with the CEO that some people were making our lives difficult. Then there would be leaks from within the building to the *Sunday Sun* or other tabloids.

There was an issue because I interviewed an Outsurance representative after it was announced by SAFA that Outsurance was going to be sponsoring referees. It was a big story. Referees in South Africa had been problematic because of Operation Dribble, when it was revealed that they were being paid money to fix games. Here was a big company investing a chunk of money. I was the MC for the event at SAFA House and I met a woman from Outsurance who I didn't know from a bar of soap. I asked if I could do an interview, she came through and obviously it was the biggest story that day.

But because there was somebody always looking out for something to be wrong, it was an opportunity to jump on. There was a suggestion that Outsurance should have paid for that interview to happen. They convinced themselves that I now owed the SABC R226 000 because I gave away the airtime. I even got a message from a *Sunday Sun* reporter asking me about this incident and the apparent transgression of SABC policy.

There were all sorts of ridiculous things that were coming up and all these obstacles. There was resistance each and every day. We were making progress on air and gaining listeners and also winning major awards. The show was growing and doing well, but there were people using their friends in the Sunday tabloids, leaking stories that were being sensationalised.

In my opinion, Chris never wanted anything that we were doing to be a success. He always had issues. We would spend so much time and effort putting together very creative promos and it was agreed that we would produce five promos every day, which was unheard of at the SABC and they needed to be played both on Metro and Radio 2000. Without exaggeration, our promos were rejected by Metro, although they were gaining financially from #MSW. Metro never played a single promo in three years.

Yet the rate card at the time shows how much money #MSW was bringing in for the SABC. It's a public document, it's not a secret of any kind. On 1 July 2020, for a 30-second advert, an ad on the Radio 2000 breakfast show was R2 730, afternoon drive was R2 490 and for the same ad on #MSW, the SABC was charging R24 600 for both Metro and Radio 2000. So they were coining it off our show and they wouldn't even let us use their studios, wouldn't play a promo, wouldn't do anything, but making all this money off us.

Sibongile and Tony, the programme manager, didn't want the promos to get any airplay. They never wanted the show to come back. They never expected or anticipated that the show would ever come back.

I knew the show was never going to last. That's exactly why I used the name Marawa Sports Worldwide, to entrench the name in the public domain so that it became the name that I could carry wherever I go. Even if they fired me, I could take #MSW and use it on any other platform. Having had so many run-ins with the SABC, I had to be smart enough to use the platform because we had been used all the time. I knew that my contract would not be renewed and that the journey of #MSW could continue wherever we went with it.

As I was facing more resistance and obstacles were being thrown in our way, I began to reach out to the CEO Madoda Mxakwe. He had enticed me back to the SABC and had assured me I would be insulated, but clearly this was not the case.

In the early months after my return to Auckland Park, communication channels between us were open. He messaged me to compliment us on the intros to our show. I reminded him about milestones that we hit when we did the 500th episode of #MSW. We discussed a potential return to SABC television after I left SuperSport.

But, over time, he began to ghost me.

As 2020 was starting to draw to an end, I began reaching out to him to ask for a meeting. I knew my contract was coming to an end mid-2021 and I wanted to get ahead of the process.

In September 2020, I asked for a meeting at his earliest and most urgent convenience. He told me he would try for the next day and would confirm. Nothing.

In October 2020, I asked for ten minutes of his time. Nothing.

The year came to an end and we had still not met. I was deliberately reaching out to him because I could sense that the Madoda that had approached me at Melrose Arch Hotel for me to come back was no longer the same Madoda that was now being evasive, not taking my calls, not returning messages, not following up on meetings.

In my mind, because I knew the landscape, I assumed the cabal had won him over and this was probably going to be the end of my time at the SABC, as I had expected.

We moved into 2021 and again I tried to reach out.

On 18 February he tried to call me but I was on air at the time so we missed each other.

On 26 February I sent him a message.

'Gmorning CEO. We ended up not connecting the other day ... I honestly just need 3mins of your time hence my efforts to try and speak to u since September last year.'

He replied: 'I'm so sorry, Rob, it's been hectic. I'll call you after my meetings at 4pm today.'

No call. In March again I tried, asking for feedback. Madoda told me that he had asked Nada Wotshela, Group Executive in charge of radio, to set up a meeting with me. He explained they were prioritising contracts that were expiring that month and mine was only due for renewal later in the year. I responded that if we were going to renew the contract for another three years then we should enter into the agreements sooner rather than later so that I was not left out in the cold. No response.

In April, I followed up with another message to the CEO asking for an update. Silence.

My patience was wearing thing.

On 9 April I sent him another message. Nothing.

Then on 21 April 2021 I had had enough.

'Gmorning CEO... When you asked me to return to the SABC you asked me to switch off the noise and focus on the work you had tasked me to do. You asked me to deliver on "credibility, increase numbers and make money for the SABC ..." I have delivered on all counts and even swayed the overall growth of Radio 2000 whilst Metro FM made money during our slot. For the last time, I'm reaching out, Sir. Thank you.'

Five minutes later he responded.

'Hi, Rob, I'm sorry you are feeling like this. I did give you feedback that Radio was focusing on shows that were coming to an end last month and that they would be engaging with you later. I'll follow up with Nada on this.'

I was not keen to leave this to the last minute. I had given the show my best shot.

Two days later I met virtually with Nada. She was given the task of doing the dirty work and informing me that my contract would not be renewed.

On 23 April I messaged Madoda:

> *Hi Sir ... The meeting with Nada has been held and concluded. At least it's good to get it officially that the show has been canned. Thank you for the opportunity. God bless.*

His response was brief.

> *Hi Rob. These decisions are at the discretion of Radio management.*

That's it.

I knew this would be the outcome, given who was in positions of power. Nothing was based on performance. That's where our conversations ended.

I was supposed to do my last show on radio at the end of July, so it would have been on Friday 30 July. But I already knew the trend of what had happened in the past with final shows.

On the morning of 30 July, I received a call from Kina

Nhlengethwa, who was programmes manager for Radio 2000 at the time and also had a marketing role at Metro. We had enjoyed a good relationship over the years and she had always been supportive of my work. I didn't answer and she sent a message asking me to call her. I immediately knew what was brewing.

We exchanged messages, I told her I was in a meeting, she asked me to call back, so I made up an excuse telling her I was in an all-day workshop until late afternoon. I was stalling her to force her hand and put what she had wanted to say in writing.

Then at 2.57pm she messaged again:

> *Hi Robert. The reason for my call earlier on was to firstly inform you about the press release that was going to go out earlier on. The second one was to further inform you that you need not come in for the show today as there will be no #MSW broadcast show tonight. Thank you.*

There it was. The fear of me doing my last show recurring. I had not had a chance to say goodbye on *SoccerZone*. I didn't have a chance to say goodbye to the SuperSport audience. It was the same again.

I was off television by then so it was just radio that was keeping me busy. I had expected this to happen and it was a Friday so we had set up Zama Masondo as our legend to come through to be on the Legends show.

In the back of my mind I knew it was never going to happen. There would be this last-minute call to say don't worry about doing the last show and, true to form, thank you very much, it happened.

I fired back several messages to Kina.

U could have mailed me.

Why is there no show Kina??

We have a LEGEND that has been booked for the Show!!

I have never heard from Kina again. That was the end of my time at the SABC. I had been fired by SMS. A statement was released that afternoon saying that we had 'parted ways'.

Obviously, there is a fear of what I will say and what the listeners or viewers will say in response. Because it was an interactive show and we opened up the lines, there would be a concern about the unpredictability. The problem with dealing with cowards is that they can't live up to their own funny tricks. They've got the power to activate whatever they want and one of the ways of doing it is not allow me my final show. They would rather end it abruptly. That's been the hallmark of my career. They don't say thank you and write a nice farewell press release and thank me for a job well done; it just ends abruptly. It is untidy, it is dirty, and it almost seems like I have committed a crime. You are almost frogmarched out of the building.

Yet on the very day I was let go, Marawa Sports Worldwide won the Best Sports Show: Commercial at the SA Radio Awards!

Then a week after I was let go, Radio 2000 was celebrating the milestone of reaching two million listeners in that period that I was on air, something that had never been achieved before. Yet they were getting rid of the person who had helped contribute to that listenership.

Obviously, the cabal had taken their decision that this is how they deemed it proper for my journey on radio at the SABC to come to an end, and it was as abrupt as that. Boom and it's done!

I was disappointed in the CEO. There's a trail of evidence showing my intention to reach out to him as early as September 2020 in preparation for the contract coming to an end. I came back on his insistence and because he had convinced me of what he wanted to achieve as CEO and how he wanted to turn the SABC around.

Sponsors had ploughed millions of rands into the show and it was much-needed money for the broadcaster and there was zero benefit to me. He was showing signs of somebody that had been co-opted. He was showing signs of somebody who was not believing in what he believed when he approached me to be on SABC platforms again. He was sending junior people to come and do the dirty work, yet he was brave enough to approach me in his capacity as CEO when he wanted me to come back.

Why couldn't he do the same towards the end and have the

courage to tell me that I had ruffled feathers or that someone in power was angry? I would have had more respect for him. He is a coward. He owes me nothing. I needed nothing from him. I just needed him to be straight up, to be honest enough, to be forthright, to reach a conclusion that made sense to me. Was it a radio decision? Were the number of listeners falling?

For me, radio is and always has been about the listener. What the listener wanted was for me to be on radio. But the people who are put in positions of authority don't want me to be. So who matters most? Why are you driving listenership when at the end of the day you don't actually care what the listeners want? The numbers show that listenership was going up and revenue was going up. No one had critically analysed the show and I had never had a snoop session either, which was a prerequisite for radio feedback worldwide.

At the end of the day, the listener is going to grow your base. If you have people hosting shows that don't succeed, it is not going to get you listenership. Then why don't you just play gospel music during that timeslot?

It wasn't just me – others experienced this too. We've witnessed the same thing happen with very highly rated and commercially viable shows like DJ Fresh on the breakfast show. We had seen it with Bonang Matheba's mid-morning show. It was the same with Tbo Touch and with DJ Sbu. They were making commercial sense for the SABC but the powers that be made it personal and got rid of them. Nothing at the SABC was ever done with the audience in mind and that's what I came to realise. There tends to be an abuse and that is why you see the SABC hierarchy always going to Parliament to get those bailouts on such a regular basis because they know they can and whatever they do doesn't really matter. They don't have to justify it to anyone. And that becomes the downfall.

I wasn't emotional when it ended. I was disappointed with the CEO, not the process.

There is no real excuse for why the relationship ended other than a form of external interference – someone didn't want me back on radio. It's that simple.

They also had to ensure that it was a clean break and that I was not 'fired'. So when journalists ask why I was fired, they can say that the contract was not renewed. That lands softer. It sounds gentler. But technically sending me a message telling me I'm not allowed to do my last show qualifies as a firing.

When I speak of external forces applying pressure on management at the SABC and SuperSport, who then am I referring to? I have said publicly that I believe that one person is responsible for having me fired multiple times.

I can never have proof. But I certainly have my suspicions.

The first time I was fired from Metro by Sully in 2017, I said to my producer that I thought The Chairman, PSL chairman Irvin Khoza, was behind my firing. She told him about my belief and he was not happy with that assumption. The Chairman requested a meeting with me one-on-one to set the record straight.

I was not allergic to having a meeting with him and said I would be happy to. He told me to choose a date and a venue and he would be there. I decided on a private room at the Melrose Arch Hotel and the meeting was scheduled for 1pm.

On the day I arrived at 12 o'clock, did some work and at precisely one o'clock, punctual as ever, The Chairman walked in.

We sat down at a six-seater table – he sat at the one head and I sat opposite him at the other head. For all intents and purposes, Dr Khoza is a gentleman in his approach. He was courteous and for the first hour or so he introduced himself, painting a picture of his character and his background. It was a soliloquy as he told me about how he was a religious, God-fearing person and a people's person, what his beliefs were and how he valued people's meaningful contributions.

I didn't say a word in that hour. I listened very attentively to everything that he had to say, because this was my first one-on-one engagement in a private environment, behind closed doors with The Chairman. We had had interviews on radio, we had meetings planning events and awards shows and anniversaries. But this was the first time we had spoken like this and I understood why he wanted the meeting because he didn't want me to have the wrong impression that he was the one who contributed towards me being fired.

I thanked him for allowing me to understand him and his principles and what grounds him as a person, that he was essentially a family man and respected. Then it became more of an engagement back and forth, with his trying to understand why I believed that he had contributed to me being fired.

I explained to him about the SuperSport intervention

around the Carling Black Label Cup, about how on occasion I had been pulled off from hosting the PSL awards and how complaints had been lodged with the SABC over comments I had made on air.

He expressed to me how he would never do that and how much respect he had for me being the voice of football in SA and that he would never want to harm another person's career merely because he happened to disagree with that person.

He laid all of those things out openly. It was a brutally frank conversation. Instead of it lasting an hour and a half, we ended up speaking for nearly four hours.

He had got the message across to me that at no point should I doubt him as a person and as a human being.

Over the years, we would exchange very courteous messages with one another and he was always complimentary of my work. Subsequent to that meeting, I did get fired from SuperSport and from the SABC. The suspicion lingered, but he had stated his case.

In my heart I believed that my repeated firings were motivated by pressure exerted by administrators of multiple sporting codes.

Rugby had also established a relationship with SuperSport and I was extremely vocal about issues of transformation. If I made comments on radio, they would run to SuperSport to complain about me. The same with cricket. I was vociferous about allegations of racism in the sport and what came out during the Social Justice and Nation Building Hearings by Cricket South Africa.

It got to a stage where I believe that it wasn't just one sporting code, but powerful forces across all three that were putting pressure on a broadcaster who has business dealings, rights, relationships with those associations.

I might have felt differently the first time I was fired and pinpointed one person, but in the end, I got to a more reasonable understanding that it was all three major sporting codes at the highest level that were going to the broadcasters to complain.

Ultimately, I have no regrets about comments I made or how I challenged authority. We live in a democracy where we engage and shouldn't take things personally. I have always loved and adored and followed the game. I've always wanted to see the game grow. Given the power of the microphone that was given to me, I had to take responsibility for how I used that power to promote and grow the sport and to openly engage with people.

I had grown up listening to Radio Zulu. It was commercial, entertainment, music, call-ins and dedications. That was the kind of radio I would listen to. I was never exposed to talk radio until I got to Johannesburg.

My journey to talk radio and my influence came with me searching for Radio Bop. I was twisting my radio late at night when I stumbled across voices on radio. People were literally shouting at each other. Back and forth. I paused and listened. I had never heard anything like this before. It sounded interesting. So I listened some more.

It turned out that after 9pm was a gentleman on Radio

702 called John Robbie. I had never heard of him and I was intrigued. I forgot about searching for Radio Bop and listened to this until the end.

Here was John Robbie being called all manner of names because he was in support of South Africa's transition into democracy. People were calling in and abusing him and I was hearing these words on radio for the first time. John was being called a 'kaffir boetie' and he was defending his position with all his might. He believed that this was the correct route for South Africa to take.

I was fascinated by this. This was my introduction to talk radio and I loved it. It was engaging. It was not just radio for entertainment sake.

In my personal journey in radio, I also wanted to bring out that public engagement that I had been taught by listening to people like John Robbie. I wanted that level of discourse on air and that it should be open engagement about sporting issues. That is all that I wanted to achieve with the platform. I didn't only want to profile players and have superstars on the show. We had to look at the real issues. We had to have a full go at it as openly and with as much transparency as possible.

The fact that people took offence to some of the things that we brought to the table is what it is. I can't be blamed for that. I can never have regrets about it because I believe we facilitated the kind of engagement on sporting issues that has brought a transformational agenda to the table.

We've challenged sports ministers. We've probably ended friendships with people who are in sports ministry positions. I was always willing to take the bullet for all of those things. Is the country better off today for having done that? I believe so.

I believe that we got people talking about transformation and we saw real tangible results. In cricket, the SJN (Social, Justice and Nation-building) hearings took place after we had run a whole series of eye-opening experiences with former Black cricket players on #MSW. In rugby, transformation resulted in the most number of black players for the Japan World Cup and we came back with the trophy and a black captain, all on merit. The word 'quota' was never used. In football, there are still so many challenges and that is why we haven't won anything since 1996, because people don't want to change certain things that are obviously in need of change and that is why we have been talking about them.

That is why I have no regrets at all. I maintain that I will never go back on anything that I've put on the platform. I would never have any regrets about any issue or topic that I have engaged the audience on or even the individuals themselves. The platform was always open.

Could it have been done differently? Probably. Would I change anything I said or did? Absolutely not. I live by everything that I said.

33
Egypt and new beginnings

After being fired from the SABC, I stayed in Durban and for the first time in my adult years I was able to spend time at our family home with my mother. As an adult I had never had that opportunity. I was always working. Even as a child, having gone to boarding school at such an early age, I had never spent a solid two months at home and that is what I did.

I wasn't working at all. I was unemployed. There was no radio. There was no television. There was no income coming in from anywhere.

Of course, you always go to the worst-case scenario and I began to worry about not having enough money to sustain myself and if I would lose my house or car. I always think about that. Even in the good times I'm always worrying about what happens when things are bad.

It was an extremely dark period for me. I was not used to doing nothing. I'm not used to waking up and having no real goal for the day or work to do or challenging myself. I was just waking up and going to sleep. It was something very foreign to me. I've always been about the challenge and stretching myself. I found myself in a dark hole and on the brink of depression. I didn't want to leave the house. I would keep the curtains closed. I had no appetite for food. I slept. I woke up. My body and my nervous system were adjusting to this new lifestyle after years of abuse.

Being at home and spending two months there gave me an opportunity to do things I had never been able to do. Some of it was administrative, like sorting out the electricity in the house and setting up an inverter to deal with loadshedding, installing an electric fence because crime was becoming ridiculous, sorting out the garden service. There were a lot of things around the house that needed attention so that kept me busy. I filled my days with the simple stuff. I was looking at my mom's needs and what I could do to help her and that gave me purpose. It became vitally important to me that her peace of mind was well taken care of and that there was extra protection for her.

Those were the things that really kept me busy and made me happy and made a big difference in and around the house.

I thought my career was probably over, at least in South Africa.

I had thought about heading to America to go and work for one of the networks in the States that I had been in touch with, but because of Covid and restrictions it just wasn't possible. I knew that the UK wasn't going to be an option because the networks there tend to be biased towards people from the UK. Going to CNN wasn't an option for me because I didn't want to be a newsreader; I loved live broadcasting and I would get bored reading off an autocue. I felt that wasn't an option for me.

In my mind I felt that those who wanted me off all mainstream platforms had achieved their desires and accomplished that. What was I going to do about not having any broadcast work to do? It was the only job I had ever done outside of studying law, which is something I did not want to do.

I'm a very resilient person and I don't fold easily.

I also realised that the way the world had evolved, mainstream broadcast platforms weren't my only option. I didn't have to look at the SABC or SuperSport as being the only options to get my message across.

My own individual brand had emerged as Marawa Sports Worldwide and that carried credibility beyond mainstream media. It meant that I could look at other options and do something on my own.

I had also learnt from an earlier experience that I had just after I left SuperSport. I was still on radio at the time but I wasn't doing any television.

In mid-2019, I received a call from Emy Casaletti-Bwalya. Her company had been approached by Brand SA to have a presence in Egypt ahead of the Africa Cup of Nations tournament. Bafana Bafana were participating and it was Brand SA's way of lending support and bringing visibility to the South African brand within Egypt.

Emy wanted me to MC a breakfast that Brand SA was doing with the ambassador to Egypt and a number of other people, including invited guests from SAFA and supporters who had travelled to Egypt. The event was a success and I was due to come back home again but I ended up staying on a little while the tournament was underway.

Emy's husband, the Zambian legend Kalusha Bwalya, is a CAF member and I had got to know him well while working on SuperSport during the UEFA Champions League broadcasts and the World Cups. I'd also interviewed him on radio as a legend. He was one of the best players on the continent.

He extended an invitation to me to stay on, so I went to a few AFCON games and had access to the VIP suites. There were big events and there was always a grand spectacle in Egypt surrounding the matches.

I have always loved using a camera to capture images and, as I've mentioned, it is something that I have always done since I was a kid. I wasn't aligned to any television broadcaster so I whipped out my trusty reliable Samsung phone and started making videos. I was also just used to working and I didn't know any different. I wasn't used to being a VIP who sits in the VIP area and claps.

Once you are a broadcaster, you want to do broadcasting things. There I was in the VIP suite with access to all sorts of interesting people. I was shooting videos with Serame Letsoaka, Mark Fish, Frankie Fredericks and Pierre Issa.

With the power of the cellphone, you just flip it around and you make great content. I was posting every single day from the venue, talking to different people, great African stars, great South Africans who were there. I wasn't being paid to do it, I just thought people would be interested and they were lapping it up. I put it on Twitter and I had no idea of the magnitude until I decided to come back to South Africa.

I wasn't going to stay for the entire tournament because I had to carry the costs of the accommodation and everything else because I was done with the work for Brand SA. I flew back to South Africa and something crazy happened because I never expected people to react that way. I did my best to try to come back on radio as soon as possible. But people wanted me to go back to Egypt. They were loving the clips I was posting so much.

It was off-season in South Africa so there wasn't much happening locally, which meant I could head back to Egypt. The fans just said that whatever I was doing there, the insights, the interviewing, the questions, was all happening in real time and it was better than what the broadcasters were doing. It was easy for me because I was just flipping the camera; I didn't have to do post production or edit or anything. People loved the immediacy of it. It was a big beautiful mess of just recording the crowds and fans.

I was left with a problem because I couldn't just go back alone. I had to try to improve on what I was doing. Somebody suggested I reach out to Kyle Westman, a videographer at Coffee Productions in Durban. He was a cameraman and editor and everything rolled into one. Kyle agreed to come on board, but I needed funding.

Through a friend, I reached out to the Chairman of Arena Holdings, Tshepo Mahloele. There was a bigger conversation to be had but there was immediacy required. I needed to get back to Egypt as soon as possible. I had a meeting with him and he made funds available for it to happen. Tshepo is an accomplished businessman, one of the leading entrepreneurs in South Africa, so we sat in his Sandton office and I told him what I envisaged. Within a couple of hours, the CFO had approved a budget and I was able to pay for air tickets for Kyle and I to travel to Egypt and back again and to stay at the Marriott and for a daily allowance and pocket money.

We bought an additional Samsung phone at the airport on the way out of OR Tambo International and Kyle had his GoPro for more effects. We had a bit of lighting and an improved sound system, and off we went.

There was a little clip of us arriving in Egypt and the driver waiting to meet us. Emy and Kalusha generously sent their driver in their black Mercedes-Benz and he ushered us in and it was all very impressive.

I always feel highly indebted to both Kalusha and Emy because they really opened up their arms and hearts and minds to my vision of starting this journey. Kyle and I immediately got to work and everything became content. People were consuming it all back home. It was living on YouTube and on Instagram and Twitter. SuperSport didn't want me so I realised that social media was the answer and South Africans responded.

With Kyle's help, we started a YouTube channel and we would tease content on Twitter. The views were increasing daily and we were hitting tens of thousands of subscribers over a short period of time. It became one of the fastest-growing YouTube channels in the country. That was Marawa TV.

When we returned from Egypt, I had meetings with the guys from Arena and they were keen for me to formalise an agreement with them. It didn't happen immediately.

I was doing my radio show from my bedroom at home in Durban and I realised that I didn't have to be in studio. I could travel with my kit literally anywhere.

So when I started doing *Marawa Moments* on Monday at Arena, it all worked seamlessly. The numbers were fantastic, the views were great. The reaction at the same time that we were going live was always great. It was also just an opportunity for people to witness the importance of allowing people to be free in terms of their speech and not to be guarded, feeling that you're going to be hurting somebody's feelings or somebody is going to give you a call and say, 'Why did you say this and that?'

Tshepo had a conversation with me one-on-one and he wanted me to do radio for Arena. They owned Rise FM and Vuma. They also own *Sowetan* and that was my Bible growing up and reading about soccer so I was jumping at the chance to do something with *Sowetan*. We struck an agreement fusing the three different platforms. Radio in Mpumalanga via Rise FM, radio in KZN via Vuma FM and then, from a global perspective, you can log on and listen on *SowetanLIVE*.

Trying something new has always excited me and being able to be on the three platforms and getting the kind of traction and reaction that we do now. It says a lot about people's loyalty and people seeking undiluted news and the kind of interviews that give them the kind of answers they want.

We're still relentless in terms of that. It's just been a breath of fresh air. It's an ability to do what you love on a daily basis, knowing that you've been given carte blanche to do it.

In mid-2021, in the midst of the Covid pandemic, I landed back in ICU for a week. This time with Covid pneumonia. I had been incredibly careful and was so strict about staying home, wearing a mask and not exposing myself unnecessarily. With all my previous health scares, I had to be extra cautious.

I holed up in my room at my mom's place in Durban. I got a pulse oximeter and regularly checked my oxygen rate. My mother says it was really bad, that I couldn't even look at her and could barely walk up and down the stairs. All she could think about was how Minister Jackson Mthembu had died and what the worst-case scenario could be. It was bad.

What started out as the flu-like symptoms quickly led to inexplicable fatigue and shortness of breath. My oxygen rate dropped to 92 and I was rushed to hospital yet again.

A chest X-ray showed extensive pneumonia. After the experience of the last time at Charlotte Maxeke, it was not something I was keen to repeat at all.

On 3 June 2021, I was admitted to ICU in hospital in KZN. It was the eleventh day of my Covid journey and my lungs were really struggling, so I needed more intensive care.

Not knowing what was to come, I took a couple of videos on my iPhone. In one I was wearing a T-shirt and the oxygen tubes were already fixed to my nose and around my neck. My lips were so dry. In another I was wearing a hospital gown and you can hear the machines beeping in the background.

I knew by then already, more than a year into the pandemic, that there were excellent healthcare practitioners who had been saving lives and they would take care of me. I was also relying on my faith. I still believed in the man above and that there would be a positive outcome to my journey. I knew that God was great. I had to play my part and just hope that, at the end of the day, I would come out of ICU and help others realise the severity of what we were dealing with. Covid wasn't a game. But I knew I would come out of it on the other side. I wanted to continue having open and honest conversations and, in order to do that, I needed to live.

Again, the attack on my body was vicious. It was a tough battle. But again, I survived and lived to fight another day. After all my near-death experiences, yet again God had smiled upon me and saved my life.

34
Sesiyayivala sithi gqimm'shelele

The fire to broadcast will always be there for me. There will always be ideas. They run consistently in my head. It's always about reinventing the person you are and were and want to be. I think the evolution has taught me many lessons. All I ever wanted to do was broadcast. All I wanted to do was what Martin Locke was doing and perfect it.

I never thought it would get to a point where people got so triggered by what I had said and what other people say on the platforms that I'm on. It almost comes across as if you have to be restricted in life. You have to say what other people want you to say and you can't have an independent voice. I don't get that, because how do we grow as a country, as a nation, as fans of sport if we're not able to interrogate issues that frustrate us as fans?

What I've realised in all of this, the lesson is that people hate to be held accountable for anything. People hate to be questioned about things that they feel you should not be questioning them about. But they are always willing and ready to be praised and celebrated in terms of saying all sorts of sweet things about their so-called accomplishments. I don't buy that. I also just feel that if you strongly believe in something, then come through. I will ask the questions, you support what you support, but don't try to muzzle me. Then why have a microphone? Why have a studio? Why broadcast?

With Nathi Mthethwa, he was appointed Minister of Sport and whatever he does, he does in that guise. I've only met him once or twice. What I communicate is what I have seen. He is a politician. I've been in sport for most of my life and I feel that the knowledge I have is enough to challenge the sitting Minister of Sport, whoever it may be. It's nothing personal with Nathi Mthethwa.

Things always need to change in sports administration. The same people have been at the helm for many years and I worry about the next generation of leaders. Both within the professional wing of football, but also within the mother body. What is their succession plan for the day that they decide they no longer want to be in those positions?

I know they always say they get voted or elected into those positions. But, obviously, there is a lot of lobbying and caucusing that happens behind the scenes. You don't just get thrust into the job. I worry about the next wave of leadership and if they will be better than the current crop.

I have crucial questions. Will they be able to grow football? Will we become that winning nation that we were under Stix Morewa? Will we get people from different race groups to appreciate football? Will the commercial entities and sponsors be as generous as they are now to pump billions into the PSL?

Will we have frequency of games for under-23 football teams as well as Bafana Bafana? Will we qualify on a regular basis for World Cups? Will we get into AFCON every two years? Where will we be and who will be leading us and will they be the right leaders in those positions?

I have battled with the current leadership but, at the end of the day, they can always show their successes by virtue of the monetary gains in the sport. We also have to admit that even prior to Covid, the number of spectators attending games at stadiums was declining. A stadium would only be packed if it was a Soweto derby. Other than that, the games were sparsely attended.

There was no real interest and that had nothing to do with that pandemic. It had everything to do with the footballing pandemic, that they had lost their fans. They were more interested in improving their income. When the game was much poorer when I was a kid, there were always great turnouts at the stadiums.

I think during the financially poorer days of the eighties, nineties and early 2000s, spectators actually wanted to go and watch live matches. There would be capacity games because there was always rivalry. They would get great value. It wasn't only Pirates and Chiefs. It was Swallows and Arcadia Shepherds and Hellenic and Cape Town Spurs. They all had a following. It was the same for Bush Bucks and African Wanderers and Celtic. They all had fans.

The modern game became richer financially, but it became extremely poor in terms of fan participation. They were not able to reinvent themselves. In the past, the public relations officers would go to radio shows and TV shows and try to promote games. There would be great banter on air. That always sparked excitement. It would get the fans interested and they would want to go to the stadiums.

Even the PSL used to have great PR people who would come on radio and talk about the matches. There would be theme songs and catch phrases. There was a theme from a song that I would play quite regularly on the show by Johnny Clegg and Savuka, *Ithikithi esandleni*. Did you have a ticket in hand? Great catch phrases always live on in fans' minds.

But clubs started dying and the PSL lost its voice and people began to aspire to different things. Rugby has drawn a lot of the fans that would go to football games. It's great to have the TV rights deal with SuperSport and there are more games on television and people are watching them on TV back-to-back in the afternoon. There's a big feast on TV but people aren't going to the stadiums. It's not matching what we are seeing in the UK. Even if it's Stoke City versus Birmingham, that stadium will be full whatever the capacity of the ground. We have lost the fan.

The quality of our football has become worse and we can gauge it from how few players are exported to other countries. You can compare from when there were players like Steven Pienaar playing for Everton and Benni McCarthy was at Blackburn Rovers and West Ham.

I think we have diluted our footballing identity because there was a South African footprint in terms of how we played the game. The South African style and identity slowly got lost. We brought in directors of football from other cultures and the clubs began bringing in foreign coaches who didn't want showboating or didn't want to improve how a player could use showboating constructively.

A lot of the players possess natural talent and the ability to dribble, but they could use it constructively in the build-up play and not just as showboating for the fans. The minute you start to limit players who can express themselves on the ball is the minute the culture goes. The kasi games that they play on dust and gravel in the off-season are packed with fans wanting to see that type of football.

That was the football that I used to watch as a kid that epitomised this. That is what the Jomo Sonos or Ace Ntsoelengoes or the Teenage Dladlas of the world were able to infuse and bring into the game. Now players play more like robots, where they are told to get the ball quickly and release. There's no expression of their talent.

Only a guy like Ted Dumitru was able to incorporate his knowledge of African football and, more specifically, South African football, to make it work during his tenure at Kaizer Chiefs. Even in his books he would always make mention of how important it is not to kill the identity of a certain country's culture, but to incorporate whatever teachings you have to better them.

In recent times, even people like José Mourinho have come out to say other countries should stop using African players to improve their national teams. When France won the World

Cup, everyone said that was Africa winning because a lot of their players had African ancestry and France then became the beneficiary thereof.

That is why we struggle to get into a quarterfinal or even a semifinal of a World Cup, because what we are left with now then becomes not good enough to challenge the dominance of the world. The fact that we still only have five African countries that can qualify for the World Cup is also a travesty.

Unfortunately, the game is just not worth the money you have to pay to go to the stadium any more.

I will never write off South African football because I think the fact that we have failed to manage it or to direct it properly does not mean that football has failed. It just means that we need fresher minds to lead the charge forward. It's always about leadership. It's always about how you turn things around. Leadership of football should also be flexible enough to allow younger, fresher minds to guide the older people who have taken this journey so far. It does not mean people being ungrateful to them. It just means that it's a new dawn, it's a new day. We can do things differently to what the old guard have been able to do.

I am proud of what I have achieved in my career and I know that I have made my family proud too.

From the very first day I left for school at the age of five, my grandfather told my mother that I would be successful. I went on to anchor the World Cup of football. Until today, my mother has listened to every single radio show since I started.

She has watched every single TV and magazine production that I've made since I set out because she also believed that I could. She supported my journey, which has made it even more worthwhile to know that she's on my side.

From the dream that I had listening to that little radio at Little Flower, wondering if I would ever see a live football match one day, to setting foot in the world's greatest stadiums. From practising in my family's lounge in front of our home camera to presenting on the global stage and being beamed into millions of households.

Part of my own personal challenge has been deciding what I want to do into the future. I want to carry on what I have been doing but possibly in a different country. I want to challenge myself outside of the borders of South Africa and I would love that. I love what the American broadcasters are doing in terms of football broadcasting.

Having been in partnership with Arena, I also think there is greater scope from a media ownership point of view for the so-called younger generation. We need to step up our ownership of the space and grow the independence, nurture the voices that want to get their points across, but be credible enough to do it because people would pay top dollar to get something that they know is credible.

Fans can always expect a reinvented product from me. They can always expect someone they can associate with, somebody who has lived his dream, somebody who is still living his dream, somebody who wants to expand his dream right now.

I will always be guided by a sense of what I feel people want and desire. Radio has helped me to keep my ear to the ground and get a sense of what people want and desire. That daily interaction has never failed me. That daily interaction with the people has made me give them a better product every day. I won't stop doing that.

I'm not going anywhere.

Sesiyayivala sithi gqimm'shelele …

Acknowledgements

This book was several years in the making. After Mandy slid into Robert's DMs in 2017 with an attempt to convince him to tell his story in a book, it took a few more years before he finally agreed the time was right. We would like to thank each other for the trust and enthusiasm that have underpinned this project.

A huge thank you to Terry Morris, Andrea Nattrass, Zodwa Kumalo-Valentine, Eileen Bezemer and everyone else in the Pan Macmillan team who has enthusiastically supported this book. Our thanks to Qhawekazi Phelakho for her meticulous work and professionalism in transcribing dozens of hours of interviews.

We are grateful to the staff and management at The Houghton Hotel for their generous hospitality and attention to detail. Each week, they took care to meet our every need and we couldn't think of a better environment to be in while working on this project.

We are greatly indebted to our families and loved ones for the patience required during the process of writing and publishing a book.

* * *

To my parents, Lynette and Frank: You brought me into this world and gave me an opportunity to fulfill a dream. You were the first to sadly leave us in 2016, Baba, but uMama did a really magnificent job under trying circumstances. Mageba, no words can describe the mother that you have been to me personally! I will forever cherish your values and consistency.

To Felicia Ntisa: If ever I had a mother in Johannesburg, it is you Madame Ntisa. I've always referred to you as such and know that all you have ever done for me or said to me has made me a better person. That infectious laugh and humility allows you inspire me in many ways.

To Luigia Scholtz: I might never have had the time to properly thank you for welcoming me and literally taking care of me from the day I first walked through the SuperSport corridors. You ably did that until the very end. I take *nothing* for granted. Your time, patience and understanding. God bless you.

To my sisters, Nomvula, Gugu and Vanessa: Thank you for allowing the only boy in the family to be just that, a boy! You took time to understand me and I hope in the end I did not confuse you too much. From saving me to supporting me and fuelling me with many ideas along the way, I can safely say that this has been *our* journey. Let's do all we can to find each other again as we enter the final lap of life agewise.

To Rob Rogers: I might have been a raw product that came into the production line, but the fact that I got on board was largely due to *you*, and as a producer, you always challenged me to step up. You always felt that I could give more, do more, create more, speak more and sparkle more. I hope I didn't disappoint you.

To Romeo Kumalo: I have no idea what was going through your mind when you decided to unleash this wet-behind-the ears chap onto a then highly respected and sought-after radio station like MetroFM. You were brave. Bold. My radio allergy and fear were healed by your vision. Siyabonga Mntungwa.

To Tshepo Mahloele: In May 2019 when I walked into your office, freshly fired by SuperSport and seeking support for my Egypt trip, together with my videographer Kyle, you had no idea that you were fuelling an independent journey in my career that I should have started years ago. That big chance you took. That risk. That trust. You and the entire team at Arena Holdings, led by Bra Pule Molebeledi, allowed us to further make history. Salute.

To my sponsors, HollywoodBets, Lexus and Viceroy: For taking up major assignments with a then unemployed chap showed your greater vision and future goals. We have certainly disrupted the industry ... Let's continue to change the many lives that you do via your products. Thank you for the faith and belief!

To my dearly departed heroes: Eddie Zondi, Vuyo Mbuli, Coudjou Amankwaa, Stephen Keshi, David Kekana, Mzimasi Mgebisa, Sibusiso Mseleku, Duif du Toit, Cebo Clement Manyaapelo, Cyril Bongani 'Kansas City' Mchunu, Joshua Mlaba, Aubrey Ndhlovu, Xolani Gwala, Father Msimango, Shakes Kungwane, Hugh Masekela, Jacob 'Baby Jake' Matlala, Nelson Mandela, Senzo Meyiwa, Steve 'Kalamazoo' Mokone,

Frank Marawa, Mam Dora. A heavenly thank you from me to you.

To Lynette Phumlile Marawa: Your journey deserves a book on its own. How you did what you did, I still don't know. Thank you for entering a technological space that you knew nothing about but you allowed me to teach you how to record a football game while I was at boarding school. The hundreds of VHS tapes that were made in the end, plus the volumes of newspapers that you stashed for me to be able to return to a holiday of reading and watching. You enabled this dream to have a beginning. The fact that you have watched and listened to every single show I've ever done on both radio and television from day one to the present (bar the times you were ill and in hospital) speaks volumes about you. It's the same support you give to all your kids consistently.

Thank you Ndabezitha, Mageba, Sthuli for loving my son Awande unconditionally, and supporting and defending him in all he does and says. He cares a lot about you and loves you to no end. A parent like you is what makes life worth living.

Words can *never* be enough.
LOVE YOU ALWAYS NDABS.

www.ingramcontent.com/pod-product-compliance
Lightning Source LLC
Chambersburg PA
CBHW070750230426
43665CB00017B/2311